The
Consolation
of Food

Sasha, thank you for peeling the thorny artichoke instead of letting me try to swallow it whole. Thank you for cleverly handing me a blunt blade when I'm busy trying to saw through my own ropes. Thank you for lining my darkest period with blossoms and small feathers. You are wise. I'm fascinated at the direction from which you approach things. You might not think I listen, but I do.

Minnie and Louis, while your mountains are far away, you are with me every hour. We are connected by warm and delicious strings of melty cheese that will stretch and contract but never snap. I have sent out a little hawk, by the way, to keep an eye over you and guard you. When not with you, in my head I'm always walking towards you.

I love you all. Let's go for a swim in the sea.

Nature, by shape colour, design and reason, you are beyond beautiful. You amaze me continually. I am never bored, you are always near.

First published in the United Kingdom in 2019 by
Pavilion
43 Great Ormond Street
London
WC1N 3HZ

Copyright © Pavilion Books Company Ltd 2019
Text copyright © Valentine Warner 2019
Extracted text, page 4, 'The Peace of Wild Things' © Wendell Berry 1968
(New York: Harcourt, Brace & World, 1968; London: Penguin Books, 2018)

ISBN 978-1-91162-403-5

A CIP catalogue record for this book is available from the British Library.

10 9 8 7 6 5 4 3 2 1

Reproduction by Rival Colour Ltd, UK
Printed and bound by 1010 Printing International Ltd, China

www.pavilionbooks.com

Valentine Warner

The Consolation of Food

Stories about life and death,
seasoned with recipes

PAVILION

The Peace of Wild Things

When despair for the world grows in me
and I wake in the night at the least sound
in fear of what my life and my children's lives may be,
I go and lie down where the wood drake
rests in his beauty on the water, and the great heron feeds.
I come into the peace of wild things
who do not tax their lives with forethought
of grief. I come into the presence of still water.
And I feel above me the day-blind stars
waiting with their light. For a time
I rest in the grace of the world, and am free.

Wendell Berry

Life, Death and Cooking

I wanted to call this book *THIS IS NOT A COOKBOOK!* but I have learnt to pick my battles.

It is not an autobiography. It's not even a memoir. It's the equivalent of a bag of groceries and household needs from different shops – leeks, light bulbs, socks, sticky moth traps, steaks and soap. What I mean is that, like its author, half magpie, half chameleon, it's a jangle of odds and sods, a collection that represents the frustrations and the joys of my life thus far.

But God forbid *anything* in this day and age does not have a THEME! And as my life, generally speaking, does not have a theme and is devoid of any obvious routine – apart from brushing my teeth – I guess it really is food that has tied it all together.

In all my cookbooks, the point was never really the sum parts of a plate of food, but the events that led up to it, by which I do not mean the completion of a recipe. Recipes are a ball-ache to write. Although cooking is a happy action, an arrangement of shapes, colours and taste, I find measurements a hassle as they often don't reflect the way I cook. No. The joy in the writing for me has always been the story *before* the recipe, the people I've come across, the surrounding and situation I find myself in. The recipes included in this book are close to my heart, certainly, just not a pedantically curated collection but more a case of this is what I cook, this is what you get.

Originally, I put forward that it should be a small book printed on psalm paper, *Consolations in Food: A Cookbook for Divorcees and the Recently Bereaved.* It was thought that this was perhaps a little grim, so it became a book about enjoyment, grief, restlessness, disasters and success. Bereavement and divorce nonetheless are still allowed to nestle among the strange fruit, smeared across these pages. But, really, I wrote it to entertain you, and in the hope it may stop you occasionally from simply 'reading on'.

Ultimately, this is a story book with food in it; and, of course, that other essential embroidery for life, music. So integral to my own daily existence and always on in the kitchen.

No doubt with certain references it will soon date, but I've written it with an openness, hoping that by sharing my idiocies and sadness as much as my frivolity, we may *all* decide to share more, admit our faults, slow down, change our minds and say 'this is too fast, slow down this mad carousel, and let me see what's going on.'

Music, food and words. A consolation surely. Maybe not the words, but I just hope you find at least one thing, maybe two, that make the purchase worth it.

Music

Music is pretty integral to this book. It has played such a big part in my life. In my experience, we all want to inflict our music taste on others, and this is my opportunity to do so. If you dislike the stories or recipes then, hopefully, you can enjoy the music and benefit from one of the three constituents.

I set myself the task of matching a song to each story and recipe, but soon realized that links via obvious association (i.e. 'I Don't Want to Set the World on Fire' partnered with my habit for burning tea towels in The Backgammon Board) meant a rather trite association between song and subject, culminating in a lot of songs I didn't really care about.

Entering songs in accordance with periods of my life would mean a distressing amount of Roger Whittaker in the early years, some nosebleed punk from my art college years, followed by a lot of questionable bleeps. So I've cherry-picked what I consider the best from my mixed bag of 700 scratchy LPs, wallets of jumping CDs, and hours and hours of combing Spotify. Most of it, bar one or two, can be found there. Some of you may be aware of My Kitchen Beets, posted bi-weekly, accompanied by a picture of beetroots wearing earphones.

So I decided to simply make a long list. To be played as and when, as it is hardly likely you will find the track to then snuggle down and read the recommended nonsense that goes with it. I mean, I certainly can't read and listen to music at the same time. No. I keep it for sulking, driving (except when trying to park), easy Sundays and dancing in the kitchen. Later at night, it is a favourite pastime to climb on my sturdy marble table (podium) wearing my earphones and boxer shorts, and bop till 1 am. Instantly preferable to exercising in that most wretched of places, the gym.

Music has been so essential to my life because, being one of life's fidgets, it fills the gaps between things. The gaps I'm not so good at knowing what to do with. My restlessness has seen me find and consume music with the same voracity I do food. A man of appetites, of which music is one. A life full of music and food ... great!

Maybe it would have been better to understand the opportunities for silence in my life more deeply than I perhaps have, but the upshot is that music has taught me a lot. Whether the words, the melodic emotion, or the fact we chose *that* song at *that* time, it carries the lurching boat of my life along on its waves. In cold, stony times, it has allowed me to cry; in warm bright times, to feel a joy I can only associate with it.

Aged ten, in the Bridport record shop, I bought my three first cassettes: 'One Step Beyond' by Madness, 'Stray Cat Strut' by Stray Cats, and Debbie Harry's *KooKoo* (because I had a huge crush in her that would see me put my arm around my pillow and ask her what she wanted for breakfast). My little cassette recorder played them again and again until each was either chewed or stretched.

(The inner leaf of *KooKoo* had a picture of Debbie with her cheeks skewered by long needles. It freaked the living hell out of me, almost as much as antlered Herne the Hunter's hairy hand snatching me in the woods.)

I was cringingly uncool for school and its musical tribes. I was dressed primarily by the shop Fosters. (Thanks, Mum!) So I'd return to school with those nylon bar-chart jumpers, Second Image jeans, not Levis, and Go Flash trainers, not Adidas. Thankfully though, I had a very cool sister who'd pick me up from school occasionally and whizz me back to her flat in London. En route we'd listen to cassette after cassette of Sly and Robbie, Motown, The Eurythmics, Fela Kuti and Mantronix.

I owe a lot to my darling sister, far more than she thinks, thank you for the music, sis. And I must quickly thank my school dormitory captain, Vere, for obsessively playing Julian Cope. It seems to have stuck.

My mother was the lead singer of the family, the musical matriarch, a passionate jazz singer. High times and evenings, when guests were round, she'd stand, hitch up her skirt, stick a foot on a pulled-out chair, throw a glass over her shoulder (once through a painting), and off she'd go. She had a brilliant voice. My dad's face would light up with his 'that's why I married her' look, while my brother and I would flash each other an 'oh no, please don't' glance and cringe with embarrassment. 'Please, don't …' She'd dismiss us with the flick of the hand.

I will never forget Mum singing at a charity event to raise money so that the Electric Cinema on Portobello Road might not close down. In she sashayed, blue sequin gown and meringue hair. She looked the crowd over with that cheeky mocking look and belted out 'Amen Corner'.

'Hey brothers, hey sisters, we got hypocrites in this crowd.'

She brought the house down.

Mum owned a lot of music and played it most of the time. Marianne Faithfull, Grace Jones, The Beatles, Django Reinhardt. If the record player or radio wasn't singing, she most certainly would be. She sang to her children regularly, often in a cockney accent, and to this day I sing those songs to my own children. 'The Alphabet of Love' and 'Little Sammy Fiddlekins'.

Little Sammy Fiddlekins the fat boy,
one day called upon his uncle Brown
just before he left young Sammy was presented
with a brand new half a crown
('Diddlyanarna')
Feeling rather thirsty he went into a shop
he drank ten lemonades a dozen ginger beers
And then there was a great big POP
More work for the undertaker, another little job for the tombstone maker
at the local cemetery they've been very, very busyyyyyyyyyyy
[slowed down and sombre] On a brand new grave for Sammyyyyyyy

9

Fish with 'airs on brown bread!

The fish with hairs on always puzzled me deeply, but I understood marginally more when I attempted to make smoked mackerel pâté while wearing an angora jumper.

Mind you, my own occasional outpourings ... now that was embarrassing. Nauseating little shit that I was, guests would be asked to turn their chairs and be politely forced to watch either a Warner Brothers performance or, worse still, a singular brother ... normally me.

I recall with embarrassment my rendition of 'Oh for the Wings of a Dove' while simultaneously doing bad robotic manoeuvres. Christ! I can just see me doing those awful jerky moves, my chubby flushed face squeaking 'Far awaaay far away wou-ould I roam ...'

Choral body popping makes for a dismal combination. I can only imagine guests driving home, one turning to the other to say, 'Darling, that Warner boy is a tragic little oaf, isn't he?'

But it was my father who was the biggest surprise. One day, I discovered nearly every seven- and twelve-inch record by Led Zeppelin and Pink Floyd. I assumed they belonged to my mother; my father was most indignant. 'They're mine,' he growled. 'You simply don't know the half of it.'

I should not have been surprised, for despite being born in 1918, my father was a most modern man. One foot in cosmopolitan life, the other in a cowpat, his interests were beyond wide ranging, which is what made him such wonderful company. There was nothing obvious about him.

Guaranteed to sob during a certain opera, he was very knowledgeable about classical music. But there was another side to him. Once, when just the two of us went to Paris, I was around thirteen at the time, he said, 'We'll just pop in to IRCAM.' A French institute for the science of music, sound and avant-garde electro-acoustic art music, he was in some curious capacity working for.

Here I sat on a stool and listened to electronic pan pipes, played from the first studio mixing desk I'd ever seen.

Simulated '60 foot long pan pipes as if blown by lungs belonging to a man 120 foot tall.'

We heard squeaks, plinks, bloobs and scratches, and I sat there wide-eyed as sounds I'd never heard or imagined oozed, squelched and boomed from that table of dials and huge speakers, accompanied by another English fellow. Named Birtwhistle. Anyway.

Ethnicity, food and music are intertwined. Music and food feed the free parts of our spirit as do art and drink. All important. Stick another sausage on, stick another record on, open the wine and I'll make you a small snake from the foil.

I sincerely hope you like Radio Val (see page 254).

Youth and
Young Manhood

Curtsey

I have never fitted in. A lone operator, I have made efforts to, but I am nonetheless what I would describe as an outsider. This is not a bad thing.

Last to be chosen for school sports' teams, first to be caught poaching at the local trout farm, I certainly found it as hard to 'follow the rules' as a boy or to 'play the game' in my adult clothes.

Nature or nurture? I'm not sure. The tracks to some extent seem laid from the very moment my parents chose each other (or I chose them perhaps. Oh the arrogance!).

When my father was the British Ambassador to Japan between 1972 and 1975, the Queen came to stay, and a hurry-scurry of preparation threw the embassy into a countdown of rehearsals and 'just so' preparation.

My father took efforts to teach me to bow and introduce myself properly and, when my moment came to welcome the Queen and pay my respects, key wound, I was pointed in the right direction and sent forward.

Few might be surprised to know I confidently walked before Her Majesty and curtsied.

There you have it. An oddity.

Baked Mackerel with Miso

Serves 2

1½ tbsp groundnut (peanut) or sunflower oil

2 medium mackerel, head and tail removed, body cut into 4 barrels

1 medium sweet onion, neatly cut to medium dice

50 ml/1⅔ fl oz/2¾ tbsp Japanese sake or white sweet vermouth

100 ml/3½ fl oz/½ cup Japanese soy sauce

2 tbsp dark brown sugar

1 tbsp honey (do not use heather honey)

2 tbsp red miso paste

1 large thumb of ginger, peeled and finely grated

2 tsp brown rice vinegar or malt vinegar

2 finger-sized strips of satsuma or orange rind

2 spring onions (scallions), chopped

Freshly ground black pepper

Heat the oil in a very small casserole or non-stick heavy-based saucepan (that owns a lid). Fry the mackerel pieces on their open flesh sides, over a medium heat, until well browned and crisp. Turn once to do the other side. Be careful not to let the oil smoke.

Remove the mackerel to a plate, add the onion to the pan and sauté. This will take 12 or so minutes as the onion needs to be lightly browned, totally soft and sweet. Add the sake or vermouth and allow to almost entirely evaporate.

In a bowl mix together the soy sauce, sugar, honey, miso, ginger, vinegar and some pepper before pouring it into the pan. Add the mackerel to the pan. Bring it all to a bubble. Add the rind and 100 ml/3½ fl oz/½ cup water. Put the lid on and simmer very gently for 1 hour, turning the pieces halfway through.

Remove the mackerel very carefully to a plate and spoon over the sauce. Scatter with some spring onion and serve with steamed Japanese, basmati or pudding rice.

Tip If you feel so inclined, very finely slice half a medium cucumber. Toss with a teaspoon of sea salt and allow to drain in a sieve (strainer) while the mackerel cooks. Squeeze out the excess water.

Mix together rice or white wine vinegar and sugar to an equal balance of sweet and sour. Add a good piece of peeled and finely grated ginger into the mix and add the cucumber to it. This works well with the sweet fattiness of the mackerel. Enjoy with Seaweed and Cucumber Salad (see page 17).

Nasu Dengaku – a Variation

Normally, you will see this served as a whole half an aubergine (eggplant), but sometimes not. I replaced some of the sugar or honey with maple syrup, given that varieties of acer (maple) tree are so common across Japan. I used the tangerine in this simply because it was there – citrus also plays a significant role in Japanese cuisine. This was once served to me with the burnt sticker still on the skin. Remember to remove it.

> **Serves 2**
> 1 large aubergine, washed and stalk removed
> 1 tbsp sunflower oil
> 50 ml/1⅔ fl oz/2¾ tbsp mirin or sake
> 2 tbsp red miso paste
> 1½ tangerines, juiced, plus a grating of tangerine zest (optional)
> 1 tbsp maple syrup
> 1 tsp soft brown sugar
> 1 large thumb of fresh ginger root, peeled finely grated
> 1 tsp fresh Japanese soy sauce
> 1 tbsp sesame seeds, toasted
> 1 spring onion (scallion), finely sliced

Halve the aubergine lengthways, then cut each half 4 times lengthways and then 'cube'. Fry in a dry pan until well charred but not black. There will be smoke, so turn on the extraction. Add the oil and continue frying until all is pathetically tender, about 7–8 minutes.

While the aubergine cooks, reduce the mirin to a syrup, then stir in the miso paste, tangerine juice, maple syrup and sugar. Reduce at a simmer until the thickness of tahini. Take off the heat and stir in the ginger and soy sauce. Tip into the tender aubergines and fry for 30 seconds or so or until all is absorbed and the sugars are just beginning to catch and caramelize.

Spoon on to plates and scatter with the toasted sesame seeds and chopped spring onion. Finish with a little grated zest from the tangerine if inclined.

Lovely with sips from little cup of hot sake and with a seaweed salad (below).

Seaweed and Cucumber Salad with Soy Orange Dressing

Serves 2
Half a cucumber, peeled and very thinly sliced
1 tbsp sea salt
15 g/½ oz mixed dried seaweed
1 medium carrot, peeled and very finely julienned (optional)
2 tsp toasted sesame seeds or toasted buckwheat, to serve

For the dressing
1 tbsp Japanese soy sauce
½ tsp Dijon mustard
½ tsp wholegrain mustard
1½ tsp caster (superfine) sugar
1½ tsp white or brown rice vinegar
Juice of a quarter of a small sweet, tart orange
Half thumb of ginger, peeled and very finely grated

Mix the cucumber with the salt in a colander placed over a bowl. Let it drip for 30–60 minutes. When done, wring out any remaining juice and discard.

Cook, or soak the seaweed in boiled water as per the package instructions. Drain. Mix all ingredients for the dressing together thoroughly.

In a bowl, toss together the cucumber, seaweed and carrot, if using, and mix gently. Place in 2 serving bowls and pour over the dressing. Scatter with sesame seeds or buckwheat.

Rabbit Droppings

No surprises maybe, but it is thought that my surname Warner stems from 'warrener', a keeper of rabbits. They were once most prized at high table (the rabbits, not the Warners), a delicacy no less for they were initially scarce, and they were primarily farmed in artificial warrens.

Introduced by the Romans[1], it took time for rabbits to adapt from the sandy Spanish soil (*Hispania* translated from its origins is 'land of rabbits'), and dig their way into the roll call of perceived indigenous British wildlife.

As a boy I hunted them hard. Lying in the grass with my air rifle as the sun dipped behind the nettles, the wheat dust and midges like sparks in the evening light, I'd not stir a muscle and move with cat-like slowness as the less cautious rabbits hopped out into the clover.

There were lots of them, and long before I understood their seasons and when best to eat them, I was never prouder as a boy than when making rabbit stews for my parents or eating my mum's rabbit pie, which she always put hard-boiled eggs in, glorious as it was.

I once tried to make a wallet from rabbit fur but was forced to throw away my grisly purse as it stank. I drew them on everything, all my school books, slowly abbreviating them over time until they became a pictorial signature that I can now draw in about four seconds.

They ran across my dreams and became my talismans. People started to give me things with rabbits on them.

Among the high hedges of west Dorset, in small dark pubs, I still hear the word 'coney' used today – the old term for a rabbit. Pockets of an old world, still in existence. I like this. It makes me smile and I use it myself.

Bunnies I call kittens, which certainly foxes my kids.

---

[1] Most likely as exotic pets – archaeologists have recently found a rabbit bone among bones excavated at Fishbourne Palace in 1964. And one without butchery marks or anything like that, hence a pet.

The farmed rabbit is a different thing altogether and the distinctions between it and it's wild cousin considerable. While delicious, wild rabbit during the warmer months can taste rather unpleasant, because primarily they're doing what rabbits do best. 'At it like rabbits'. Loving in the grass, sexed up and funky, their bodies fizzing with amorous chemicals that taint the meat. It can be tasted. It's unpleasant and they should be avoided. Have a sausage instead.

Secondly, with barely any fat on them, adult rabbits can be very stringy – a muscular requirement from having to leg it so frequently from stoats, weasels, cats, foxes, dogs, owls, buzzards, farmers ... and me. This means that their meat is easily dried out, so using a pressure cooker would be a wise move.

Most you will find in a butcher's shop are arguably too large, and often there at the wrong time of year. This is simply because there are a lot around and the butcher pays very little for them. So, even if inspired by River Cottage (or maybe even me), don't be too hasty. A big summer rabbit is best avoided – more sustenance for a wandering traveller, shivering in his cloak and turning his coney over a hissing fire, an unlikely sight these days, but who knows how our future will unravel?

Soaking adult rabbits in milk can mellow the grassy flavour. Mature rabbits, best bought in winter, are better when paired with strong flavours such as bacon, anchovies, vinegar, wine, tomato, preserved lemons, green olives and turmeric. Mincing them can be a good trick; the minced rabbit can then be incorporated into ragùs or lasagnes.

If you know someone who shoots, as cold-hearted as it may sound, ask them for small rabbits. They are tender and indeed lovely, deep fried in breadcrumbs, with a little fresh lavender, and eaten with aioli and lemon or salsa verde.

The farmed rabbit on the other hand owns plump white meat, is easy to cook and quite fatty. However, there are pitfalls here, too. European practices when it comes to animals are significantly behind our own, and still leave a lot to be desired. And it's Europeans like the French and Spanish who have a voracious appetite for farmed rabbits. Sourcing good farmed rabbits is essential and not easy. So, if you're inclined to try this recipe, please really look into it.

All this writing just for one recipe. I love farmed rabbit.

Not so long ago some silly butcher tried to hoodwink me into believing the wild rabbit he was trying to sell me was a farmed one. Give over, he picked the wrong guy. Famous butcher's shop, too. So for your information, it should be a very pale pink, chicken-like colour and still have the head attached with the pink eyes glaring. You may find this disturbing, but see past that as, ultimately, it's delicious.

My Favourite Dish – Roast Rabbit

Serves 3–4

1 fat *farmed* rabbit, jointed (each back leg cut into 2, saddle into 3, plus the rib section and 2 front legs – 10 parts in all. Liver and kidneys and heart reserved)

25-g/1-oz bunch of sage

6 x 5-cm/2-in lengths of fresh rosemary

4 sprigs of fresh thyme

1 large head of garlic, unpeeled and split horizontally

Rind from 1 small unwaxed lemon, removed in strips with potato peeler

½ tbsp fennel seeds

1 tsp coriander seeds

2 small red (bell) peppers, deseeded and sliced lengthways, then across

75 ml/2 fl oz/¼ cup olive oil

2 tbsp capers, rinsed, drained and dried on paper

1 tbsp red wine vinegar

Sea salt and freshly ground black pepper

Lemon wedges, to serve

For the offal (optional)

Butter, for frying (optional)

Olive oil

Fresh thyme

Red wine vinegar
Sea salt

In a large bowl, place the jointed rabbit and its offal. If there is no chance of you eating the offal, then at least pass down to the dog.

Mix ¾ tablespoon of sea salt with the rabbit, then add the sage, rosemary, thyme, garlic, lemon peel and fennel and coriander seeds, and toss to coat. Cover with clingfilm (plastic wrap) and leave for 2 hours.

Preheat the oven to 180°C fan/200°C/400°F/gas mark 6.

Place the rabbit on a baking tray. Let anything stuck to it come to the tray with it. Lift out the garlic, herbs and lemon from the bowl and dump them on the rabbit. Leave as much remaining salt in the bowl as possible. Add the peppers to the tray. Pour over 3 tablespoons of olive oil and mix everything together well. Let it fall loosely back into the tray but don't cram it all in.

Put into the oven and roast for 45 minutes –1 hour, turning once or twice. The rabbit should be well browned, the herbs and peppers beginning to char.

For offal lovers, divide the heart in 2. Melt some butter in a small frying pan (skillet) and fry the liver, heart and kidneys with a little oil and butter, thyme salt and pepper. Deglaze the pan with a splash of red wine vinegar. Push on to bread, or better still some fried bread, and enjoy with a glass of cold sherry.

With 10 minutes before the rabbit leaps from the oven, pour 2 tablespoons of the olive oil into a small saucepan and over a medium heat fry the capers until they become crispy and split. Just before removing them splash the rabbit meat all over with red wine vinegar and return to the oven for 2 minutes. Note: don't overcook the rabbit meat as the pieces are small, and will dry out.

Take to a plate and serve with the pepper, leaving most of the herb branches behind. Spoon the crispy capers over, and garnish with a wedge of lemon.

Eat with the Anchovy Salad below.

Anchovy Salad

Simple but delicious. This will make enough dressing for two salads.

Serves 4

300 ml/10 fl oz/1¼ cups whole milk

1 x 4-cm/1½-in sprig of fresh rosemary

3 fat garlic cloves

8 good-quality salted anchovies in oil, drained (I like Ortiz brand)

125 ml/4 fl oz/½ cup olive oil

1 large endive and equal parts treviso, radicchio, watercress, dandelion, rocket (arugula) – whatever you like – enough to make a medium helping of salad

Juice of half a small lemon

Fresh chilli, finely sliced

Pour the milk into a small non-stick pan and pop in the rosemary and garlic.

Over a low heat, slowly reduce the milk, taking great care not to burn, until reduced by three-quarters and both faintly creamy and a fraction ivory coloured, too.

Meanwhile, put the anchovies in a steep-sided, medium-sized bowl. Remove the rosemary stalk from the milk, leaving any detached leaves and the garlic. Pour the milk over the anchovies. With a stick blender, purée the mixture, then very slowly trickle in the oil. The mixture will gradually start to thicken.

Once the oil is used up, set the dressing to one side. It will keep well covered and in the fridge for 2 or 3 days but seldom lasts that long.

Take the endive and cut off the base in a thin sliver. Divide it lengthways, then break up all the leaves into a bowl. Add 2 handfuls of whichever other salad leaves you have.

Take 2 big serving spoons of the dressing and blob it over the salad. Mix together the lemon juice and chilli and pour over. Mix gently until combined. Kapow! This is my favourite salad.

Feel free to serve with a couple of soft-boiled eggs, or scatter with toasted pine nuts or fennel seeds.

Cut Down in Their Prime

My view is that little boys break things for two reasons: to find the boundaries and limits of others and themselves and, in a perverse sort of way, to break the world around them to understand how the sum parts come apart, how they were put together. A kind of textural experience.

My brother and I were pretty naughty growing up on the farm. There was a lot of mischief to be made. Raiding the fruit nets was not too bad, I guess, but for the fact we could do the work of a hundred blackbirds in five minutes; throwing apples at windows a little worse, but poking holes in multiple fertilizer bags just to watch the mesmerizing cascades of white beads fall out reduced even the toughest farm manager to watery-eyed frustration. The discovery of a petrol can and an uncontrolled explosion in the bonfire tip was a lucky escape that could have seen me blown into Devon. We thoroughly tested our surroundings.

Around the age of eight, I was outside with my father, watching him plant trees, tiddling around as kids do once bored with the initial keenness to help. He was planting an avenue of apple saplings, carefully spaced out on each side of the road leading up a hill to the farm cottage. It had taken him most of the day. A lot had been planted. Twenty trees or so. He needed something or other, and headed back to the garden shed to get it.

There I was alone, when I saw a pair of grass shears in the wheelbarrow and so quietly got on with methodically chopping every single tree in half. Even now I remember surveying my handiwork, tree heads lying at the roots, my blank feeling overlaid with at least some idea that what I'd done was perhaps not such a great idea. A kind of 'fine for now, but this is not going to end well' notion.

My father returned and came across the fallen. Shocked, there were no words, there was no furious explosion. It was not necessary. He just looked me straight in the eyes. Deadpan on the outside, raging within, purse-lipped but barely contained. It was the deafening quiet between us that saw me drop the shears and run.

I ran and ran to my secret place by the stream where I wept for my crime, for upsetting my father, for the utter confusion of it all.

It was not discussed. It didn't need to be. No spanking the world over could have had a effect of that stare, that look of 'Are you really my son?' or 'What are you in fact?'

It's all as crystal clear as I write it today. So why is it in here? Simply a weird device for an apple recipe?

No, I think I just needed to say sorry for the last time. Even though he's up there and laughing kindly at the irrelevance of my earthly apology.

Chicken and Apples

My girlfriend Sasha's recipe, this is always a fine welcome home. Bags dropped at the door and, like the Bisto Kid, I follow my nose to the kitchen in the happy knowledge that chicken and apples is what I'm going to get.

Serves 2

2 large chicken leg and thigh portions, divided

1 tbsp flour or rice flour (optional, see Tip)

50 g/2 oz/4 tbsp butter

Dash of sunflower oil

2 large onions, chopped to a medium dice

2 sprigs of fresh thyme

3 large garlic cloves, halved lengthways

1 tbsp cider vinegar or apple balsamic vinegar

1 large Bramley apple, peeled, cored and chopped in 12 segments

500 ml/17 fl oz/2 cups medium (hard) cider

300 ml/10 fl oz/1¼ cups chicken stock

1 tsp mustard

Sea salt and freshly ground black pepper

Season the chicken pieces generously with salt and pepper.

In a heavy casserole (that owns a lid) over a medium heat, fry the chicken legs in the butter and oils. Do not hurry this on a high heat, as the butter and chicken will burn. You want to achieve a deep golden brown on both sides.

Remove the chicken legs onto a plate to rest. Add the onions to the fat with the thyme and season with pepper. Sauté gently until the onions are soft and deep golden. This should take 12–15 minutes.

Add the garlic, then the vinegar, stir, and let it evaporate. Reintroduce the chicken with the apples and pour in the cider, followed by the stock. Simmer gently for 1 hour.

Remove the lid, stir in the mustard and continue to reduce at a rapid simmer until reduced by half. Check seasoning and serve with mash.

Tip In order to get a creamier, more wintery sauce, dredge the chicken legs in generously seasoned flour. Pat off the excess.

Hares

My mother's jugged hare was a legendary dish in the Warner family, and we ate it regularly through the autumn and winter due to the voracity with which I hunted the poor things. A rich, glistening mahogany colour, it was a luscious, dark pool of jointed hare meat, red wine, lemon zest, bay leaf, ginger, garlic, brown sugar, rowan jelly, butter, bacon, onions, celery and carrots, all thickened with cocoa powder and the hare's blood mixed with vinegar. It did not smell nice during the cook, but it was unctuous and eye-rollingly delicious by completion. Always served on Sunday, it featured regularly in thank-you letters from guests.

I knew our fifteen acres like the back of my hand – those ash branches on which wood pigeons would pause, a preferred holly the pheasants would roost in, where the rabbits emerged at dusk, that patch of clover wandering ducks went to, where a covey of partridge was sure to play King of the Castle on a rotting haystack, and the favoured places of the mysterious hare, an animal now most dear to me.

I will not lie: when these creatures were hard to find, young and bloodthirsty and with my heart thumping in my ears, I'd crawl under the barbed wire or cross the road that separated our three fields from the land that was not ours, but where hares could be found in greater numbers. The jacket I used to wear was a testament to my forbidden inclinations. The torn back and liner around the shoulders told the tale. With the intent of a hungry Inuit, I was also armed with an early understanding of perspective and foreshortening that would see me use even a fence post as cover for a stooping approach. I was a deadly little bugger.

I remember the smell of the gloomy apple shed where my quarry would dangle, one leg pushed through an incision in the other leg to make a fur fastening to hook over a nail. Apples, damp, musty newspaper and dust mixed with the gamey smell of pelt, feathers and blood fills my nose as I write this. It shapes a memory so clear I could be standing there right now.

My father knew, I think, of my poaching, not least because he worked in his beloved garden as often as I'd slip out with my gun. And so it seems most likely that he saw me slip beneath the fence or slowly disappear through a hole in the hedge. But he said little on it and, in hindsight, allowed me to shoot far too much. I patrolled those grounds like the most fervent, ruthless sentry. I would not allow my own son to do so with the same appetite, if indeed that time should ever come. And I have never understood why I was allowed to shoot so much, for my mother certainly disapproved.

If my father were alive today, he'd now be 101. He fought in the navy during the Second World War and had, no doubt, seen a lot of death. He disliked killing, adored plants and birds … all nature … and had himself stopped shooting shortly after the war. I've come to think that, as a lonely child growing up in rural Dorset, he'd learnt to depend on his own company, and had thrown himself into learning as much as he could from books and fields or wherever learning could be found. For the same reasons, I think he was loath to separate me from something I loved, perhaps amplified by feelings of guilt at being absent for a large part of his sons' lives. It was his old gun I used, an implement that belonged to us both, part of a wild world we both loved, and a rawness that we both found so essential and that could only be found outdoors.

There was an unbroken understanding between us which was, quite simply, if you kill it you eat it. There were a few exceptions, of which the less said the better. I think it is particular to growing boys to try to break with the world, almost as if it's a requirement to understanding how it's put together. But nonetheless, boys can be horrors, and I have since been stung by regret.

If he did indeed know of my offences, to my luck I don't think it was by way of the two keepers who did catch me. One simply caught me up under his arm and gave me a thorough thrashing I can still feel the vibrations of today. The other took my brand-new game bag and said, 'Let's be having an exchange then, and let it also be a lesson, you silly boy.' I was so upset to lose my Christmas present, and pretended I had mislaid it in forgetfulness.

I have stopped shooting hares now, and for good. Though I nearly wavered this last year. There had been a lot of talk of cooking on a rough shoot in Scotland and, taken by an urge to cook hare, I asked my host if I could kill one. They were more plentiful than I have seen in a long time, yet even as I asked I was wrestling internally with my request to break my promise to myself. But permission was granted, and the moment soon arose when one broke from the grass and out over the new wheat shoots, cantering in that strange lolloping way. Even before my gun reached my shoulder I knew I would not follow through.

I have come to believe that hares rub against the calves of mother nature as she stares down at them lovingly. They hold answers we would all be wiser to know, and keep secrets with which we should never be trusted. And to explain this, I shall repeat a story I included in my first-ever cookbook, not out of laziness but because I think as many people should read it as possible. (I hope neither publisher feels swizzed.)

Some time soon after Christmas, my father and I were on the home stretch of a well-known walk we'd often take, likely after a big lunch. As we came off the Berkshire Downs, passing under the grim icon of Combe Gibbet, the sky was as chalk white and flint grey as those fragments that litter up the plough. The air felt muffled and bitterly cold, and you could feel snow coming on. At the bottom of the hill, knees shaken by the steep incline and sheep ruts, we strode out onto the flat, wide track that lined up, almost, with the top of our garden in the distance. Hares were a common sight here; we could see a gathering of many some distance away, but something immediately struck us as odd. An unnerving, witchy disturbance settled on us both as we noticed a distinct formation to this gathering.

Some thirty metres away, nine hares formed an almost perfect circle, probably five metres across. And within the circle, two hares stood back to back. Was this a court passing judgement on the two in the centre, or were those two talking to the circle? We did not know.

We walked slowly ever closer, the hairs on our necks prickling and tingling, our eyes wide, our steps careful. Too close. With a discernable air of annoyance, they broke their coven at our disturbance, and each went its separate way.

We were silent. Struck dumb. Both quietly unsettled.

Thinking the same thing, we turned to each other, put our arms on each other's shoulders and swore not only had we both seen the same thing, but that should either of us tell the tale and it be doubted, we would back each other up on the truth of it. We then walked home in silence through the dusk, holding hands as the snow began to fall.

If You Haven't Tried It, Then How Do You Know You Don't Like It?

I once handed a teenager a globe artichoke. The astonished, almost scared look on their face would have not been out of place if I had handed them a pangolin.

I've taught cooking to a fair few young people over my career. But for four years, once a year, I taught at Jamie Oliver's Fifteen Foundation, and enjoyed it hugely. I'm sad that it no longer exists.

Every year the lesson unfolded the same way. I'd walk into a room of kids larking about or fiddling with their phones, a few hoods up, and the reception not exactly warm. A posh voice and a silly name serve as a cold starter. That is until I open my boxes to tip out six dead rabbits in fur or reveal a clicking, tangled mass of live crayfish, claws raised in defence against a strange new world.

'Wicked!' or 'Siiiiic!' would be their collective outburst. And the atmosphere in the room would change immediately. Those sulkier students, who tend to sit at the back, would then rise from their chairs to have a look.

I start going on about rabbits and how their summertime jiggy-jiggy makes them unpleasant to eat, and start to hear giggles; how the watercress and wild garlic I've bought along were pulled up near the crayfish, a meal produced from an hour spent outside, and now I have their total concentration.

I explain about the invasion of these American signal crayfish. 'Melt butter and declare war,' I say. They like it, and ask if they can come to catch crayfish with me. I tell them that if they come then it might mess up their trainers but that I will have a think. (We did in fact later offer just such a trip as a prize for best student.)

29

Unwrapping the fish, I explain mackerel can be caught using flowers superglued onto hooks ... and all of a sudden the phones are ignored. When possible, I want them to eat things raw before they're cooked and explain the differences they notice between the chillies they try. Most of them want a go at grasping the crayfish without getting nipped, while another backs away: 'No way, man, no way! I is not touching that!' Others are already trying to skin the rabbits before I've even explained how.

They're IN!

While claws and fur are helpful, storytelling is key.

I never remembered much from my years of history lessons, but what I do remember is everything taught me by Mr Parks. His King Harold never just got an arrow in the eye. No. There was a spurt of blood, a tumble under the pounding hooves, mud flying as the battle clanged around. The breath of his princes' stank with rotten meat while the great hall smelt of roasting boar, leather, spilt mead and dog farts. He was an eighties precursor to *Horrible Histories* and I looked forward to his lessons.

Kids like stories, as they embroider and illuminate otherwise dogmatic lists of facts. Stories are more personal, convey more care, and keep the orator as entertained as the student. What better place to find never-ending stories than in nature and food, that the link between them be planted deeply?

In their pairs, they interpret the cooking instruction I've shown them.

'Valentine can I put hot sauce in mine?'

'Of course you can.'

They want to know of the stranger things I've eaten. An easy win.

Timid at worst, straight in at best, by the end of these cooking sessions they'd be eating boiled crayfish, rabbit stew and fried mackerel and, better still, they enjoy them. They taste each other's cooking, mark each other with tenderness and teasing. Always a hard start, it was always a good end.

As I left that final class, I told them that by not paying attention to food and nature, or not looking after their world, they might find themselves trying to spit roast their Nike trainers over a small fire of melting iPhones, crouched together on a bald rock.

'Oi, mate! You're crazy!' they jeered warmly and, to tell the truth, I was sad to leave them.

Kids of a young age, while often squeamish, will one hopes become inquisitive as they get older. Yet I often witness quite the reverse. I've frequently found, with all types of kids, but more in urban society, that to be adventurous or to ask questions is to be a smart arse; to enjoy something new, superior; while not knowing is failure. So better just keep quiet. In this edited world of aspiration and success, failure particularly seems to rock confidence in a way it should not. What a shame, as Christ only knows how many disasters I've cooked over time. So I think it important, outside any hilarity, to share such catastrophes.

That cooking is no longer taught in schools I find madness. Cooking is a life skill. If you can't cook, you are not a grown up and that's that. Self-sufficiency not dial-up convenience.

Teach computer sciences, teach Mandarin and Spanish, teach them to look after their money, teach them that their wits, charm, manners and common sense will get them further than they ever used too, but don't leave out cooking. Just call it Nature and Flames, as who wants to sign up for Home Economics?

'How do you spell satsuma?' asks my son, as he pens out his Christmas list for Santa.

'Why?' I ask.

'Because I want to tell him please can he not put one in my stocking.'

My children live in the Spanish Pyrenees, where cooking is a large part of everyday life. Their mother insists they sit at the table to eat three times a day. I agree with this. They live in an almond orchard where last week the farmer unloaded a boar he'd shot. They are growing up to the sound of sheep bells. So I will not worry yet.

Crumbed Bone Marrow

To my delight, I found bone marrows in Waitrose. Supermarket equals 'accessible' – a word I dislike as it tends to make all books and recipes supermarket driven, but hey ho!

Anyway, publishers like it, and I like marrow. Everyone wins, so into the book it goes.

Serves 6 as a side for beef; 2 for a main
40 g/1½ oz/⅔ cup shelled walnuts
6 x 15 cm/6 in beef or veal marrow bones, sawn lengthways
30 g/1 oz /1 cup dry, loose proper white or sourdough breadcrumbs
Zest of half a small unwaxed lemon, finely grated, plus wedges, to serve
2 tbsp baby capers
2 garlic cloves
25 g/1 oz fresh parsley, finely chopped
25 g/1 oz fresh tarragon, finely chopped
25 g/1 oz/⅔ cup Parmesan cheese, finely grated
Lemon, cut into wedges
Sea salt and freshly ground black pepper
1 punnet of watercress, to serve
Dijon mustard, to serve (optional)

Preheat the oven to 180°C fan/200°C/400°F/gas mark 6.

In a small dry pan, roast the walnuts until darkened, but not burnt. Allow to cool and then finely chop to the size of mouse teeth, but not to dust.

Put the marrow bones flat side facing up. Season well with salt and roast for 20 minutes or until the pinkness has most gone from the marrow.

While the marrow bones are roasting, mix the breadcrumbs in a bowl with all the other ingredients, including the toasted walnuts but except for the watercress. Squeeze over the juice of one or two lemon wedges to sharpen the mix and season.

Take 3 tablespoons of the rendered marrow fat, and mix it through the crumb mix.

Load the mixture onto the marrow bones and stack loosely. Don't pat it down. Roast for another 10 minutes or so, or until browned and crispy.

Serve with the watercress, lemon wedges and perhaps some Dijon mustard.

Coconut

While I'm grumbling about something as I put the children's breakfast on the table, my son, aged five, catches my gaze with a fixed stare. He says resolutely, 'You crack the nut, you drink the juice.'

Coffee comes out my mouth, I laugh so hard.

I don't know which of us says it more now.

Butterscotch Pancakes with Hazelnuts

Serves 4

150 g/5½ oz/1 cup plus 2 tbsp plain (all-purpose) flour, sieved

1 large pinch of sea salt

300 ml/10 fl oz/1¼ cups semi-skimmed (low-fat) milk

2 large eggs

25 g/1 oz/2 tbsp butter, plus extra for frying

For the sauce

2 large handfuls of hazelnuts, finely chopped or blitzed

Finely grated zest of half an unwaxed lemon (optional)

150 g/5½ oz/¾ cup caster (superfine) sugar

75 g/2 oz/⅓ cup fridge-cold butter, chopped in small chunks

125 ml/4 fl oz/½ cup double (heavy) cream, plus extra for serving
   (optional)
1½ tbsp whisky

Place the flour into a bowl. Add the salt and then whisk in the milk. Beat in the eggs vigorously and thoroughly.

Melt the butter in the large non-stick frying pan (skillet) you are going to use to cook the pancakes. Remove from the heat and beat it into the batter mix. Pop the mixture in to the fridge until cold.

While the batter is cooling in the fridge, heat a dry pan over medium heat and toast the chopped nuts and lemon zest, if using, constantly swirling them about. Toast until deep golden in colour, and put to one side.

Pour the sugar into a small clean saucepan. Add enough water to cover it. Place over a high heat, and as soon as it starts to turn brown at the edges, start swirling it. Take the colour to a deep nut brown. Whisk in the cold butter, then pour in the cream, whisking all the time. Stir in the whisky and set aside.

Preheat the frying pan and flick a dot of butter into it. Swirl the sizzling butter around the pan.

Add a ladle of pancake batter and rotate the pan so it goes right out to the curve of the pan edges. Fry until patches of deep gold appear and it crisps at the edges. While it is cooking, smear the top of the pancake with a bit more butter, then flip and cook as you have the other side.

Move to a plate and smear generously with the butterscotch sauce. Fold in half, and fold again into a triangle. Dust with the toasted hazelnuts and splash over a little extra cream, if you like.

Repeat with the remaining batter.

Christmouse

None of the Warner men has ever exactly been famous for saying the right things at the right time. More likely, they will say the first thing that comes to mind. I do however feel it important to add, so as not to draw a line through us, we are capable of occasional fits of sympathy.

Christmas time 1987, like every other Warner Christmas was hectic as expected. Guests staying, drinks, parties, and a lot of food to prepare. I'd never describe such a time of year, as those famous carols propose, as still, silent or peaceful. Mind you, come 12.30 am, leaving the cold church for a colder night, a shake of the vicar's hand and feet crunching on the gravel under the twinkling stars, *that* was the dot of peace we were yearly afforded.

Christmas Day mid-morning and we heard hysterical shrieking coming from the other end of the house. So alarming was this shrieking that my brother and father and I dashed to the kitchen and, on bursting through the door, were met by the sight of my mother, tears pouring down her cheeks, wearing oven mitts and holding a tray of spitting, hot goose, doing a demented can-can in front of the Aga, wide eyed in terror.

I remember that mask of horror as she furiously shot out a leg towards the fridge, simultaneously yelling and sobbing, 'Fred, there's a mouse in my trousers, its gone right up inside!' before breaking out in another frantic leg kick and sobs.

With a look of consternation, my father simply replied, 'Christ, we'd better send the cat up.'

My brother and I burst into giggles and my mum into a full flood of tears. Perversely, this comment had the desired effect. Her fury at such wild insensitivity saw her leg lash out again, most likely to kick my father, and the tiny petrified mouse, its teeny claws dislodged from a 100-denier gusset by sheer force and fury, jettisoned from Mum's trouser leg at high speed, hitting the fridge door with critical impact and a barely audible tiny thud. It fell to the floor and lay there briefly before dragging itself under the fridge and out of sight.

My mum was furious.

I got it into my mind that, because of this episode, Mum left the house and drove to Greenham Common, only returning to pack more clothes. I have since been corrected. 'I did indeed go to Greenham Common that year, but out of interest, darling, not to provide you with a better story.'

Rats! How inconvenient.

The mouse died in the darkness. Its last revenge, a terrible little pong emanating from beneath the fridge.

Duck with Potatoes

Perfect for two, I cook this often. Make sure the rack in the oven is clean as you will be putting the duck directly on it with the potatoes underneath.

Serves 2

6 medium potatoes such as yellow Cyprus, scrubbed and sliced
   lengthways
1 large onion, halved and thinly sliced in semi-circles
20 garlic cloves, halved
2 tbsp olive oil, plus extra for rubbing
1 duckling (*not* a full-size duck)
1 tsp dried rosemary
½ tsp dried oregano
½ tsp dried sage
25 g /1 oz fresh curly parsley, chopped
Sea salt and freshly ground black pepper

Arrange the racks in the oven so that the duckling sits as high up as possible. If you have two racks, put the second just low enough that it can fit the oven tray for the potatoes with a 5-cm/2-in gap. If there's only the one rack, then the potato tray can simply sit on the bottom of the oven with the rack for the duckling at mid-height.

Preheat the oven to 140°C fan/160°C/325°F/gas mark 3.

Mix the sliced potatoes with a little salt, the onions and garlic cloves in a roasting tray. Turn 2 teaspoons of olive oil through it all.

Rub the duckling all over with a small splash of olive oil, then scatter all over with the dried herbs and a generous amount of salt – at least 1 teaspoon, don't be shy. Put the duckling directly on the rack, and the potatoes directly underneath, so that the fat drips into the potatoes, not on to the oven, where it will smoke and cause a mess that you will not appreciate having to clean!

Roast the duckling for 45 minutes before turning the heat up to 180°C fan/ 200°C/400°F/gas mark 6 and then cooking until crisp – about 30 minutes.

The potatoes will need turning often, so that the duck fat coats them, the garlic doesn't burn and the onions and potatoes take on a lovely golden colouring and a kind of squidgy crispness ... if that makes sense.

Remove the duckling from the oven and allow to rest for 7–10 minutes, leaving the potatoes to roast on.

Remove the potatoes and stir the chopped parsley through them.

Carve the duckling and serve on top of the potato.

Serve with French mustard, and eat with a good bottle of aired red Burgundy. You will need its mineral edge and rapier slashes to cut the fat.

Lance

Although a popular and successful diplomat, my father was probably of some frustration to the Foreign Office.

Keen to find out what was going on in the surrounding communities, mountains or wherever, once he had quickly settled into his post, he then thought his time far better spent outside the office than in it.

Dad was restless and inquisitive, and so it came as no surprise to recently see a black and white photo of him, dressed in linen trousers and white shirt, receiving a gift from tiny village elders in the middle of the Laotian jungle. Six foot five Dad almost resembles Gulliver in Lilliput, his forehead level with the top of the hut he stands beside.

He would have found today's continual stream of emails most frustrating. Back then, you were chosen for the very reason that you were trusted to make the correct decision as a representative for your country without constant interference from back home.

'To understand anywhere,' he'd say, 'if you see a little path wiggling off to a curious place you must go down it and see where it leads. Treat a goatherd as you would a king, and your life will be more rewarding.'

My father told many stories of his adventures, all of which took place in a time when it would seem the world was travelled more safely and freely than seems possible today. One such story would get him into a state of high excitement as he approached the punch line, simply because he knew how much it thrilled my brother and I. It's a silly story really, but how we would howl with laughter. What's more, as a deeply serious and acrobatically intelligent man, I loved that he could be such fun, and indeed silly, as well.

Dad was built for the tropics; he was very strong, had the constitution of an ox, and a permanent biscuit-coloured tan that blocked out the sun, which served him well as the Chargé d'Affaires in Burma in the fifties.

A spell in Moscow had taught him that most symptoms of ailment could be seen off with a measure of spirits. He didn't suffer from hangovers (which was handy for outdrinking Russians not inclined to divulge anything until drunk), and with little effort was one of the fittest men I've ever known.

Were you to find him covered in bleeding scratches inflicted from a 'walk' that included getting lost and ended in sharing a delicious morsel with a bewildered goatherd, you would see him at his happiest.

With this seemingly endless energy, enthusiasm and excitement, a man of stamina, he didn't suffer laziness or 'limp wristedness', as he called it. And this saw him somewhat frustrated by Under Secretaries sent out to him from London. 'Pale and wimpy, they'd eat something and within hours fall to pieces,' he'd tell me. 'Either that or they simply couldn't take the climate. Floppy and damp things, they would fold up like bath towels no sooner had they stepped off the plane.'

So one is returned and another 'string-like fellow' is collected from the airport. I've called him Lance, in the same way my father seemed to change the name each time the story was told.

Lance got off to a good start, but when removed outdoors from under the muggy movements of overhead fans, soon looked no more qualified than his predecessor. As predicted, he quickly fell victim to the inevitable stomach complaints and a clammy forehead, but he nevertheless made noted efforts to remain useful. So, since he was looking increasingly miserable, Dad decided to prescribe him a night out in Rangoon where he'd heard Helga, an Austrian roller-skating giantess, was performing to sell-out crowds.

Likely insisting they should eat and with a restorative glass or two drunk, they later found themselves sitting in a ring of seats within an excitable crowd as the lights dimmed.

Lance was quiet and ashen when Helga zoomed into the room. As Dad put it, 'She was huge, at least seven foot tall, dressed in a white leotard and sequins with great Danish pastries of hair plaited on each side of her head. Both fearsome and attractive she circled the crowd fixing each of us with a stern gaze ...'

Helga leapt, jumped, pirouetted, juggled, cartwheeled and overall amazed. And, come the final act, skirting the rink in casual loops as she inspects the crowd, she shouts out: 'I vont a volunteer.'

Lance, arms folded and shrinking at the utterance, tucked his head down just as Helga zipped by. And, seeing this, with a strong arm she wrenched the wretched Secretary from his chair. Standing him up in front of all, she took him by both hands and, moving backwards, dragged him into the centre of the rink to announce, '*Die Windmuhle!*' ('The Windmill!'). Lance glanced back toward my father with a look of pleading terror.

His wrists clamped in her hands, Lance found himself forced to turn with tiny steps as she skated around him and, just as he stumbled, unable keep up with the speed, his feet flew off the floor and straight into a flat spin.

Faster and faster they went until, 'soon they were simply a sparkly blur of sequins and brogues.' The speed was apparently jaw dropping.

But in the eye of the cyclone, it was all too much for Lance. His nausea and poor stomach could take no more. With his wrists locked fast, the rest of him simply let go.

'And from his trouser legs, anyone close enough to take the force of it was sprayed in a terrible mist of shit!'

So there you have it. What recipe would you like after that?

Rebel Pizza

Over my time in restaurants, working here and there, I became very interested in that overlooked caste of the kitchen underdog, the dishwashers.

99.9% of the time, they were foreign and, generally speaking, worked damn hard. They were grafters. Most of them came from humble backgrounds, trying to make a better life for themselves in London or wherever they found themselves. Sometimes with their families, most of the time they were separated from them.

There were some though who looked curiously out of place, and it was likely they were older. Two in particular: a sixty year old who'd been the head of economics in an Eastern European college during the war in Yugoslavia, the other a solicitor from South America – both had fled their respective countries to wear Marigolds and aprons while younger chefs with shitty attitudes rudely bombarded them with dirty pans and took the piss out of them with stereotypical crass humour.

It saddened me to see the mix of pain, cracked smiles and the toleration it demanded.

In the changing room, a very silent Somali man I got on well with, while changing his jacket, revealed the most horrific and brutal assortment of scars I thought it better to not question.

While I chatted with them often, I knew very, very little of their lives, perhaps drawing the wrong conclusions from the bit I did know. Many wonderful stories, normally reminiscences of life before their new-found discomfort, masked a lot of sadness that once or twice turned into tearful eruptions of anger. The worst I witnessed was while working in Dubai.

I took it upon myself to act with particular respect towards those at the sink. A two-way thing, they were good allies to have as they made my own kitchen life easier in return.

Two such had done better for themselves, working above ground and as pizzaiolas for Pizza Express. As an art student working in the Islington branch, I befriended Hassan and Mehmet. It was the nineties and I was in my early twenties. Hassan was an immensely tall, muscular, shaven-headed young man, also known as 'Hassan the Bear', the name given him back home. Mehmet was older, small, wiry and black-haired with pointy features and stubble that certified a thorough shave was required at least once daily. Friends from the same village in Kurdistan, in their Pizza Express uniform and paper hats they'd most likely always be seen making pizzas together, side by side as they preferred to be. I liked them a lot and the feelings were mutual I think.

Asking them why they had come to London, they said because of the fighting, that as younger men they'd had to leave. 'We will go home soon and fight,' they would say with increasing frequency. They were proud Kurds, bright eyed and joyful, despite their worries. They told me many times of their beautiful hills and mountains, delicious food and how much they deeply missed it.

'You will be our guest one day, you must come,' they'd offer with sincere generosity. 'You may meet nice Kurdish girl. Nice girl like Alice [the waitress they knew I fancied rotten]. Hassan, Mehmet, crazy Val, we all live there together, no?' they'd say.

One night after work I was handed a bag of Betamax videos and told to watch them but not share them and that I must give them back the following morning. All of them!

'Why?' I asked.

'Watch,' they said. 'You ask us a lot about our country and then we have question for you.'

So I went home and watched some of the footage (as, luckily enough, I was one of the few who'd also backed the wrong horse and gone for Betamax over VHS). The content was similar throughout, militia walking in silence along broken tracks against a stunning backdrop of trees and grand mountains. I distinctly remember the radio operator in one, the long bent aerial bouncing out to the side of him as the group trudges through dust. Then all hell breaks loose. There is crackling gun fire and the video violently shakes around as the cameraman breaks into a run. There is a lot of shouting, the filming pretty blurry and unwatchable but for snippets of recognizable chaos, the scramble of feet or someone returning fire. In one, someone is screaming off camera and it's pretty obvious they're hurt. Collectively the videos explained little more than the documented struggles between the Turks and the Kurds.

So I returned the videos and over staff dinner, an American Hot – I don't forget such things – they asked if would I put my art student skills to work and build a rallying poster for the PKK (Kurdistan Workers' Party) to be hung in the Kurdish centre which I think was in Stoke Newington.

'Sure,' I said.

I'm a naïve student, they're oppressed and the Kurdish plight is being reported often in the news. It's all the thought I seem to have given it.

So I go home for the weekend and make my poster. Using sheets of coloured sugar paper, scissors and Pritt Stick, it's a collage.

On a sky-blue backdrop there is a red star sitting in its own green circle and, in the middle of the star, a circle the size of a Royal Doulton side plate.

On it I've pasted a cut-out relief of the mountains of Kurdistan with clouds and sun behind them. Around the landscape are flames, burning out towards toward each point of the star. A bullet heads each of the five points. A dove flies out from the tip of each bullet. Underneath are three large letters, PKK, spelt in the same typeface as my Brigade Rosse The Clash T-shirt. I had no idea who the Brigade Rosse were either back then.

Riddled with clichés, certainly, as I remember it, the poster was pretty striking nonetheless.

My father sees me making this giant collage at the dining-room table and suggests I do more research before throwing myself into such things. 'Are you sure you know what you are doing?' he asks. 'Sense over enthusiasm equals?' he asks with a raised eyebrow.

Snapped into a long roll with an elastic band, back in London I take my poster into work and hand it over to Mehmet and Hassan. They do not unroll it on the white marble dough top or on a table in front of the other staff but are thrilled and invite me the following week to visit the Kurdish centre. They've already arranged I get the same day off as them.

The Kurdish centre is busy when Hassan and Mehmet introduce me, and there is a feverish shaking of hands or patting the palm to the chest with a nod and smiles. Most people we come into contact with seem aware of my commission. I'm then shown my poster. It's Blu-Tacked to the wall high up for all to see. Everyone seems genuinely chuffed with it and I suddenly realize I haven't got a clue about what I've involved myself in, outside of friendship.

We sit at a table and drink weapons-grade small coffees and eat flatbreads and lamb koftes. I'm looked at a lot while they speak Kurdish. I feel self-conscious. Nearby a small group is gathered on plastic chairs around a radio while a fax machine 'chizz chizzez' out a message which is torn off, read and delivered with some urgency to our table. Hassan sees I'm confused by it all and tells me fighting around his area is bad and they've been by the fax for days.

And that's kind of it. I leave as they all huddle up close over their coffees again. Within days, as you will read later, I get fired from Pizza Express. I go back a month or two later to eat with friends and ask after Hassan and Mehmet, who are not there spinning dough.

The manager tells me they've left. Alice the waitress, plugging 50p into the jukebox to play Bassomatic's 'Fascinating Rhythm', for what must now be her five-hundredth or so time, informs me more specifically that they have gone back to fight and that she misses them.

I feel very sad.

Good luck Hassan.

Good luck Mehmet.

I wonder if my now-sun bleached bullet star still hangs somewhere in London.

Fired

Sometime in the early nineties, a sofa-surfing art student, watching the mid-afternoon Western, plate of crackers and Primula cheese spread (prawn flavour, I think it important to add) resting on my chest, I thought, 'Christ I've got to get a job.' I rolled off the sofa, brushed off the crumbs and tiptoed across a carpet strewn with sleeveless vinyl.

I walked into Pizza Express and asked to see the manager. I was sat down with a coffee and, after a few sips, I had a waiting job. I returned home triumphant. My housemates all laughed at me and immediately started shouting, 'One Margarita and dough balls, pronto.' 'Idiots,' I thought.

Soon after starting, on a hot summer's day two women arrived for lunch. I think they could be best described as the kind of friends or sisters that might be found in a Roald Dahl novel. One all elbows and nose, a kind of walking coat hanger. The other, an immense woman, who following the path of most resistance, barged through the jungle of red chairs like an elephant through the undergrowth .... but less graceful.

Seated, they were in my section. Notepad in hand, I bounced over to serve them.

They ordered their pizzas, I served them their pizzas, I cleared away their pizzas. Business as usual.

A stout arm was raised.

'How can I help you madam?' I enquired.

'Well,' she said, 'I'll have one chocolate fudge cake and one strawberry cheesecake.'

The absence of her friend would suggest she'd repaired to the Ladies'. But ... out of sight, out of mind! And, with what I honestly thought was a deeply practical and helpful suggestion, replied, 'And would you like those both in the same bowl?'

'What did you say?' she roared.

Deeply perplexed and anxious, with an inkling something had gone wrong, and in defence of what I thought to be considerate service, I repeated myself just as her friend reappeared through the door.

It all got rather heated. The woman repeated my impertinence to a nearly sympathetic manager who, purse-lipped, was barely able to keep himself from giggling. It was awful.

In the back office and leaning into the wall, my manager was crying with laughter. I wasn't.

'You're crazy, you're very crazy,' he said. Something I've never liked being called.

'I'm not crazy, I'm leaving,' I said.

He agreed it might not be such a bad idea, saying that over the past couple of weeks he'd thought that perhaps waitering was the wrong line of work for me.

The next day I started at a different branch of Pizza Express in West London and promptly dropped a tray of wine glasses in the first ten minutes.

Cut from the Same Napkin

My daughter is full of pie, she's had thirds and is tucked up in bed and settling into drowsiness. I stroke her head and say, 'Daddy is going downstairs now to make a cup of tea and warm up the rest of that chicken pie.'

'Not the chicken pie,' she says, mustering a droopy-eyed stare and a surprisingly strong grip on my wrist.

'Choose something else,' she whispers. 'Just not that chicken pie.' And then falls asleep.

That's definitely my girl!

For What We Are About to Receive

Bless my grandmother, but she was not the kind to knit you a jumper, share secrets, give you sweets and cook a lovely roast. While I loved her, she'd decided to lock away fun and the world, replacing it with devout faith. One of Mary Baker Eddy's crack troops, she was a militant Christian Scientist.

I can vouch that none of my own joy in eating could be ascribed to my grandmother, except perhaps my joy at being clever with leftovers. Perhaps I inherited a bit of that from her. She was very frugal ... to say the least.

Her devout faith meant that food to her was primarily sustenance and little more. She regarded our approach to eating as overindulgent and frivolous, endeavouring to improve us fractionally by insisting upon saying grace when she came to stay.

These visits were gloomy times. My favourite programmes *Monkey* and *The Dukes of Hazard* were deemed 'wicked and unkind'. She would turn off the telly, open her *Christian Science Monitor* and make us, furious and fidgety, sit through its teachings. On saying goodbye, she'd occasionally give us a five pound note from her three-fingered left hand, probably, over time, working out at about 20p per reading.

She did not enjoy cooking remotely. My brother and sister and I did not appreciate her food when staying with her. Her dog Poly was the best-fed soul in her house. It seems mean to say it but I was likely more jealous of Poly's food. Those tender rabbit chunks with chicken jelly ... Although my grandmother was a vegetarian, one who survived on a diet of Polos, taken hourly, she was a vegetarian who could always be counted on to order breaded plaice if eating out.

What used to fascinate me was the inside of her fridge. Unlike Polos, a box of Black Magic was an extravagance not to be eaten in one sitting. She would nibble a half of one chocolate, then wrap it up in clingfilm (plastic wrap) and pop it in the fridge to be enjoyed at a later date. Weeks away.

Next to the box of Black Magic would be green eggs (not with ham), some stale sliced bread and a jar of marmalade. Otherwise it was as bare as the Arctic. I had a vivid dream about her once. She was sitting downstairs under her chair's side standing lamp eating a pizza. Draped over her knees, it was as big as a carpet. In real life, she must have existed on virtually nothing.

On visiting her, I would be both worried and astonished to watch her eat an alarmingly discoloured boiled egg, having removed the clingfilm (plastic wrap), or pop some mouldy bread in the toaster. 'Nothing wrong with it at all,' she'd snap when I made a face. 'One should be thankful.' While I will certainly scrape a fungal bloom off the top of the jam, she took what could be scraped off to a new level. Fresh was not to be thought of as a given; fluffy penicillin-type flora were.

Once I had a job and some money, I'd insist on either eating out or shopping in the frozen section for ... breaded plaice. A few times, she caught me sorting her store cupboards and fridge and throwing stuff away. She'd get cross and upset, and say, 'I do wish you wouldn't interfere.' And then she would put the things back.

Tiny and thin as she was, she must have had the gut of an iron-smelting works as she just didn't get ill. And to her credit, her refusal of medical intervention in the place of prayer saw her accept pain relief only in her last weeks. Her faith was everything. It was remarkable and, while I do not believe in God (but for an enjoyment of taking quiet time out in churches), I have some kind of strong belief nonetheless. I thank my grandmother for that.

And I thank her for her 'absolute' that nothing, not a blue crumb, browning leaf, wrinkly carrot, fizzing tomato, weaponized plaice fillet, green egg should be wasted. Even now, thoughts of her are a yardstick for good kitchen practice. When in haste or through lack of thought, I catch myself binning something carelessly, I stop myself and think 'Mer-mer would not throw that.'

However, if I think 'Mer-mer would probably eat that,' I'll continue to scrape it in the bin.

She would be most upset to read the statistics of how much we throw away today, and rightly so. She'd pray hard and regularly that it stopped. I had the pleasure and privilege to work alongside the extraordinary Marguerite Patten on two TV programmes called *Ration Book Britain*. Marguerite had worked for the Ministry of Food during the war, and also penned well over a hundred cookery books. Both women shared the belief, purposefulness and requirement to make a little go a long way. To both of them, wartime or not, waste was simply unacceptable.

Once, chopping a carrot in front of Marguerite, I made the cut too far away from the stalk. With flashing eyes, she immediately jabbed out an arthritic finger and said, 'What's wrong with that bit? Save it!' My grandmother would have read Marguerite's books and recipe ideas during wartime, so I was sad that, when asked to include my own family in the programme, my grandmother was no longer around to contribute. She'd have had a lot to say and to talk about with Marguerite while I'd hope to see that glint and sharp wit that only very occasionally darted out across her otherwise godly manner.

My mum contributed and was fantastic.

While I snigger that my grandmother's cooking could be seen as a sin against God's creation, it was in fact quite the reverse. She just wasn't interested in food, while going out of her way to waste none. About as opposite as you can get to the blasé way we eat and treat food today. All that was missing was deliciousness.

I should end this here. But I can't write about my grandmother without mentioning one of her habits that, as a family, we've now exaggerated into an absurd joke. Whether she were in the Antarctic, with dogs barking through a whining blizzard, or in dense, sweaty jungle with Indian arrows zipping overhead, or docking '*CLANG!!!*' into the deep-space Zargon Station 6, she'd be sure to look around and say, 'This looks just like the Lakes.'

Roast Cauliflower

Serves 1, or perhaps 2
2 tbsp pine nuts
2 tbsp olive oil, plus 2 tsp
2 large good, hard garlic cloves, sliced paper thin
1 finger-length mild red chilli, halved lengthways and finely sliced
1 x 47-g/1¾-oz can salted anchovies in oil (preferably Ortiz), drained
Half medium-sized cauliflower divided in two, through the stalk
A little sunflower oil, for rubbing
25 g /1 oz bunch of fresh coriander (cilantro)
¼ tsp ground coriander
Juice of half a small lemon
Sea salt

Preheat the oven to 180°C fan/200°C/400°F/gas mark 6.

Take a small frying pan (skillet), and dry toast the pine nuts over a medium heat, swirling them often until deep golden (not brown). Tip into a small bowl.

Pour 2 tablespoons of olive oil into the same pan. Over a low–medium heat, fry the garlic and chilli until the chilli pales in colour and the garlic is cooked but not coloured. Melt the anchovies into the oil until totally collapsed, taking care not to burn the garlic.

Rub the cauliflower with the sunflower oil, season with salt and put in the oven on a metal tray to roast hard for 30 minutes or until unmistakeably golden brown all over. Turn to ensure stronger colouring on the two flat sides.

While the cauliflower cooks, very finely chop the coriander, or better still grind it to mush in a pestle and mortar, with a little sea salt. Add in a pinch of ground coriander. Mix in the lemon juice and add the remaining olive oil.

Take the roasted cauliflower to the plate.

Warm the oil again if needs be and stir the pine nuts through it. Pour this over the cauliflower and pour the coriander sauce at the base of it. Eat it.

Baked Celeriac with Romesco Sauce

Serves 2
2 medium vine tomatoes, rinsed and quartered
2 red (bell) peppers, deseeded and quartered
1 small whole garlic head, unpeeled and cut through horizontally
1 small red onion, unpeeled and quartered
150 ml/5 fl oz/⅔ cup olive oil, plus a little extra for roasting
Handful of crusty white bread, torn
1 small celeriac, peeled (see Tip)
A little sunflower oil, for rubbing
25 g/1 oz bunch of fresh sage
40 g/1½ oz/¼ cup shelled almonds or hazelnuts, or a mixture
2 tbsp sherry vinegar
1 tsp smoked sweet paprika
Sea salt

Preheat the oven to 180°C fan/200°C/350°F/gas mark 4.

Place the tomatoes, peppers, garlic and onion in a small roasting tray and add a liberal splash of olive oil. Scatter generously with salt.

Roast for 30 minutes, or until the contents of the tray are well coloured with golden brown tinges. Add the bread for the last 15 minutes, but be ready to remove at any point if it starts to become too dark. The faintest dark brown/blackening is good, but don't take it too far.

Meanwhile, divide the celeriac into 3, rub lightly but thoroughly in sunflower oil and season generously with salt. Place on a small baking tray with the sage snuggled between the pieces. Put into the oven below the tray of vegetables, moving to the top shelf when they come out. Cook for 40 minutes–1 hour, turning occasionally, until all sides are richly coloured, and blackened in places (mainly the edges).

While the celeriac cooks, pop the nuts onto a small tray and transfer to the oven and cook until deep golden, about 5 minutes or so.

Meanwhile, pinch the skins off the roasted pepper segments and tomato halves and discard. Squeeze out the garlic and discard the skins with the onion skins.

In a food processor, blitz together all the ingredients with the olive oil until as smooth as possible, before adding the vinegar and smoked paprika and blitzing again. (This can be done with a stick blender, too.) If the mixture is too thick and stiff, add a little water. It should only just hold its own, but spread with ease when pressed.

Take the roasted celeriac to a plate with any dried sage that is crisp but not too dark. Put a good amount of the sauce next to the celeriac and serve.

Tip When peeling the gnarled celeriac, you must go deep with your knife as the skin is very thick.

Earthy Veg

A late entry – I can't believe I nearly left out two of my favourite vegetables. Beware the Jerusalem artichoke! Knight of the hovering duvet.

6 Jerusalem artichokes, scrubbed
6 baby beetroots, scrubbed
Sea salt

Preheat the oven to 220°C fan/240°C/475°F/gas mark 8.

Having scrubbed the veg, place them in a roasting dish. Throw the salt all over them and roll them around in it – the water you've rinsed them in will make the salt cling. (Don't worry about the amount – a lot of it will fall off.)

Roast the vegetables like you hate them, by which I mean until dark brown and coloured, and beginning to char – you'll have to keep watch. Dress with a little extra virgin olive oil and enjoy as is.

Sink a Pint

Cleaning out my office today, I have found a picture of myself standing by some tents. I have red eye, the photo taken at night and most likely on those throwaway cameras I used to be so fond of. My legs are spread wide, my hands are clenched on each side of a gigantic pair of Y-fronts, and I'm pulling them up as high as I can over my anorak and laughing.

It was that year of the solar eclipse, 1999, and my sister invited me to go to Cornwall with her. We were camping in Prussia Cove, a most beautiful place, belonging to her friend. The idea is to enjoy the eclipse and then a party on the beach afterwards.

I in turn invited my friend Jamie. We picked him up on the way out of London. He had a duvet over his shoulder and was waving a toothbrush over his head. That was Jamie, great fun, total chaos. My sister was annoyed that he was coming. She kind of liked him but, as with everyone, you have to be in the mood for Jamie. Jamie went where the wind blew him or where a girl fluttered her eyelashes.

Arriving in Cornwall, the weather was glorious. Many had gathered for this auspicious event and soon we were all in the warm sea.

Night fell and we ate well in the kitchen. Sausages and rolls and salad, that kind of thing. Around midnight, most were dancing in the kitchen when our host came in and announced over the noise that he needed volunteers to help take the beer to the beach so it could settle overnight.

I volunteered, Jamie said he'd rather stay at the house; I told him to think differently (registering that our host was a little miffed I'd brought him along).

So it's pitch black, and Pete is very excited because he's secured two barrels of beer from the local brewery, two barrels from a small batch made only once a year or something to that tune, and it's very hard to get even one barrel, let alone two. We don't know how lucky we are, etc. etc. I'm looking forward to it too. It's called something like Nettle Rash or Wizard's Sleeve or something along those lines.

In his Land Rover, we bounce down a coastal track with the barrels nestled in a large blanket. We stop, get out, heave them over a wall and then start to roll them down a narrow footpath with a sharp drop into the sea on our right. Moving slowly, the barrels are touching and rolling together, Jamie at the front, me at the back and Pete ahead lighting the way with one of those big, black, rubber torches farmers like.

Jamie stops. 'I need to readjust,' he says tugging on his jumper.

'NO DON'T!' I bark and it's all downhill from there. For a split second too long, his sudden fidgeting combined with neither of my hands on the back barrel sees them both swivel in unison and roll off the edge of the path.

And away they go out of view but momentarily, then found by torchlight as they hit a tussocky rock ledge and with an odd dull *goyoing* to then lift off into the inky black. There is a short silence amplified by dread and then kersploosh! kersplosh!

I remembered being called a stupid ***** and ******** and 'You two are complete ******* **** *****!' Thinking of those expletive speech bubbles of fists, skulls and thunder from an *Asterix* comic, I remember desperately trying not to laugh as, like my father, I'm prone to inappropriate giggles.

'What on earth were you doing,' I say, attempting to throw it at Jamie, 'trying to take you're jumper off?!'

It was a very bumpy ride home, angry driving, cross darkness. Everyone was still dancing when the lights were flicked on and it's announced to all what 'complete ****** idiots, these two are.'

My sister is mortified, the uninvited guest more uninvited than ever.

Party over, we all go to our rooms or tents. 6 am and I wake Jamie and make him get up. We walk back to the site for the party and traverse the pathway scanning the water, which is thankfully clear. For an hour we trudge up and down, hands shading our eyes as we hopefully look to the sea. It's hopeless.

'Come on, let's go home,' Jamie says. 'I'm tired.'

I want to thump him. 'Err... you appear to have mistaken me for someone who gives a shit. I'll give you tired,' I say. 'No way we aren't going to find those barrels. We are not going anywhere until we do.'

Then two things happen that I can only put down to some kind of divine intervention. No sooner have I uttered the word 'do' than, like a giant stage curtain, the seaweed below us swishes to one side to reveal the barrels glinting in the sun. We stare at each other, grinning like idiots. But they are too deep and too heavy to recover.

Divine intervention two happens when a squat blond man in blue budgie smugglers, lean and muscular with a grappling sort of physique, walks past. And, will you believe me if I tell you, hooked over his head and across his beautiful chest is a good thirty foot or so of coiled rope? The golden rope of salvation carried by a wondering hero.

'Hi,' I say, 'If I give you a tenner will you dive for those barrels?' I ask.

'Nope' he says.

'Twenty?'

'Nope.'

'Twen...'

'Let me stop you there,' he says. 'Thirty, and it's a deal.'

I ask Jamie if he's got any money on him. Of course he hasn't. Stupid question. So I pay up. And Baywatch dives in and saves both barrels. We load them onto the drystone wall where rocks have been removed and inlayed with moss to support them.

The barrels are a bit bashed and dented but okay. My host is calmer and I feel we are semi-forgiven. We walk to the beach. The eclipse is starting, the seabirds are squawking and anxious as we all stand there in our special glasses, looking up like the front of some eighties album cover.

The sun returns, the birds settle and Pete starts grumbling about the beer. 'Go look over there,' I say. The eclipse is eclipsed. I cook 80 mackerel over the fire and all is good.

Hedge-stuffed Mackerel

Serves 2

2 whole very fresh, iridescent blue-green shiny, stiff mackerel (not sunken-eyed and gloomy grey), gutted with gills removed

As many of the following you can find would be good: Large handful of watercress, taken from a fast-flowing bit of water, thoroughly washed in salty water and chopped very fine; Small handful of the smaller wild chervil leaves (cow parsley leaves), chopped very fine; Small handful of wild garlic leaves and flowers, thoroughly washed in salty water; Handful of wild fennel fronds and some seeds or flowers if possible; Handful of sheep's sorrel; Handful of black mustard leaf

1 tbsp Alexander seeds

2 heaped tsp hot horseradish sauce or Dijon mustard

75 g/2½ oz/¾ stick softened butter
A small handful of stale breadcrumbs (optional)
Zest and juice of quarter of a lemon
Oil, for rubbing
Sea salt and good grind of black pepper

Prepare your fire, or turn the grill (broiler) on to full heat.

Place the mackerel on a board and wipe down both sides with paper towel. Taking a sharp knife, cut from the tail to the head, keeping the knife flat against the spine. Snip out the whole spine and tail and discard. You will now have a head with two flappy fillets attached.

In a bowl, put the chopped greens and Alexander seeds, the horseradish or Dijon mustard and the butter and roughly blitz together. Stir in the breadcrumbs, if using. Grate in the lemon zest and squeeze in the lemon juice. Stir it through and season with pepper and salt.

Open the mackerel and thickly spoon the stuffing into the middle. Tie the mackerel behind the head in the middle and near the tail with three lengths of kitchen string. Lightly oil and season the skin side.

Grill on both sides until brown and blistered. Eat with new potato salad.

La Strega – a Witch Song

During my time at art college – in my second year I think, just before a term end – I somewhat surprisingly, certainly for my frustrated tutors, was offered a month scholarship to the Brera Academy in Milan.

I'd sent off a painting, and had received a letter. The academy would be delighted to further my portrait-painting skills under their famous guidance.

I was thrilled but nervous to go alone, as yet to find confidence and a somewhat awkward twenty-something. I accepted.

It was a fractious time in Italy's political shenanigans, with accusations of corruption wobbling or toppling many an administrative or associate. A lot of finger-pointing in exchange for lenience. It certainly made life interesting, as I seem to remember, and the principal of the college himself was in trouble. 'Out for a very long lunch,' I recall someone joking.

Subsequently, on my first day, no one seemed to be expecting me nor had any idea what to do with me. My letter of acceptance only met with sucking teeth and a perplexed shaking of the head. I was passed around and around with the letter until one teacher, with the sweep of the arm and a grimace, reluctantly gestured for me to help myself to the place and left the room.

Teachers over all seemed thin on the ground and it struck me over my first week that some of the 'students' were no more than enterprising pedestrians using the college facilities without any worry of detection.

The courtyard, a gathering place, was full of far more overtly confident students than myself. The girls chewing gum and flirting with the boys, who all had mopeds. I remember the wallflower I felt.

I found it hard to be noticed but one Italian girl, Maria, who observing two days of my loitering and glances, decided to take me under her wing, show me around town and eat lunch with me a few times. She spoke great English.

I fancied her so much I couldn't speak. Not particularly exciting company. After two days, she became unavailable.

Every night I'd wander back to my apartment, eating in the same restaurant on the way, ordering tagliatelle with porcini and garlic sausage sauce. Thinking back, already deeply interested in food and a mad keen cook, I was most uninquisitive, given my location.

One night I thought to myself, 'Bugger this, I'm not going back to the apartment.' It was stark, empty of pictures, strip lit and had furniture that scraped and clattered on the marble floor throughout its tiny space. Typically

Italian, as I've come to understand. It was cold and only amplified feelings of loneliness. In my mind my father would have felt disappointed by such inactivity.

'Go and know the world, understand this time that sees you here.'

'Come on Val,' I thought to myself.

It was a Tuesday evening and, avoiding my usual route back to the flat, I'd soon found a street that seemed to be solely the territory of soothsayers and mystics, tarot reading and palmistry. Traversing its length, unconvinced by tilted fedoras and beckoning curls of a finger, I ignored those who I decided were bogus or clichéd.

I walked it twice and, about to turn out of it, at the end of the street I noticed an immensely large woman sitting on a box, her round face startling, actually unnerving, due to the thick application of white foundation. She wore crimson lipstick and a huge mink coat. Odder than her overall look, was a pair of huge Onassis-style sunglasses sitting tight round her face. It was night-time.

I had no wish to see behind those sunglasses then, and still don't.

She had a card table in front of her, cut to knee height. The three women with her seemed to be there to make sure her every need was tended to. An entourage.

'Do you speak English?' I enquired. 'Inglesi?' I followed on clumsily.

'Yes' she said.

'Will you see me?'

'Only if you take out the earrings,' she replied flicking a pudgy finger in their direction.

'What difference does it make if I wear them or not?'

'What difference if I read you or not?' she returned, gruff and impatient.

Fair enough.

I took them out, two small hoops from my left ear. One silver, one gold. I put them in my pocket and waited.

'Would you like nice, or all?'

I presumed 'nice' to mean unchallenging.

'You tell me,' I answered, feeling somewhat confrontational.

'Difficult,' she said laying out the cards

The first card was a house on fire.

'You live with three other boys,' she rightly claimed, 'you are not happy there, you have outgrown them.' 'When you return, next week,' (this was odd as I was meant to be in Milan for three more weeks) 'soon you will be fighting. These friends are no more for you.'

The next card, as I faintly recall, had a maiden, or at least as I remember it, with yellow hair.

'You will meet someone. She is not English. She will be your first love.'

'Yeah right' I thought cynically ... but 'great!' I thought hopefully.

I cannot remember the symbol on the next card, but things took a sharp down turn.

'Your father is living in Italy, no?'

'Yes,' I said. 'In Rome.'

'He is apart from your mother. They are both sad.'

I was troubled to hear this but thought this was probably true.

'Your father will soon become ill. He will pass.'

'Enough,' I said irritably, upon which she laid a hand on mine. Oddly calmed, I remained seated and she continued.

Walking home that night I felt terribly lonely, and the next day decided not to attend college as I had a splitting headache. An axe in the skull, that I could only imagine was a migraine. I have never had one since.

Rudderless, I would probably not see out my time in the academy. I would decide in the next few days.

This is where it gets very weird. Some days later I received a postcard from my mother. It read something to the effect of:

'Darling Val, I hope Milan is going well.

The reason why I am writing to you is because last night (Tuesday) I had a dream about you and tried to call you today but you were not in ... What was so significant about the dream was that you'd taken your earrings out. This was so vivid that it prompted this card.'

I returned home the following week.

I almost immediately met an American girl, fell out badly with my housemates and moved. My parents told me together that my father had terminal cancer and about a year to live. He came home from Italy.

I never wore those earrings again.

We are best to forget such things as fortunes told. We are not meant to live by them. I have never used them to find hope in low moments. I have forgotten what she went on to tell me about the rest of my life. Perhaps I will remember when these punctuations crop up. This is the right way. Love, dispute, death, work, children, hope, struggle, the preoccupying flow of existence has thankfully faded the forecast.

Often as I write, I'm inclined to look up towards the empty corner of the room and say 'Hi' out loud to my father. He visits from time to time.

An Aside

I was born in 1972 and asigned to five godparents, George Weidenfeld the publisher and Picasso's engraver Aldo Crommelynck, among them. Three out of five were Jewish.

This raised an issue with the Church of England. As kind, accepting and forgiving as we are meant to believe them, they refused three such godparents on the grounds they couldn't make the appropriate vows.

My father, ever the quick thinker, called in on the Greek Orthodox church on Moscow Road in West London. He explained his dilemma.

Simple, they said. A donation towards gilding the ceiling, and we'll see you all on Wednesday.

Last Suppers

My father spent his last week alive at home with all of us around him, plus his best friend Harry (see page 198), who'd come from America and was staying in a hotel just around the corner. We knew what to expect and, for the main part, treated each other with tenderness and delicacy, despite the devastation, strain, and our very separate thoughts as children or spouse.

Keen to give him something special, I cooked him dinner one night, making him a little salad of beans with walnut vinaigrette and a dish I'd seen Keith Floyd cook and would often repeat for myself.

It was a beaten out escalope of veal lined with Parma ham and two sage leaves, a fat peeled langoustine in the middle, all rolled up and stuck with a tooth pick and sautéed in butter. The sauce was finished with cream and marsala. The veal was sliced in little rounds and prettified with a feather of chervil. I took it in to him on a tray.

He smiled weakly and attempted to eat a few bites but could not finish it.

The day after, my brother and I were required to bathe him, a not so easy task as, although able to move his legs, he needed supporting in and out of the bath. He was 6ft 5.

I will never forget the touching remembrance of my father in the shallow warm water, his grey hair floating out around his head, staring at us, blinking, a very gentle sweet smile on his face. It was similar to bathing an infant, that look, one of helplessness, trust, and a nervousness of the element it cannot command. Our trouser legs rolled up so we could work around him, it was a preparation for death and 78 years after his baptism.

We lifted him up, dried him, and returned him to his bed.

That evening, my mother made him dinner but, delirious with morphine, he rejected it.

'But Fred, it's important that you eat,' she said.

'Nonsense,' he replied. 'Neither my troops nor I have eaten between the Battle of Bosworth or Agincourt, and we are all perfectly fine.'

It was sad, but at the end of his bed, we laughed, and with love.

Overcome by watching someone so slowly 'move through', I needed a break and left the house the following day for a friend's down the road. Twenty minutes after arriving there, my mum rang to tell me my father had died.

Walking back along the Portobello Road was like travelling a tunnel but never taking your focus from the destination in the distance. The world around me had simply vanished as, step by step, I drew closer, stern and numb. Thinking about it now, that 100 metres seemed like a mile.

Back then, there was an Afro-Caribbean man, dressed in a black suit, who would trudge the length of Portobello Road carrying a 6-ft, collapsible white cross over his shoulder every day.

He passed me just as I reached the door.

Dry Hot Prawn Curry

Please don't be dissuaded by the list of ingredients here. Most are spices and, after just a little preparation, the actual cooking is very quick. I've committed a few crimes due to my limited knowledge of curries. I'd like to thank Vivek Singh for setting me straight on tempering spices.

Serves 2
1 thumb of ginger, peeled and very finely chopped
1 medium onion, very finely chopped
4 garlic cloves, very finely chopped
⅓ of a cinnamon stick
1 tsp each of fennel seeds, mustard seeds and cumin seeds
10 cardamom pods, bashed
6 peppercorns
3 cloves
1 bay leaf
15 fresh curry leaves, or 20 dried

2 tbsp each of vegetable oil and butter or ghee

2 generous tbsp tomato purée

1 tsp light brown sugar

2 tsp red wine vinegar

½ tsp hot chilli powder

1 large ripe vine tomato, rinsed and quartered

1 tbsp Dijon mustard

1 tsp sea salt

200 g/7 oz large Atlantic peeled prawns (and any juice)

Before doing anything else, place the ginger, onion and garlic in three piles. Put all of the whole spices on a plate. In a wok, get the oil very hot until the first wisps of smoke may be seen, then throw in the spices. Swirl them around until they darken considerably with a strong, rich, toasted smell coming to the nose – this will take little more than 30 seconds. Do not burn them!

Wasting no time, throw in the ginger and cook for 30 seconds stirring often. Add the onions with the butter or ghee and cook for 12–15 minutes until totally tender. Stir in the garlic and cook like this for another 2 minutes.

Stir in the tomato purée and sugar, then cook until it catches, then stir and let it catch again; do this for 2 minutes or so. Add the vinegar and evaporate it completely. Now add the turmeric and chilli powder. Stir in the mustard and salt. Add a splash of water to loosen the consistency. Add the fresh tomato, stirring occasionally, until collapsed. Add the prawns and cook for no more than 2 minutes. Eat with rice or hot black pepper poppadoms.

An Adult

A Peculiar Stance in Underpants

Shortly after my father died I returned to Dorset. I drove from London straight to the cemetery, and sat with my back against his gravestone eating a cheese and pickle sandwich and a packet of crisps. I was there for some time and, on rising, felt my gloom might be alleviated by a trip to the pub. I called a friend and there we sat consuming pint after pint of cider, punctuated with shots of Golden Cap whisky (not a recommended combination).

Although the chat was constant and cheery enough, my state of gloom returned with pint five.

My usual inclination, in such a state, is to think under the moon and roam in darkness across the fields. This time I chose to go home and sleep.

The vultures were sure enough hopping at my bedpost the following morning. I went down to breakfast in my boxer shorts, missing my father and filled with jangling discontentment. On glancing out the window, I was suddenly overtaken by the strangest urge to shock my hangover and mood from their very skin.

Returning the butter and eggs to the fridge, I walked straight from the front door of my sister's cottage into a large bed of healthy, muscular stinging nettles. I roamed around this small bushy space that I be vigorously bitten and my God, I was, legs burning as if I'd climbed into a laundry basket of wasps.

I guess I was simply trying to shake the illness that comes from pub work and chase out the oddness I generally felt over the weeks since my father had died. A hardline approach, I know.

My plan on nettle-patch exit couldn't have been clearer, directing me quickly into jeans and then into the car for an excruciating drive to West Bay beach.

Here, I immediately stripped and dashed into the cold sea.

Pleasure and pain produced the most extraordinary and uplifting fizzing in my legs, amplified by the cold salt water and goose bumps.

Equivalent to attempting a whole can of icy cold Coca-Cola in one go, I felt a similar carbonation overload in my legs rather than in the back of the throat. It quickly flushed out my hangover, like a heavy animal from thick brush, and I remained hopping in the waist-high shallows until only a sensational faint tingling buzz remained.

Smiling, I was clear headed. Exhilarated in fact.

I have revisited this hangover cure in happier times since, and in smaller nettle patches that can be found nearer the sea.

Dare I recommend this cure for the foolish? Highly!

(Note: don't substitute the sea for a cold bath, it does not work.)

Pleasure and Pain Soup

This is best made with nettle tops picked in the early spring months. Use gloves unless otherwise inclined. Try to pick leaves only, not stalk, and wash them thoroughly in cold very salty water, rinse well and repeat. If I want to luxuriate this soup, I add a dollop of crème fraîche to the bowl.

Serves 2, with crusty bread
30 g/1 oz/2 tbsp butter, plus extra for frying, if needed
1 medium onion, finely chopped
12 quail eggs
1 good, pert, garlic clove
250 g/9 oz stinging nettle tops, rinsed (see above)
300 ml/10 fl oz/1¼ cups good, tasty chicken stock
Generous scratching of nutmeg
2 rashers of smoked streaky bacon (optional)
1 tbsp large porridge oats (optional)
Sea salt and freshly ground black pepper

Melt the butter over a low to medium heat and sweat the onions until very soft. Stir often, don't let them colour, and cook until meltingly tender. This will take about 8–12 minutes.

While the onions cook, place the quail eggs in a small pan filled with just enough cold water to cover them. Bring water to a boil over a high heat. Once boiling, count to 25 and immediately drain them before plunging the eggs into a bowl of cold water. Get them cooled quickly then drain again and peel. Crack them thoroughly by rolling them on a work surface under slight pressure. This will help the skin come away on peeling.

Stir the garlic into the onions and cook for a further minute or so. Add the nettle tops and cook for approximately 5 minutes or until tender, but still bright green.

Add the stock and bring to a simmer. Allow to cool slightly, then blitz in a blender or food processor until totally smooth.

Reheat if needs be. Season with nutmeg, salt and a good bombardment of pepper. Pop the desired number of quail eggs in to the soup and gobble the rest at a later date, dusted with celery salt.

If further garnishes are required, while the nettles cook, fry the bacon with the porridge oats in a dash of butter until the bacon and oats are browned and crispy. Drain off fat on paper towels and scatter over the soup and eggs.

Taking the Paper

I was in less than a good mood. My breakfast had been ruined on finding two newspaper articles that had swelled my despair for both the animal kingdom and mankind.

In one, I learnt of a six-inch long, Barbie-pink slug called a Kaputar slug. I never knew such a splendid slug existed, and was sad to learn that, while it resides on a single mountain in Australia (Mount Kaputar) it also resides on a list of forty other critically endangered species.

Bizarre as this creature was, without doubt it served some crucial employment under mother nature's bequest.

Thumbing to a nearby page, flicking from famine to Epicurean dog food, a story of total inconsequence: Sinitta and Simon Cowell's relationship or diet or some such.

I have no room for this, I thought.

Closing the papers, I headed out food shopping for a change of scene and mood.

In the veg section of my local Co-op, small joy came in a reduced-price bunch of dill slapped with a bright orange sticker, REDUCED!

The dill was vibrant and bushy, no reflection of its use-by date, or sell-by date or lurid warning. At the till, I'm told that, despite the label, the scanner reading means the dill must be handed in for destruction and the reduced offer has, in fact, expired.

Destruction is such a strong word.

'Just let me buy it anyway,' I say.

'I can't do that,' the checkout girl replied. 'It has to be handed in.'

I wonder what she was like at school.

'Why? So you can destroy a perfectly healthy bunch of dill? Can you see anything wrong with it?'

'I wouldn't know what to look for,' she replied.

'So: it's been picked to be thrown away?' I ask. I've snatched the dill from the counter during this exchange.

'I'm going to have to get the manager,' she says.

'Great,' I reply.

'Just sell him the dill,' a voice chips in from behind. A small queue is waiting to pay. Supportive or exasperated, I can't tell. They can see I'm in for the long haul though.

The manager comes and I explain the situation to him. 'I still want the dill on the bill ... at the till.' He sees no humour. It meets with a dead look. 'It's pert, it's toned,' I continue, 'It's still happy, not so much as a drooping leaf of ill-health. No yellowing fronds, no withered tips; this is vigorous, teenage dill, still loving life,' I put forward.

I do remember continuing into 'not going anywhere' and the words 'cold dead hands', but I don't remember at what point the manager snatched the dill back from my grasp.

'Why don't you just give me the dill and also pay me to take it away?' I suggest with flaring nostrils

'Give him the bloody dill, I need to get home,' a local tattoo enthusiast with a loaf of bread mutters.

'Will you go if the dill goes with you?' I'm finally asked.

'Yes, that's only been my intention for the last ten minutes.'

On the way out, a lady in a headscarf clutching her wallet and the *Daily Mail* in one hand, cigarettes and car keys in the other, taps me with her one free bony finger and says, 'You did well, I completely agree with you.'

I thank her and follow it with 'You should give that up ...'

'Too late to stop now,' she laughs with a wheeze, shaking a jingly-jangly full hand of keys and fags.

'Puff away', I say to her. 'I meant the paper.'

Phone Manner

Touch screens are complicated. Having a nose and chin like Punch, I tend to inadvertently exit a call with a brush of either.

I have also realized a passive-aggressive tendency to start eating crunchy things like apples and tortilla chips once certain conversations are underway, more likely to crunch more at points when I do not like what I'm hearing.

It gets worse. I've been busted taking a conference call from the bath.

I do, however, seem to conscientiously place a strategic flannel before such calls. I also eat crunchy things in the bath.

Shoal

Many tides ago, I was at a Save the Ocean event in London. All the great and the good were there, environmentalists, chefs, philanthropists, marine biologists, journalists, authors, sashaying celebrities and an otherwise glitzy rent-a-crowd. All gathered, the volume was high in what was no less than an amazing marine theatre set. Replica polystyrene tuna fishes and sea creatures hung from the ceiling, while below the guests picked at trays of sustainable canapés like shoals of exotic fish pecking at coral.

Two women beside me were standing next to some fish tanks. Obsessed by each other's clothes and stroking each other's sequins in studied, pouting admiration. One turned to me and said, 'Don't you think she looks beautiful?'

Never being one who likes to be pushed towards a desired answer I replied, 'In truth, I think the colourful fish behind you are far better dressed.'

They looked me up and down with flaring nostrils and slid away.

Immediately behind me I heard, 'Darling, do you know what this event is for?' and turned to see a smartly dressed couple jiggling away to the music.

'Some sea thingy,' came her reply, followed by, 'I've had enough, shall we go and get some sushi?'

Like laughing into a snorkel and mask it went wrong, and snorting Champagne all down my shirt, I was met with another frosty stare.

The pelagic wanderer, I'd taken my fill of this super shoal. I flicked my tail and headed to a friend's house for baked potato and beans.

Crispy Haddock with Morels and Bacon

Serves 2

1 small packet of dried morel or porcini mushrooms, about 20–30 g/
  ¾–1 oz
25 g/1 oz/2 tbsp butter
50 g/2 oz smoked lardons
150 ml/5 fl oz/⅔ cup double (heavy) cream
2 tbsp plain (all-purpose) flour, sifted
2 small eggs, beaten
70 g/2½ oz/1 cup white breadcrumbs
150 g/5½ oz haddock, skinned and cut into medium-sized chunks
Sunflower oil, for frying
1 tbsp finely chopped fresh parsley
Sea salt and freshly ground black pepper

In a bowl, steep the mushrooms in just enough water to cover them, and
leave for half an hour.

Melt the butter in a pan over a medium heat and sauté the lardons until
nicely golden brown. Drain the hydrated mushrooms and pop them into the
pan with the lardons. Add the soaking water, strained if you like.

Bring to the boil and rapidly reduce the sauce until all the liquid has gone
and the mushrooms start to colour. Remember to stir the mushrooms and the
lardons together so you get a nice even cook and colour all over.

Pour in the cream, stir and then simmer for barely a minute. Season with salt
and pepper and put to one side.

On a plate, season the flour with salt and tip the breadcrumbs on to a baking
tray. Line up flour, then egg, then breadcrumbs in a neat row. Lightly flour
the fish, then dip in the egg and then roll thoroughly in the breadcrumbs.

Pour the oil in a small to medium frying pan (skillet). It needs to be about 1 cm/½ in deep. When the oil is hot enough, the fish should frizzle on entry. Fry on all sides until the chunks are lovely and golden. Remove with a slotted spoon and set aside to drain on paper towels.

Gently reheat the sauce. Stir in the parsley and then spoon on to plates. Put the pieces of fish on top. Accompany with a cold beer.

Oop North

We had left London to the 'chink, chink' of blackbirds at dawn, in a car full of musty waders, rods, two bulging rucksacks, dry bags of tackle, coats and Mossy, a long-haired lurcher, curled in the back seat.

To a Haribo sunrise, we chewed up both gummy bears and the M1 as we rushed towards Cumbria and the town of Cockermouth or 'Knobagob'. I'd recently learnt this (to my delight) from a coven of Cumbrian sisters, all three running pubs in Sussex and a long way from home.

We laughed and hid our jealousies as best our competitive natures would allow until, aquaplaning into a ninety-degree skid across the motorway just past Coventry, we crept into a lay-by to blink at each other in startled, shocked silence but for heavy panting and exclamations of 'Jesus Christ!' I quietly thanked my father, keeping an eye from above.

I was with my friend Rowan and his dog, off on a salmon fishing trip on the River Derwent.

In the rod room the next morning, I told our hostess we were one rod short as I had loaned mine to Rowan and would need one for myself. (I'd actually lent it to a friend who'd managed to break it in his flat. So excited was he pre-fishing trip that, either posing or worse still role-playing on his carpet river, it'd somehow ended badly for my rod. Something to do with a free-standing lamp and a pile of books. Idiot.)

'Well you'd better choose one then,' came the gracious reply of Pamela, Lady Egremont, one of my father's oldest friends and a woman I eternally thank for my love of salmon fishing.

One rod struck me particularly. I remember how distinct looking it was. With its black finish and purple whipping it stood out, papal almost, among the browner, humbler rods.

'Could I use this one?' I enquired.

'Wise choice,' came the reply, 'that happens to be Cardinal Hume's rod.'

After bumping and rattling over the fields, the rods fastened from bonnet to roof, we pulled up alongside the River Derwent to a waiting line of huffing cows.

The Garden Pool is a long pool, a waist-high, sturdy push of clear mahogany water moving beneath a bank of alder, beech and oak.

After climbing into waders and assembling ourselves, I ended up with my own rod and, Rowan with Cardinal Hume's. I saw no problem with this other than, as my friend had never used such a rod (or caught a salmon before), I'd prefer any accidents befall my own rod than another's but I left things as they played out. Richard, the ghillie, was coaching him after all.

Into the river I waded, and as the water pressure pushed my waders against me, so London seemed squeezed out to swirl away in the eddies with the fallen autumn leaves.

Second nature was now piloting, my confidence uplifted by the gurgling current, river smells, and that well-known anticipation – the relaxed concentration that comes with fishing fluency.

A jet formation of mergansers raced passed me. I always find such things symbolic, and store them while never really knowing the meaning.

Upstream, Rowan was into a fish. He landed it and I was delighted to see his excitement. He was trembling, the ten-pound salmon as rewarding as that first trout twisting on the pebbles is to a determined five year old.

I walked back to where I'd left the river and started casting again. Within minutes there was another whoop as Rowan lifted a second, larger fish. He landed it. As the fish, a twelve pounder, was unhooked I felt a pang of jealousy and guilt.

If indeed this holy rod was blessed I had been foolish not to stay with it! With this arrived neurotic feelings of infidelity to my own rod. Suddenly my belief was gone. It is hopeless to fish in such a state. I have always believed such negativity travels the length of the line to the very fish you seek.

God damn it! Five minutes later and 'Ha ha! Another!' came the yell.

Sighing, I left the water again and trudged upstream to go and show my support, albeit reluctantly. I joined them as Richard sternly said, 'Be careful now, this is a huge fish.'

We saw its tail, and I also saw the ghillie's deeply nervous look, his desire to see an historic fish banked. 'It might be the biggest fish I've ever seen in the river,' he sighed.

All of a sudden, there was a huge judder on the rod, an almighty surge, a brief whizz of line, a thunderous splash. And the fish had gone.

Over lunch, I skipped the fruitcake and orange and stole ten minutes with that rod. Bless my soul, I caught a small hen fish.

And then the rain came ...

Part Two

It rained solidly and hard all that afternoon and night with the intensity of a tropical monsoon but for the bitter chill in the air. A trip into town early morning to check the river, and it was a torrent of chocolate milk under the bridge. Fishing was off, so I returned to our B&B where, like Ernie and Bert, we sat in our single beds in our pyjamas, and spent the morning talking, squabbling and smoking out the skylight.

The rain continued.

Perusing the local paper, Rowan suddenly laughed, jabbed at a page and said, 'We've gotta go to this!'

'Go to what?' I asked.

'Ben & Jerry's International Gurning Championship.'

We certainly needed to do something. The central heating was making the room stuffy while our rucksacks resembled bin liners, their rubbish tugged out by midnight foxes. Besides, I had cabin fever.

Brilliant, we had a plan.

We set off that evening with Mossy the lurcher, me in the usual jeans 'n' jumper, but Rowan wearing a pair of baggy, terracotta silk combat trousers cut at a peculiar angle, some lurid trainers and a colourful jumper with a zip that ran at a diagonal from neck to hip. He looked like a tots' TV presenter.

Through the pitch black and rain, getting very lost, we reverse a million times as we searched the lanes. Mossy remained curled up on the back seat, snout on paws, content.

We finally arrived at a village hall with one Ben & Jerry flag flapping and slapping in the downpour and wind. A row of SUV and Hilux trucks was pulled up outside. It did not seem remotely international. A creeping nervousness seemed to settle on me, despite the warm glow and chatter coming from within.

We walked in, me feeling at odds, my friend dressed like a twit. The room was filled with about 150 people, mostly men, mostly bald men, hard men, Northern men. Men you would not like to see standing on a battlefield thumping their axes against their shields and jeering.

They were all facing the stage but as the door swung shut behind us an announcement declared 'That ladies and gents, is the end of the clay pipe-smoking competition.'

Turning away from the stage to fall into shouting chats with each other, they suddenly noticed us.

Shit.

While most then turned away with a glance or a chuckling whisper, a group broke away and approached us.

Circling around to us, one said to me, 'What's yer name, man?' They were a tanked and edgy bunch.

I paused for too long before uttering, 'Errr ... Valentine.'

Another pause.

'That's a fookin' girl's name,' came the reply with a stare.

I blushed, then surveyed his head, saw the glint of gold left and right, and answered, 'Mate, you're the one wearing earrings.'

Things got a little tense; Rowan dropped in to his Chi kung stance. But it was the dog that saved the day, as in trotted Mossy and nuzzled against Rowan's leg.

'D'ya like hare coarsing?' one of them asked, and quick as a flash in unison, we both replied 'Yes!'

We knew nothing about it.

They drank pints and stayed with us from that moment on. We paid no attention to the gurning on stage.

'That dog's as wet as you two. You know jack shit about hare coarsing!'

'Course we don't,' I replied.

'Tell ya what: we're all going on a lads' trip to London next week, shall we come over yours for a laugh?'

'Why not?' I replied ... at which they collapsed in laughter.

'You should seen the look on your face.'

'How disappointing. I thought we could all go have a kebab and a Turkish bath together.'

We all cracked up laughing again.

'Yer look weird but yer not bad lads.'

Making to leave, forgetting myself and prone to displays of affection, I hugged the one I liked most.

'One word of advice,' he said.

'What?'

'Never hug a Cumbrian man and definitely never bloody kiss one as I guarantee it'll not end well'.

'See you in London!' I threw over my shoulder.

'Unlikely,' they all said together.

Lady Tacos

About ten years ago, and with one television series, perhaps even two, under my belt, I was invited to do a talk in Dorchester. Dorset was my childhood stomping ground, and I think they were proud of this local boy done good. I'd certainly mentioned how growing up there had a huge impact on me.

The room was full. About eighty people or so jostling each other. There was quite a buzz. And I distinctly remember the crowd was mostly comprised of older ladies, WI officer class, and similarly elderly besuited men, the genteel type who hand out the hymn books, walk around with the collection purse or otherwise ready the church in those quiet, cold hours of early morning when everyone else is having their first cup of tea.

Always good at talking about myself, I rolled through my young life in food and random thoughts on things ... A few risks, some laughs and the hour passed quickly. They clapped heartily and I felt happy.

Pleased, I asked if there were any questions. One octogenarian lady with a lilac rinse asked me what the strangest thing I had ever eaten was. Moving too fast, I replied, 'I don't think that would be appropriate for this talk.'

Another elderly lady banged her stick on the floor and shouted 'Go on young Valentine, tell us, tell us!'

I was now locked in.

Thinking they might not be as conservative as expected, and that she perhaps enjoyed ringside seats at the wrestling, I answered her.

'Well then, it would have to be the pig's vagina tacos I ate in Mexico City.'

A hush fell across the room. Hurriedly filling this void, I continued with a second truth: 'They were tender and giving and I ordered another.'

I might have continued, had not the Rotarian jumped up to interject, 'Well, thank you Valentine for a most entertaining ...'

There were no more questions. And certainly no sherry.

Happy Valley

I once spent a lovely weekend in Dorset with Miles Irving. Miles wrote *The Forager Handbook* – as complete a work as one could hope for on the edible wild plants of the UK. It sits in the good company of Richard Mabey's *Food For Free*, and all the books of Roger Phillips, that scarlet wizard of the woods.

For my weekend with Miles we were tasked with eating only what we'd hunted and gathered. Driving down, I told Miles I had brought some good butter, that it would lay a golden foundation beneath our cooking.

'That's deviating, Val,' he said. 'Keep the butter under wraps for the while as I've bought something too.'

'What'? I replied.

'You'll see,' he said.

Refuelling the diesel tank with petrol, the weekend got off to a slow start but as we waited in the narrow lanes of Marshwood Vale for help to arrive, Miles took up his fork to turn over the tangled bank beside the car, bending down to shake the earth away, methodical as a rice picker, and he'd soon gathered enough to fill a large portion of the boot.

Lesser celandine and silverweed, both plants were new to me. I asked why we needed so much. Pointing to the teeny-tiny nodules clinging to the thread roots of the celandine he said, 'They look like nothing but they're delicious. We'll remove these and eat them as tiny potatoes, but will need a lot for any idea that we have eaten at all.'

'Silverweed, we need the roots. Know you will like them.'

Having barely travelled more than ten steps from the car, over that hour alone, he filled the boot completely and with many different things, leaving little sign we had been there at all.

While mushrooms on toast, blackberry crumble, wild garlic and rose hips should all be considered treats, in order to gather enough to support the modern English family we would totally have to reorganize our way of life.

It struck me how far we've come, how quickly, how utterly beholden we are to the easy food we have today; among the scribble of UK roads, a supermarket in every gap.

Out on the hill that afternoon with my gun, I shot a young rabbit. Turning homeward, we had retrieved some sweet vernal grass. That the two existed side by side was reason enough to cook them together. The grass has a wonderful sweet flavour you'd recognize in Zubrowka Bison Grass Vodka.

I wanted to fry and brown the rabbit first, so retrieved the butter.

'Wait!' exclaimed Miles, rummaging in his knapsack. He produced a honey jar filled with pale, buff-coloured contents, a little like wax.

He unscrewed the lid and held the jar towards my nose.

I had a good deep sniff and quickly decided that whatever it was reminded me of the smell of linseed oil, and reminded me of my earlier life as a painter. I was baffled.

'Take some for the rabbit,' he said.

'What is that?'

'Guess,' he said. I couldn't.

'Badger fat! My friend found one on the roadside not that long dead. He rendered the fat and filtered it.'

I was overjoyed and astonished in turn, before recalling that a few cookbooks of mine talked of badger hams in West Country pubs of yore.

Melting the fat in the pan, we fried the rabbit, at which point the nature of the smell changed, becoming a savoury tang, mixed with scent of mechanic's grease. It was not bad exactly, but I nonetheless mellowed it with butter. I only had one rabbit, plus the obvious task that all dishes must be good and the means of cooking fairly accessible!

While the badger fat was an acquired taste, once transferred to a pressure cooker with sweet vernal grass it all came together nicely. The punch from the fat gave a pleasant depth, the sweetness and flavour of the vernal grass took the lead and was luxuriated with cream. Yes, I'd snuck in some cream too.

It was sensational. I remember the smiles and the rolling eyes. That such a fine thing be part badger, rabbit and grass thrilled me in the way such cooking always does. The overall expense: the price of a shotgun cartridge, 40 grams of butter and 100 millilitres of cream.

I would add that the badger fat also made for excellent dubbing when waterproofing my leather boots.

It was a magical weekend. Moving Japanese knotweed with the care taken with nitro glycerine, so as not to spread it, we braised it like rhubarb and baked it on puff pastry to accompany a custard flavoured with unripe rowanberry. We cured trout with salt mixed with the clove-tasting root of the easily ignored wood avens, a wondrous plant.

We made broth from seaweed, wild mussels, limpets and wood ear mushrooms, while salads of sorrel, cleavers, jack of the hedge and dandelion bounced into the bowl. We made many things but oh, oh, oh! those tiny sautéed celandine nodules mixed among the silverweed roots we'd roasted. Nutty with a sweetness, sustenance for a pauper maybe, they provided a kingly dish for the intricacy of their preparation and the delicacy of their taste. With only the tiniest portion each, they gave me as much joy as would caviar.

Over dinner I joked the salad be called apocalypse mix and, while Miles frowned, I immediately regretted this comment. But for those who once relied on such things, these were far from desperation ingredients, their flavours delicious, varied and remarkable – sweet, peppery, sour, bitter.

The weekend over, Miles had already been added to the bard, the blacksmith, the seamstress, the engineer, the saddler, the distiller and the mechanic. My fantasy Outsiders' League.

I was sent a letter once that read something to the tune of, 'Valentine you are an idiot.' I could not argue with that but could the following 'while gallivanting around the countryside banging on about foraging, do you really think, on getting home, I have time to then set off with a bucket gathering nuts for my dinner? I work hard and have three children to feed. Your posh ramblings are annoying and impractical ...'

Gosh I thought, now there's a cross soul, and with no desire to anger him further wrote back to him to say that, with respect he had appeared to miss the point.

Foraging is rarely more than a contribution to my table and that, should he ever pass a watercress bed or a cobnut tree, some horseradish or a stand of mushrooms, then is it not better to know than not know that something as pleasing as a country walk may also result in bounty? To know simply gives you options.

In cases where nature does supply me with the whole meal, then all the better. It is not a way of life, just an extra string to my bow.

To show such things to his children might mean a lovely time spent together, or alternatively, he could send the little brutes out foraging and take some well-deserved time to write more letters. Should the jets streak low one day, leaving the Pot Noodle factory a smoking ruin, it might indeed be useful to remember where he put the bucket and where those nuts grow.

Apologies for my posh accent, but to try and impersonate a Stepney barrow boy would look ridiculous.

Thankfully that was the end of our correspondence.

And that really is it for me. This is where I am from. These fair isles. I speak the English language, behave by most of its rules and enjoy its traditions. As a cook and an Englishman, I want to know my countryside that I can use it best, as we did long before the first avocado rolled into town. I want to pass this on to my children so that the cycle of nature continues.

So pull away at blackberries, cut the cep from beneath the pine, make rose hip syrup and nibble the Alexanders. Put meadowsweet in your shellfish soup, and elderflower fritters in the deep fryer.

Which twit said nothing in life's for free?

Deep-fried Elderflowers

Fairy food!

As this recipe uses gluten-free flour, it can happily be consumed by coeliacs too. Yipeeeee!

Serves 6–8
3 tbsp light wildflower honey
1 tbsp elderflower cordial
1 tbsp lemon juice, plus a few scratches of finely grated lemon zest
100 g/3½ oz/¾ cup gluten-free self-raising (self-rising) flour

Some good fizzy (hard) cider

Pinch of sea salt

3 elderflower heads, plucked from a bush (not after rain as it will have much reduced perfume, the pollen having been knocked away by the raindrops)

Sunflower oil, for deep frying

Vanilla ice cream, to serve

In a large bowl, mix the honey, elderflower cordial and lemon juice. Set aside.

Place the flour into a large mixing bowl and add just enough cider, folding it in gently, that it becomes slightly thicker than pancake batter. We want it to cling to the flower heads, but not be claggy, nor should it run off the flowers exposing the green stems.

Let the batter stand for 5 minutes or so. Just before using, add a pinch of salt.

Heat a deep-fat fryer to 180°C/350°F.

Using tongs, dip the flower heads in to the batter and coat thoroughly, wiggling off any excess batter. Carefully lower the heads into the oil, suspending them with the tongs for a few seconds rather than simply dropping them in. This will keep them from sinking and sticking to the cage.

Fry on both sides until golden brown. Remove and set to drain on some paper towels.

While still hot, transfer to a plate and put a scoop of vanilla ice cream on the flower heads. Pour over the honey, elderflower and lemon syrup.

Ideally, munch on this while sitting outside. Delicious served with a cold glass of pudding wine.

Wood Ear Mushroom Salad

The wood ear mushroom is very common in British woodland, and is to be found growing on dead elder trees. Obviously the shape of ears (be they more like a bat's ear), they appear a translucent tan colour and, although more a textural experience when eaten (as are many ingredients in Chinese cookery), they nonetheless have a mild and pleasing flavour.

At largest they are little less than a human ear and are very unlikely to be mistaken for toxic fungi. *Please* thoroughly cross-reference or simply avoid if unsure. To the feel, they are soft and skin-like, very pliable, flexible and softly rubbery. They are not brittle or crumbly like other brackets and cups.

If in doubt – move on. Or you could replace the wood ear mushrooms with the same quantity of shitake mushrooms.

This salad is a very nice balance with, say, deep-fried sesame lobster or roast pork belly or any other such fatty delights.

Serves 2–4

200 g/7 oz wood ear mushrooms

2 tsp fresh Japanese soy sauce

1½ tbsp Chinese black vinegar (very easy to buy in Asian supermarkets. I have not tried to replace it with balsamic but this would probably work)

1 tsp lemon juice

1 tsp sunflower oil

½–1 tsp fresh sesame oil (be careful not to use ancient bottle as, once off, it tastes foul)

1 good, hard garlic clove, grated

1 large thumb of ginger, peeled and finely grated

1 long hot green or red chilli (how violently hot is up to you), finely sliced

25 g/1 oz roughly torn fresh and tender young fresh coriander (cilantro)

Third of a small red onion, very finely and neatly diced (chopped as needed to avoid it getting tainted)

Good grinding of black pepper

Remove any mossy feet from the mushrooms and wash them in very salty water. Avoid any with a green and dusty appearance, as these are old. Rinse them well and drain them.

Bring a medium-sized pan of water to the boil, then drop them in and cook for 4 minutes before draining and allowing to cool.

In a large bowl, mix together the soy sauce and the black vinegar with the lemon juice, oils, grated garlic, ginger and sliced chilli, and toss this mixture with the mushrooms.

Give a good grinding of black pepper before stirring in the torn coriander and freshly chopped red onion.

Tip into a serving dish bowl and eat with chopsticks.

Tip Cucumber is a common addition to this salad. Thinly peel and slice half a medium cucumber. Mix with 1 tsp sea salt and leave to drain in a sieve for about 30 minutes before squeezing out as much of the remaining water as possible before adding to the salad.

Chestnut Soup

Serves 4
1 large sweet onion, very finely diced
50 g/2 oz/4 tbsp butter
5 garlic cloves, finely grated
50 ml/1⅔ fl oz/2¾ tbsp grappa, brandy or Calvados, plus a splash more
Approximately 600 ml/1 pint/2½ cups good tasty chicken, ham or
    vegetable stock
2 x 180-g/7-oz packets of cooked, peeled sweet chestnuts
50 ml/1⅔ fl oz/2¾ tbsp double (heavy) cream

6 paper thin slices of lardo or pancetta (optional)
Small block Parmesan cheese
Sea salt and freshly ground black pepper
Extra virgin olive oil, to serve

In a saucepan, gently fry the onion with the butter until totally, pathetically soft, 8–10 minutes or so. It should only just be beginning to faintly colour.

Stir in the garlic and continue to cook until softened. Take great care not to burn the butter, onions or garlic while completing this delicate operation for the soup base. Add the grappa, brandy or Calvados and allow it to evaporate completely. Pour in the stock and then plop in the chestnuts. Simmer very gently for 10 minutes or so, allowing the chestnuts to soften.

Let the mixture cool before popping into a food processor and blending. If impatient, make sure to drape the food processor with a dish cloth to avoid getting splattered with hot soup. The texture of the whizzed chestnuts will give the soup a super-silky smoothness. If the soup is too thick, loosen with a little extra stock. It should be a little thinner than a pea and ham soup.

Return the soup to the pot, season with salt and gently reheat.

Meanwhile, fry the lardo or pancetta until crisp.

Just before serving, add a last dash of booze to the soup, just so it keeps that raw alcohol taste. Stir through the cream, then season very generously with salt to expose the full flavour of the chestnuts. Spoon the soup into bowls. Add a slash of olive oil over the soup followed by a sleeting of Parmesan cheese and the crisp lardo or pancetta. Finish with a good grinding of pepper

Tip Any leftover soup is good as a sauce for parboiled and then charred Brussels sprouts. An excellent lunch. Also very good to eat with roast apples, ceps and pan-fried duck breast.

Anonymous

I go to a restaurant with a famous chef. He has chosen it. I do not want to go there. I want to go to a different one nearby. But I give in and go because I like him. He's got Michelin stars in his pocket, and wants to investigate the high rating this place has ranked on the World Top Fifty list.

By course five of a twenty-plus-course tasting menu, I'm really hating the meal. Most dishes are born of a flimsy idea or come with snot-like gel attachments.

It's mean as well. If you're going to use cheap cuts and the humbler ingredients, you'd better know what to do with them. I'd rather eat such ingredients at the tables of international grandmothers. Don't get me wrong: I don't want asparagus tips and fillet. Far from it. But I'm feeling ripped off and we've hardly started.

We are however getting quite cheery on the wines. We deserve to find something we like and the wine flight is good.

Another course arrives and it's truly weird. Tragic in fact. We are given a table game to play, the winner getting the caviar. It's a pathetic idea and we start to get the giggles but play on as instructed.

The waiter returns and asks, 'Who's won?'

'Not me,' I say, 'but I want my caviar too.'

'Sir, that is not the game,' he says.

'Well, given the price of dinner, I'd like it anyway, if that's okay,' I reply with a deadpan and direct stare.

He looks pinched and minces off in his *Star Trek* outfit. We both get the caviar. Hooray, a course I can savour.

Twenty or so courses of misery later, my companion and I nevertheless have had fun dissecting each course. In fact, I have not laughed so much in a long time. We've both found it more than hard to keep a straight face as the dishes are delivered. At worst, with gritted jaw and mouth clamped shut, the uncontrollable giggles attempting to exit via our noses, we've had to suffocate such outbursts with napkins. Quite obviously, in fact, but I'm past caring.

We listen to the minute detail of the ingredients and the ingenious cooking methods used, an agony when simultaneously trying to suppress Chief Inspector Dreyfus-style whimpering. It is my belief, in these situations, that if I want to know, I'll ask.

So when, at the end of the meal, the waiter asks, 'Any questions?' I reply, 'Yes, I have one.' Only to receive a sharp kick under the table. So I amend my response to, 'Actually, no, I don't.'

The waiter then invites us to see the kitchen. Personally I'd prefer to bob for apples in boiling oil, but we smile and tell him it's a fine idea.

'Smile and wave,' mutters my friend, as he pushes his chair back, 'Smile and wave.'

We trump around the kitchen and see the sections and implements our food was prepared in and on, where the dearly departed ingredients were depleted, their goop extracted, their fibrous remains so expertly tortured. My friend is given a signed book. We pay an eye-watering bill and leave.

For such money, I would prefer to eat at my favourite Moroccan stall a hundred times. I could have bought two cashmere jumpers, a new fly rod, had a wild night out with my lady or taken my kids to Center Parcs. Hell, I could have eaten a far bigger tin of caviar than I can ever afford and devoured it in front of back to back episodes of *Vikings*. Now, there's an evening well spent.

I do not have good thoughts towards the judges of the World Top Fifty, I can tell you that. They owe me!

We go back to the hotel and, sitting in the chef's room emptying the mini bar, flick olives into our mouths. I use the bathroom and re-enter the room to hear giggling and smell traces of smoke. The book is in the metal waste paper bin, burning from one of its corners while chef judders with mirth and points his phone at it.

As you'd see in a movie, all goes into slo-mo, my voice drops to a deep bass as I slowly lean forward to run, hand stretched out, a deep bass 'NOOOOOOOOO!' escaping from my mouth.

I grab the phone from him. Jeezuz, the Instagram is already up!

I throw my gin and tonic on the book, open the window and usher the smoke out.

I'm shocked as my friend is one of the nicest people in the whole wide world. But still ... we crack up laughing and move onto the crisps, almonds and chocolate.

We have hangovers at breakfast.

'That was touch and go,' he says.

'Provincial granny cooking tonight, and my choice,' I reply.

Asparagus with Anchovy, Lemon and Chilli Butter

Serves 4

30 g/1 oz salted anchovy fillets, drained weight (preferably Ortiz)

Zest from 1 unwaxed lemon, finely grated

Juice of half a lemon

2 medium garlic cloves, very finely grated

Pinch of chilli powder for a discernible kick but not extreme violence

3 bunches of British large green or white asparagus stems (*not* jetlagged varieties from Peru, eaten in winter)

100 g/3½ oz/1 stick unsalted butter, at room temperature

Good grinding of black pepper

Very finely chop the anchovies and smoosh them to a paste with the side of the knife. Pop them in a bowl. Mash the anchovy paste with all the remaining ingredients, except the asparagus and butter, and leave to one side.

Individually bend each asparagus spear until it snaps at its natural break. (Keep the stalks – if you are eating as much asparagus as you can while the season provides, they can be turned into a respectable soup.)

Steam the asparagus spears until they reach a perfect balance of tender yet firm. Drain and leave to one side.

Heat a large frying pan (skillet) and melt the butter, taking care not to burn it. Once foaming, let it gently cook for 30 seconds or so before tossing the asparagus through it.

Transfer to plates or put the whole lot in a pile alongside plenty of napkins.

The Smoken Word

If I were to cook but one way, it would be over wood. If I were to open a new restaurant, it would be made of wood, and set in a wood, with all the cooking done over wood, and with no doubt an insurance premium that matched my propensity for setting tea towels alight.

Let us dispense with the outdoor gas grill. It is a pointless contraption, akin to wheeling your gas cooker into the garden. Black griddle lines on your rib eye do not equal deliciousness. They simply mean black lines. You might as well draw them on with a Sharpie.

To cook over wood is to use smoke as an ingredient. And the wood matters. The incense notes of juniper are completely different from the gentler ones of silver birch, different from old vine wood or oak. It creates a cosying and strong sense of environment – in more rural quarters, ingredients will likely be cooked over the very branches they lived beneath or grew nearby.

A wood grill demands the simplicity I look for, a decluttering of ingredients and method, a requirement to understand what's available from my surrounding location and community. It requires me to impose on the food as little as possible.

Cooking with fire is a far cry from drunken Saturday blokes with a set of tongs and an aluminium Bar-Be-Quick pack. Concentration is essential. The fire needs tending and adjusting, as do the ingredients if they're going to go over such direct and raw heat.

Cooking on wood warms me with a sense of self-sufficiency, often in scenery no restaurant can match. Whether I've yomped a côte de boeuf into the middle of nowhere, or driven to an echoey tiled and panelled family-run restaurant in the Pyrenees, it's the wood grill itself that affords me a state of true relaxation. The fire is an un-complication, and the cooking is not hectic. In fact, the combination of setting and smell and circumstance makes each occasion all the more memorable.

I recall that Arctic char I pulled from a hole in the ice, with its spotty olive back and apricot-sunset belly. In temperatures pushing −40°C (-40°F), we built a fire on the shore as the snow floated down through the forest by the frozen lake. Justin used his knife to shave and raise curls along the edges of the wood, leaving them attached to it, good catch-points for the flame. With an encouragement of lichen and moss, our freeze-dried pyre was soon a dancing rush of heat and sparks. We unzipped, splayed and cured those fish with pine needles mixed in salt, pinned them to a board propped near the heat and smoke. And, when they were done, while drinking coffee and aquavit, we ate them with greasy fingers and bread.[1]

Africa has seen me cooking guinea fowl and gourds in hot ash as a giraffe wandered past my field kitchen. In the Indian jungle, I have reincarnated chickens into curries, bubbling in a dented pan over a campfire. In the Mediterranean, I've cooked goat on a boat. In Britain, I've cooked grayling, eating it with young cobnuts and watercress; cooked a strip loin of roe deer with chanterelles over which perhaps it had walked; grilled mackerel over driftwood on Chesil Beach, watching the sun go to bed as I eat. And at Hepple, my roasted Northumbrian lamb over twisted lengths of dead juniper, with the distillery in view, has become a staple meal.

These memories are not just reserved for the meals I've cooked myself. I have waited expectantly for yakitori gizzards and crispy chicken skin wood-cooked in Tokyo; sat with my father watching our veal chops spitting on a grate over the fire in a restaurant on the very edge of Rome.

---

[1] Cooking over fire is not just a summer activity. There's as much pleasure to be found in it in the cruel months as in the warm.

Cooking over wood represents to me the complete opposite of the precious, worried, regulated, nannying and squeamish way we have come to cook in the West. While cleanliness and care are essential to anyone who loves food and cooking, there is something deeply tactile about cooking with bare hands and open fire, hair volumized with greasy smoke. That pulse and glimmer of white ash and orange ember, that smell of charcoal-sooted fingers. Food and fire are people gatherers. Stood with soot on my jeans, knife in my hand, as sparks fly up the flue or into the night sky, I think the more complicated world can go to hell in a self-basting foil bag.

Plank Fish

1 tbsp dark muscovado sugar
2 tbsp sea salt
Finely grated zest of half an orange (optional)
6 juniper berries, ground
1 tsp coriander seeds, coarsely ground
1 tsp fennel seeds, ground
White pepper
1 tbsp Douglas fir leaves, finely chopped (optional)
1 kg/2 lb 4 oz trout, filleted but with the skin on

12 x 4-cm/1½-in nails
A hammer
A 75 x 30 cm/28 x 12 in wooden board of untreated oak, birch, beech, pine or apple

Mix all the ingredients, but the fish, in a bowl.

Take the board and, with 6 nails per fillet, attach the fish skin side down to the wood, pinned at the outer reaches of its flesh. The nails need be only deep enough to be secure.

Distribute the cure over the fillets, remembering that the thin end needs less than the shoulder end. Leave to cure for 1 hour.

Lift the board to a standing position so any excess cure falls off. Leave the rest on the fish. Prop near the fire where it will pick up a lesser heat and, if the smoke is drifting, directly in its path. If using a barbecue, shove the coals to one side and prop the board opposite them.

Cook until done to preference. This is a touchy feely experience – pick out little bits of flesh to decide when and if it's done. Remember that the nails will be hot.

Eat with aquavit and bread.

Greece, 23 April 2017

Another night of hotel buffet unhappiness: the bewildering choice annoys me. And so I've asked reception where something simple, off the beaten track, can be found. Something local and uncomplicated. 'Go to this village and ask anyone there for the place with the cook who has a pony tail. They will know.'

I like this. Many adventures begin with this kind of instruction.

'I cannot drive *and* read the map. Can't you just hold it in the direction we're moving in?' I moan at my girlfriend in a lay-by. I'm hungry and she's exasperated.

'Theseus wouldn't have said that,' she says. 'He could drive, read a map and beat someone up and be adored all at once!'

I'm torn between laughing or continuing to sulk.

We arrive in the quiet mountain town clinging to the rock face. I wind down the window and interrupt two men, one on a moped, one leaning on a wall, to ask for the taverna with the cook with the long hair, while playing out an odd charade about the hair bit.

The man on the moped shouts, 'The chef is bald, but if you mean place where the proprietor has long hair, follow me.' He hastily bids his friend goodbye and, beckoning with one hand, zooms off up a steep hill where he slows outside a tiny door, points, and then zooms back to his friend. This is the Greek hospitality my father spoke so fondly of. 'They will go out of their way for you,' he said.

The place is small and very busy, but I'm dismayed as no one is local but for the staff. Some one says, 'Basingstoke.' Everyone is British, it seems.

I'm cheered again when the man with long hair appears, seats us and immediately returns bearing stewed peppers, lilac and brown olives the size of cherry stones, wilted beetroot tops swamped in vinegar and oil, and some hard local rusks that need a good soaking.

I order a bottle of cold retsina and food. A seemingly endless succession of rustic treats starts to arrive from the tiny kitchen. As the plates jostle for space, I'm quickly aware I've ordered too much, spurred on by an inquisitive nature, a fear of missing out and a certainty I'll want things my girlfriend doesn't.

Thankfully, it's a very cheap menu. Yeeeahah!

Local sausage, yellow split peas dressed in olive oil with raw onion scattered over, grilled smoked pork, steaming hot stuffed vine leaves, more beetroot tops, smoked pork, this time cooked with wine and lemon, twenty-five snails in a clay pot, and a radiant golden-yellow omelette shining with local goat butter, gleaming like the chariot of Helios.

This omelette gets me very excited. I swoon as yolk orange rays shine out from behind my eyes. Incidentally, the eggs are stirred with local clarified goat butter and mixed with barley flour. The omelette is flat and open and browned, but soft, tender and giving within. The inclusion of flour gives it the faintest blanket-y pancake texture while also retaining an almost runny egg luxuriance. It's fantastic, rich and I gulp down the whole thing. My girlfriend has that look of 'thank God he's found happiness'.

I'm full and cannot finish all the plates. This dismays me. Any two dishes would have been perfect satisfaction for tonight or any other night. I feel joy. I feel swelled with a love for food and cooking that I occasionally lose sight of when it seems like just a job.

It strikes me that, were I to lead a life following goat bells over hot fields of rocks and spiky plants, or surviving the cold, damp Cretan winters, what wonderful food this would be to return to. This little omelette dished up with beetroot tops, or maybe the split peas and slices of sausage, or simply a bowl of broken rusk soaked in oily peppers would taste no less to me than a reward.

This is food not only for shepherds but also for those mythical heroes I am reading about. As they go about their dangerous travels, such wonderful plates of egg, small pieces of pork, herbs and honey are the very sustenance for strength and sinew needed, that the club may fall with shattering effect or that arms may strangle the clenching cabled necks of giants in their death throes.

Nourishing in mind, body, spirit and wallet, my dinner is fine, honest food and I'm more than happy to pay the bill in ways I so often am not in grander restaurants of sophisticated mediocrity. Yes, I pay with pleasure and ask more questions about the omelette.

'Foodies' would be wise to remember to travel with an open mind so that, rather than navigate by Michelin stars, they may try opening a small door to simple pleasures. And I would be wise to remember that my fellow countrymen on surrounding tables were only looking for the same thing as I and, that throughout mythology, the haughty and the arrogant only come to a sticky end.

Watermelon with Olives and Goats' Cheese

This is so often made with feta, and while I do like feta, I think to work best the salad needs a softer cheese.

Serves 4

2 large slices of ripe but firm and tasty watermelon, peeled, deseeded and
    chopped into big chunks
Half a small red onion, halved and thinly sliced
Big handful of interesting little purple-black or Kalamata olives (devoid
    of any disgusting garlicky, citrus or chilli marinade), pitted
Good handful of picked fresh, pert mint leaves
Good handful of young flat-leaf parsley, leaves only
Small tub (150 g/5 oz) soft creamy tangy fresh goats' or sheep's curd or
    cheese
Smallest pinch of dried oregano
Good handful of toasted pumpkin seeds
Enthusiastic passing over of preferably Greek extra virgin olive oil
Whizz of squeezed lemon juice
Dusting of piment d'Esplette or mild chilli powder
Sea salt and freshly ground black pepper
Crusty bread, to serve

Place the watermelon in a large bowl. Scatter over the onion. Let the olives
fall where they do. Let half the fresh herbs wander down on to it all. Blob
the curd or cheese here and there. Scatter the dried oregano here and there.
Scatter over the pumpkin seeds and remaining fresh herbs.

Season well with salt and freshly ground black pepper.

Go over with the oil and lemon juice. Scatter over the d'Esplette pepper or
chilli powder.

It should all look buoyant before it gets muddled up at the table.

Eat with good crusty bread.

Fish Eggs

Many moons ago, I found myself on the street just off Scrubs Lane, in swirling drizzle and wild wind that shook and rattled the glowing orange street lamps. It was 11.30 pm.

I met a man there who handed me a parcel. I handed him an envelope containing a large amount of cash.

I'd been sent to buy caviar, and while the darkness and the very time would make anyone think this a shady deal, a good source like was obviously a closely guarded secret in my world. The money was in the thousands, and the 500 gram tins enough to form a considerable height, one similar to a tube of whisky, stacked and wrapped neatly in waxed brown paper.

All this clandestine behaviour for a catering job was for a well-known and respected fashion house who were opening a new store on Sloane Street. I had been given three colours to work with. And those colours were to be reflected in the canapés.

I was a small outfit at the time, but a sample tasting had been approved and I was now left with the gargantuan task of producing 4,000 little bites of cutesy perfection, the most important being a thin, black rye bread cup holding warm, perfectly cooked and slightly oozing scrambled eggs with caviar spooned thickly on top.

The evening of the party arrived. We assembled our kitchen workspace, carpeted the floor in roll-out plastic, plugged in the fridges, installed the ovens. All that for two perfect hours of canapés. My rank of chefs would deliver a seamless procession of nibbles into the soft-skinned hands of 'sleepy giraffes' (how I miss you, A A Gill) and bespoke toad clientele.

The waiting staff were really, really ridiculously good looking.

In my experience, male models and good waiting don't always go hand in hand. Within an hour some gorgeous hunk had managed to drop a tray of beetroot, fig and hot foie-gras tarts all over a white goatskin chaise longue.

The waiting staff were thankfully nothing to do with me.

Anyway. Rewind. Just before the first tray was sent towards the rich, famous and downright spoilt, I thought it time to open some of the caviar in preparation. I removed the seal and untwisted the lid to hear that wonderful faint 'slotch' as the roof of the tin came away from the eggs.

And there they are, green-grey, large, fat eggs in their thousands, and there am I, master of them all. There am I, surrounded by large spoons. There am I, soon to be found climbing into a broom cupboard where I have upended a bucket and am sitting on it, with the bare bulb on, surrounded by cleaning materials and spooning caviar in great, generous, sliding piles into my mouth. I only meant to take a taste. But I'm a caviar Pooh Bear.

Despite eating these generous mouthfuls with a somewhat nervous urgency, the enjoyment is hardly diminished. My mouth and brain are in rapture as those perfectly salted, faintly greasy, plump, popping eggs from heaven are bursting all about my mouth and soul.

I've spilt some down my front; I pick them off my jacket and nibble them as a chimp would termites.

150 or so grams in 'just the one last spoon', and all of a sudden the door is pulled open and before me stands my client. I look up mouth closed around large catering spoon, grey pearls on my jacket, while he looks down with what I can only describe as contained but intense irritation.

'It better be good,' he says. Luckily, realizing he means the job I've been hired to do, my inclination to say, 'don't worry, it's delicious' is only just caught by its toe. He closes the door and I hear him say what sounds like, 'your boss is in the cupboard if you need him'. I wait until I think he's gone.

I walk out of the cupboard with tin and spoon to see my staff all looking at me with raised eyebrows.

'As you were,' I say, 'and send out the beetroot and hot foie-gras tarts, it's 6.30.'

He returns later that night and asks if there is any caviar remaining. There are two tins. To my astonishment, he gives me the opened one. It is still pretty heavy. I feel inclined to decline it. But then again.

Tea-pickled Cucumber with Crème Fraîche Salmon Eggs

Bursting through the front door to remove my trousers and to cook in my boxer shorts, this recipe is a cooling oasis for a sweltering hot summer's day, soothing my agitated soul from an idiotic decision to wear jeans in 31°C/88°F.

Serves 2

1 medium cucumber, washed and peeled so that you leave alternate stripes of skin and peeled flesh down it's whole length

1½ tsp sea salt (*not* table salt!)

1 tsp fennel seeds

75 ml/3-fl oz/¼ cup white wine vinegar

10 g/⅓ oz dill stalks, plus extra top fronds, finely chopped

1 Earl Grey tea bag

Caster (superfine) sugar, to taste

1½ heaped tbsp crème fraîche, double (heavy) cream or creamy yoghurt

1–2 jars of good-quality Keta (salmon eggs)

Freshly ground black pepper

Pinch of fennel pollen or ground fennel seeds, to serve (optional)

Swedish rye-bread crackers (such as Peter's Yard), to serve

Take the peeled cucumber and slice into thin rounds. Put in a sieve (strainer) over a bowl and stir in the salt. Leave to drip drain for at least an hour before collecting up the slices in your hands and squeezing them like a flannel to finally force out as much of the remaining juice as possible into the bowl beneath. Retain the juice. Flop the cucumber back into the sieve over the bowl of juice.

Take a small saucepan and dry toast the fennel seeds in it until their smell comes to the nose (avoid burning them by swirling the seeds often). Add the vinegar and the dill stalks and gently heat with the tea bag. Then stir in enough sugar until it is sweet enough to balance the vinegar but not overly so.

Remove the pan from the heat and the tea bag from the vinegar; it must not be overly stewed with Earl Grey.

Allow to cool before adding half the cucumber juice to dilute it a bit.

Add the sliced cucumber to the vinegar mix and leave for 10 minutes. Squeeze the liquid from the cucumber slices once more, reserving the vinegar mix for anything else you might want it for – it can be used to dress grilled mackerel, mixed with a little Japanese soy sauce.

Splay a pile of the cucumber slices across a plate. Add a large dollop of crème fraîche, double cream or creamy yoghurt and scatter with a little extra finely chopped dill before putting a dollop of sticky salmon eggs on top.

Season with a generous grind of black pepper and maybe a little fennel pollen, if you have some.

Other nice additions can be hard-boiled egg and the leaves of wood sorrel.

Eat with Nordic types of crispbread or crackers.

Warm Leek with Egg and Smoked Salmon Mayonnaise

If you don't have, or don't want smoked salmon – just leave it out and you will have a gentle herb mayonnaise.

Serves 2
4 eggs plus 2 egg yolks
2 tsp Dijon mustard
2 large slices of smoked salmon, chopped (optional)
150 ml/5 fl oz/⅔ cup sunflower oil

50 ml/1⅔ fl oz/2¾ tbsp good extra virgin olive oil, plus extra to combine
   with vinegar

Juice of half a lemon

2 small to medium leeks, peeled of any tough outer stem and trimmed,
   root end left intact

1–2 tsp vinegat

1 tbsp finely chopped fresh chives

1 tbsp finely chopped fresh parsley and chervil

Sea salt and freshly ground black pepper

Hard-boil the 4 eggs and allow them to cool. Liking the yolks more moist
than hard, I would advise 5½ minutes then instantly into a bowl of ice water.

Place the egg yolks into a large bowl. Using a stick blender, blitz the yolks
with the mustard and the smoked salmon.

Combine the sunflower and olive oils in a jug. Very gently and slowly,
in a barely continuous thin, thin stream, pour in the combined oils. The
mayonnaise will soon begin to thicken. If very thick and stiffly ribboned,
relax it with a splash of warm water. Continue until all the oil is used up then
sharpen with a little of the lemon juice. Season with salt. Taste. Add more
lemon juice if required. Set aside.

Bring a large frying pan (skillet) filled with water to the boil and poach the
leeks until very tender. Using tongs, pick them up by the root end and dangle
them so as much water as possible comes out. Pat them dry in a tea towel.

Combine the vinegar with a little olive oil on a large plate. Roll the leeks on
the plate and then lay them on a serving plate. Season with salt.

Peel the hard-boiled eggs. Cut a flat patch from the curved side of each so
they can sit steadily on the serving plate with the yolk facing up. Go over
with a grind of pepper. Halve the eggs.

Spoon a large thick dollop of mayonnaise over the egg halves and then completely cover the mayonnaise with a thorough scattering of herbs. Transfer the egg halves to sit next to the leeks and serve.

Any remaining salmon mayonnaise is delicious in a new potato salad or an egg sandwich.

Smoked Cods' Roe Crudités

'Traditional' crudités can be one of the greatest joys or a miserable affair of 'kiddy stick' batons with some gruesome dippy yoghurt splodge. So we are going to take this on from scratch. Leave out the cods' roe if inclined.

The mayonnaise will freeze well. It is also delicious shaved onto pasta to join toasted pine nuts, parsley, garlic and lemon zest, with a good slug of oil or, more simply, spread on toast with butter and pepper.

Serves 6–8

For the mayonnaise
3 egg yolks
1½ tbsp Dijon mustard
2 large fat garlic cloves, finely grated (optional)
50 g/1¾ oz smoked cods' roe, deskinned and chopped into small blocks (optional)
Good splash of white wine vinegar
150 ml/5 fl oz/⅔ cup sunflower oil
50 ml/1⅔ fl oz/2¾ tbsp good extra virgin olive oil
Juice from half a lemon

For the crudités
1 lovely oversized Sicilian red pepper from a laughably expensive West

London greengrocer (shop is optional)

1 endive, thin disc of brown stalk end and any damaged outer leaves removed and quartered lengthways

1 head of fennel, preferably with lovely green fronds

6 hot long radishes, served with tops

3 whole young carrots scrubbed, not peeled, with bit of stem and the root whisker still attached

Young turnips, scrubbed and tops left on (optional)

Handful of young broad beans in their pods

2 semi-hard-boiled eggs (boiled for 5–5½ minutes, stopping cooked immediately with a plunge into cold water)

In a small processor bowl, or in an open mixing bowl and using a stick blender, blitz together the base of the mayonnaise: the egg yolks, mustard, grated garlic, if using, and cods' roe, if using, and the vinegar.

Combine the sunflower and olive oils in a jug. Slowly incorporate the oils in a thin stream. DO NOT rush this. If, before the oil is all used up, the mayonnaise is ribboning and overly stiff, let it down with a splash with warm water and continue.

If the mayonnaise splits, do not discard. Take a clean bowl, add another egg yolk and slowly feed in the disaster version as you would the oil. It will come together again. You will however need to bump up the other ingredients as it can taste 'over yolky'.

Near the end, add in the lemon juice and, on judging the consistency, add a little more olive oil to get the correct thickness. The mayonnaise should be stiff and hold its on but not be soldier rigid.

Then, and especially if not using the roe, season generously with salt as the mayonnaise can be bland if you are too timid.

Enri Eurice

Twelve years ago, or perhaps a little more, I was taken to Racine on the Brompton Road, alas no longer there. I loved everything about the place, the leather banquettes, old mirrors, panelling, wall lighting and, above all, the thick curtain behind the front door you had to find the cut in to duck inside. It felt as if, when you did, you'd suddenly gone to Paris.

(I once got so tangled up in that curtain, I must have looked like someone panicking and thrashing their way out of a body bag.)

We dined on the fattest snails in parsley butter, fried brains on toast, brandade de morue, veal chops with Roquefort and walnuts, all accompanied by wines from a shockingly good list, and followed by a crème caramel that boasted a caramel made by someone with the confidence to take it to that precise shade of dark brown that happens just before it becomes bitter.

So I went back the following week for another blinder of a meal, including a mussel and saffron mousse that proved a warm, jiggling epiphany of joy, followed by a giving, succulent, gelatinous tête de veau, its richness punctuated by little barbs of caper from the ravigote sauce. I hailed the waiter. 'Can you tell me who the cook is here, because his food is delicious! I've eaten here twice in a week, and would every night if I could!'

'Mais oui!' he replied. 'Ze chef is Monsieur Enri Eurice.'

I paid my bill, made my thanks, gulped down my last pale glimmer of Sancerre, and made straight for Books For Cooks on the Portobello Road to ask the young assistants for any works by chef Enri Eurice.

They couldn't help me. But then, they didn't know of Racine either. And I was left wondering: was this talent a complete newcomer to London?

I told many others of Enri Eurice, and my mother started going to Racine once a month. A few months later, I found myself drinking martinis with Mark Hix in Soho, when his attention was drawn by a tanned, twinkly-eyed and prosperous-looking fellow in a flowery shirt who, for some inexplicable reason, reminded me of a grey heron. Mark shook his hand warmly, turned to me and said, 'Val, do you know the owner of Racine?'

Before he can go on, I leapt in. 'Ah ha! Yes! Monsieur Enri Eurice! Enchanté.'

Came the reply, 'I'll take the compliment, but I'm actually called Henry Harris.'

Mark guffawed. 'God, Val, I really don't understand how your head works.'

Neither, if I'm honest, do I. But now I refer to Enri Eurice, in pure Bermondsey, as Enry Arris.

Veal Chops with Roquefort Butter and Walnuts

Serves 1

1 unwaxed lemon

1 veal chop

½ tsp each of fennel seeds, coriander seeds and dried rosemary

A few stems of fresh sage

5 garlic cloves, 4 unpeeled

40 g/1½ oz/⅓ cup Roquefort cheese

1 tbsp butter, plus extra for frying

3 drops red wine vinegar

1 tbsp finely chopped fresh parsley

½ tsp Dijon mustard (optional)

Olive oil, for frying

Handful of shelled good-quality walnuts

Salt and freshly ground black pepper

1 bunch of watercress and lemon wedge (optional), to serve

With a potato peeler, strip the lemon rind from half the lemon and put in a plastic container together with the chop. Add the fennel seeds, coriander seeds, rosemary, sage and the 4 unpeeled garlic cloves, roughly chopped, and some pepper. Work all this into the chop, making sure it is evenly distributed on both sides. Pop the lid on the plastic container and banish it to the fridge. The longer the better.

Chop the peeled garlic clove very finely.

In a small bowl, mash the cheese, butter, vinegar, chopped garlic, parsley and mustard together and put to one side until ready to cook the chop. If too soft, firm up a little in the fridge. But remember to bring to room temperature before using.

Put a large frying pan (skillet) over a medium heat. Add a little butter and olive oil.

Season the chop well with salt. Put in to the pan with the walnuts around it. The chop should sizzle on entry. Add any loose odds and ends, like garlic and herb trimmings, from the marinade to the pan too – around the chop, not under it, as to avoid burning. Keep an eye on the walnuts – you do not want them to burn. Remove when nicely coloured. You want the meat to be browned and the fat crisped. I like the meat pink inside, but a veal chop is forgiving so you can overcook it if you enjoy such things as mercilessly cooked veal ... but I don't advise it.

Put the chop onto a warmed plate. Make a quenelle with the butter, or just blob a dollop of it on top of the chop. Scatter the walnuts over the chop.

Serve with a pile of watercress on the side, and maybe a wedge of lemon to dress it.

Catsuit (feat. Pat Llewellen)

Coast to Coast is nearly a wrap but for the last shoot.

It's been a genuine laugh, as I love the crew. Travelling from west to east, from the sea into the River Severn then into the Tamar, Avon, Itchen, Test, Kennet, Thames, then across to Essex and Norfolk, I've cooked pike, grayling, dabs, crayfish, indeed every fish we've caught. Met many fine folk along the way, enjoyed a few memorable pub nights too. The fug in the car is just bearable, stinky with rods and damp kit. We've all got pretty feral.

Joining us has been Duck Cam™, two mallard drake decoys fixed together behind a duck. Each is drilled with holes made for the lengths of sawn-up fishing rod that hold it together in a convincing triangular formation. Clever, no?

The director, Joe, must be given full credit for Duck Cam™, born on his kitchen table and built over a week. Early trials tended to sink, but Blu-Tack and a lot of epoxy glue prove successful.

Inside are the remote parts from a toy car. Outside, a GoPro fixed underneath.

Devastatingly effective, despite the din from the motor. Oh, and the forward/reverse being the wrong way around, which has made for some confusing steering.

Fish we expected to flee find Duck Cam™ curious. Barbel no less than show off in front of it. Trying to film chub one day, it got stuck in some reeds, but lo and behold, a West Country girl walking her dogs on the far bank, strips down to her pink camisole and knickers and wades in to get it. Genius! And on film too. She doesn't think twice about signing a release form.

Later that day, however, Duck Cam™ stalls and bobs out to sea through the Itchen estuary. We are devastated. Worse still, the rushes sent back to London are accidentally recorded over – I think with Bill Granger squeezing some lime onto something healthy and delicious.

A week later we have to drive back to do the scene again. This time, no luck fishing, no stripping, no Duck Cam™, nor does my puff pastry for my trout and pernod pie rise to the golden heights it had the first time round. A damp squib.

Anyway, it's minnow day. I ask our runner, who's already been sent off to look for something or other in Bristol, to go to a fancy dress shop and hire me a cat suit. Head, tail, ears and whiskers.

'Err, why?' she enquires.

All will become apparent. 'Just get me one and I'll refund the kitty.'

Preparing for the next cooking sequence, I take a two-litre water bottle, cut off the top quarter, drop a rock in the bottom and put the top back, but inverted, to form a funnel. I gaffer tape it all together, more gaffer to attach a string, poke in the last of my cheese and ham sandwich and launch it into the river. I secure my string end to a willow. I won't have to wait long.

The idea is to catch minnows, toss them in flour and then fry 'em up and peddle them as 'fresh water white bait'.

I only need to give it half an hour before hauling up the bottle, now teeming with minnows. I can't fry them live so kill them all with a sharp pin. It's a bizarre micro-morbid task.

My cat suit has arrived and I put it on. It's rather fetching. Black and white with a pink nose and long, silky whiskers. I'm just wearing my boxers inside, and have to admit, I'm feeling rather frisky.

'This is not a good idea!' says the director.

'Trust me,' I say, 'she'll love it.'

'Who's she?' you may ask, 'The cat's mother?'

Well, yes. My telly mother, the great Pat Llewellyn, she who begat Jamie Oliver, producer of *Two Fat Ladies*, Gordon, Heston and many others. Visionary, inventor, the grande-dame of modern food television.

On starting out Pat once said to me, 'It's important not to get a reputation for being hard to work with.' I logged this while also interpreting it as, 'Please do what I say.'

Today I have no intention of asking permission for what I am about to do.

'Will you be talking?' asks the sound man.

'Miaow,' I reply, licking my polyester wrist. Audio department is laughing enough that we have to restart a few times, while I also have to peel the paws back as they make holding a frying pan quite hard, and are prone to smoke over the camping stove.

I cook, chase my tail, paw a sun spot on the table, roll under the table, lick my arm and occasionally toss a shoal of minnows in the pan. Miaowing all the way. I might add that I do a very convincing purr, using my tongue behind my teeth.

Minnows go to the plate, the plate to the grass and, on all fours, my face to the minnows

'Cuuuut!'

'Well Val, that was fucking weird,' says Joe the director.

Because we're filming while the series is already being aired, the rushes are rushed back to London.

Sure enough, a little later, I get Pat on the phone: 'Val, can you explain yourself?'

'Did you like my fat cat, Pat?'

'I'm being serious, Val, please tell me you filmed a normal take.'

'No! I wanted to end with something special and what could be more appropriate than a cat on the riverbank cooking fish?'

'You are joking?' her voice has raised. 'Do you think that anyone turning the programme on and seeing a cat will know what the hell is HAPPENING?'

'Yes. A cat eating fish. I don't think you are thinking about this the right way,' I continue.

'I don't care what you think, Val, you are not producing this ser ...'

Joe the director can only guess at what's going on, and can't take any more. He dashes forward and blurts down the phone, 'Yes! Pat, we did film it normally.'

'Oh, Joe, you are such a Nancy,' I chide. Truth is we did film it twice. Feline and un-feline version. I just wanted to extend play a little longer.

Sea Bass with Herb Oil

1 fresh 1 kg/2 lb wild sea bass or a large gilt head bream

Wild fennel tops, plus some fennel leaves for the oil (wild fennel is a common and easily identifiable plant growing near many roadsides and verges)

2 sprigs of fresh rosemary

1 tsp fennel seeds

5 tbsp extra virgin olive oil

40 g/1½ oz/3 tbsp butter

1 finger-length strip of unwaxed lemon rind

8 large fresh sage leaves

1 large bay leaf, torn

4 good, hard garlic cloves, very finely sliced

Sea salt

A squeeze of lemon, to serve (optional)

Dried chilli flakes, to serve (optional)

Stuff the stomach cavity of the fish with wild fennel tops or 1 rosemary sprig.

In a pan, dry toast the fennel seeds until their smell comes to the nose, swirling them occasionally to avoid burning. Pour in the extra virgin olive oil and drop in the butter. Pinch the strip of lemon rind and add to the pan. Add the remaining rosemary sprig, the fennel leaves, the sage and the bay leaf. Add the garlic to the oil and cook for 5 minutes or so, very gently so as not to burn the butter or oil. The garlic should be tender.

Preheat the grill (broiler) to full blast.

Put the stuffed bass under the grill and cook for 6–7 minutes per side. If not sure if it is cooked through, poke a knife into the thickest part of the meat, behind the head, where the tip of the blade only meets with the faintest resistance at the spine. The skin should be bubbled, browned and blistered.

Lay on a plate and spoon the herbs and oil over the fish.

Delicious accompanied by steamed fennel, well seasoned with salt, and served with a little dried chilli and lemon juice.

Part One – Big Chub and Head Hunters

There are relatively few trips in my life I could ever truly describe as a proper adventure. And by that I mean an adventure in the Victorian sense of chairs, equipment, food, boats and tents carried in procession over tricky ground.

A trip into Arunal Pradesh with three of my closest friends, Richard, Tom and Ben, was one of them.

We had gone to fish the Mahi-Dehing River for the golden mahseer, loosely speaking a huge type of chub that live in the raging rivers of the low Himalayas.

Camp was made on a sand patch at the river's edge, where great clouds of butterflies came to drink, delicately wobbling in the breeze.

On the far side the tall tree line of trunks were draped and hung with creepers and led into thick, dark jungle, amplifying a mesmerizing cacophony of whistles, trills, whoops, a strange water-drip noise and the peculiar see-saw sounds of birdsong. Creeping out into the cold mist on the first morning, I'd seen two maroon-coloured jungle dogs licking the water on the opposite bank. Romantic? Lyrical? So far. But, done on a shoestring budget, the trip had to come with issues.

On the not so serious side, there was no fishing kit outside what we'd bought ourselves. Even our heaviest fast-sinking fly lines were simply swept aside by the torrents of water. We gave up on our salmon rods, and switched to spinning. While resulting in the desired effect, it now illustrated the immense power of these fish. Even more powerful when multiplied by the force of the river. Many were lost to bent-out hooks and weak ring clips, while general spares had not been sufficiently accounted for.

The relentless heat of the midday sun meant that we kept the same hours as the fish. Early morning and late afternoon to nightfall. The largest landed was forty-five pounds, despite the attempted removal of a jacket mid-battle that met with a resounding 'Nooooo!' from all of us.

We tried for the mystical goonch, a huge and hideous-fanged bottom dweller and swallower of children, but even chicken heads and feet stuffed into a sock and bound to a shark hook got no moonlight interest. There were no children to hand.

Cutting my leg quite badly on the second day, falling while trying to leap athletically over the rocks to grab a net, I discovered a medical kit contained only a dead moth and pair of nail scissors.

Nothing, however, compared to what could have been the end to it all when Tom, the most eager of us, rowed over to a huge, deep pool of racing water, overhung by a flat, sloping boulder the size of a house. We'd all agreed it was there where the bigger fish lay.

While his studs had worked well along the boulder-strewn shallows, they were like skates on the rock. We cheered as he reached the summit to raise his rod in victory, then gasped as he took off down the slope like a ski jumper, only to disappear 'sloop' into the pool in full wading gear.

We'd become careless with life jackets as the heat had made wearing them uncomfortable, while the terrain had kept us fishing on the safer shallow side. So Tom wasn't wearing one.

Terrified, the porters, who couldn't swim, ran up and down hands on heads, while a dinghy was launched and those of us who could swam out in search.

I thought he'd drowned, and was grasped by a growing anxiety and dread. After a period of time that could only mean despair, I heard a very faint 'guuuuuuyyys, down heeeeerrre!'

Some 200 metres downstream and there he was, spluttering around in the shallows. The currents were so strong he'd been whipped past us and deposited exhausted on to a sandbank downriver.

'Crystal clear down there,' he said wiping his wet hair while miraculously retaining not only his rod but sense of style... if YSL ever made fishing kit.

The food prepared by our cook was spectacular, if rather monotonous. Namely ten ill-fated chickens in a crate. He would disappear daily into the tangle of jungle and emerge with great armfuls of edible greens and banana leaves. He turned the breasts and legs from said chickens into the most delicious curry, the jungle greens he simply fried with a little ghee, cumin, and garlic. But it was chicken innards that I will remember forever.

Dragged through thumb and forefinger, the intestines were emptied and cleaned in the river. These guts, the heart and the liver, he chopped finely together with charred spices, ginger, chilli and garlic. Mushed with ghee he then rolled them in an A4-size cutting of softened banana leaf and rolled them up. This green parcel he then pushed down inside a similar length of bamboo. The ends were blocked up with mud and the package tossed casually into the embers of the fire. After a while, the bamboo split with a crack and a hiss – a rudimentary kitchen timer-cum-meal rolled into one, to be poked from the embers and broken open. The leaf unrolled, we consumed the contents hungrily, squatting by the river, picking the chicken innards from the floppy leaf, occasionally reaching for a sip of Scotch from a plastic cup. Heaven.

The fishing had been amazing. Many fish over twenty pounds, a few in the thirties, the one over forty and a fish so huge it broke Ben after a fight of forty minutes.

We floated away from camp five days later, having been visited the previous night by barefoot men with AK-47s. We knew of local unrest, so this moment reasoned that it was time to go. What we were moving towards however I could never have imagined ...

Part Two – Nagaland

I am crouched next to a huge cast-iron pot. In it lies a large mass of chopped pig, the hairs pickling up from the hacked daubs and sticking out through the two inches of blup-blupping oil that sits on top.

This does not faze me one little bit. I've eaten far more frightening things, and the smell is delicious. The sauce below the slick is a warm orange colour, a sign that chillies and turmeric lurk within.

There is around me a wooden fence erected in a curve, with benches against it. Hung at head height, along its whole sweep, are woven caps fixed to the wall at exact intervals so that, when someone sits, their head comes to rest naturally in a ceremonial cap, from which feathers protrude like sunrays. It strikes me that, through them, when all residents are slotted into place, they share some kind of unspoken communications.

Nagaland is not easy to get into. Relations between the Indian government and the otherwise ferociously independent Nagas are fraught, and we have been lucky to get visas. It has been a long journey to Kohima, packed with fellow travellers and an infestation of cockroaches of *Indiana Jones* proportions. When we pulls the beds down, the cabin turns suddenly into an infested tomb. But exhausted from the fishing we have left behind, plus several sleeping pills, I am immune to the scuttling. On awakening, I am told I missed quite the hexapodic party on my chest.

But no matter: we are here for the Hornbill Festival, a heritage event held by the Naga tribes to keep their traditions, dancing and folklore vibrant. It is named for the hornbill bird, as its feathers are included by the tribes in their traditional costumes.

This first night, and God knows how, Ben has managed to get us invited to the Miss Nagaland beauty pageant. It goes on for ages, and I fall asleep thanks to the plentiful gins and tonic at the hotel, only to be nudged awake – apparently, I'm getting stern looks from local councillors, who are not impressed.

We arrive the next day at the festival itself, where I am immediately confronted by an elderly man. He resembles a raisin in a tail coat, and he dashes up to me, stops dead. And flashes me. His beady black eyes flash too, as he reveals (thankfully) not what I'd expected to see, but the inside of his coat, embroidered in bright thread. It reads:

Britain

We helped you in WWII

Where are you?

You have deserted us.

He smiles, glances to the side and exits pursued by a rather lacklustre policeman holding a banana leaf with his rice lunch inside it.

The Naga men are tall and proud looking, muscular and fearsome. In their traditional dress, they carry spears and knives hang from their belts. Boars' tusks and brightly coloured beads adorn their necks and wrists, and criss cross their bare chests. Black and white feathers crown their heads. And long, narrow nets, framed at the mouth like small basketball hoops, sit at their buttocks – the head baskets that once carried the bodyless grimaces of their enemies. The women wear largely white or navy blue dresses, and are more beautiful for their traditional dress than they seemed in their pageant frocks the night before.

Watching the dances, their stamping and formation, I am mesmerized. I want to give up my London life and marry into a Naga tribe right now. I've decided I like the costume of the Angami tribe the most. This is convenient because, quite coincidentally, I strike up a conversation with a friendly old man called Kevisu, who so happens to be one of the Angami elders. Which is how I find the pig pot.

Crouching there, Kevisu tells me a little of our combined history, and how by the 1880s the British had pretty much outlawed and abolished most of the head-hunting for which the Naga were notorious.

'But then,' he says, 'you have problem with Japanese and we help British.'

(During the Second World War, the British were dealt significant losses in Kohima by the Japanese. Should you visit the area, there's a place called the Tennis Court were some of the bloodiest fighting took place. And under the backdrop of the hills lie the serried rows of gravestones – among them so many from the Dorsetshire Regiment. It's very moving.)

'So headhunting okay again.' And Kevisu points to the supporting beam of the long house, where a cluster of heads are fixed together by their hair, like grim party balloons. I don't ask who they were.

Kevisu tells me that the Naga operated in small groups or alone, taking heads under cover of night. He crouches and demonstrates their stalking methods, then sharply pulls a hand across his throat with a grim-faced 'chkkk' sound. The British paid by the head. He encourages me to act out the movement too, and while I do, I ask about the man and his coat.

'We help you a lot,' Kevisu says, 'but when war over, you do not look after us, and we have many problems.'

By dark, I am smashed on palm wine. My coconut-husk cup has been topped up continually, and I appear to have bought a lot of Naga blankets. The rice and pork have proved memorably delicious, thick, rich and warming, and leaving the faintest growl of chilli on the back of my throat. I have eaten a lot of it yet I am still undone by the wine, and have come to the conclusion that its fermentation has continued in my insides. It is a strange drunkenness. I feel as though I can hear everything, the evensong of the insects, the whole jungle.

And then the tribal singing starts. Delicate. Rhythmic. With lulling clicking noises and harmonic pings. I've never heard anything like it and, lying on my back looking at the stars, I feel as though I am floating away into the night sky.

Until suddenly Kevisu shakes me awake. 'You sing the next song with us. Up! Up!'

'But I can't sing like you. I don't know the song.'

'No, no. Listen ...' he says as most of the eldest stand and pick up their spears. They stand straight and stiff as ramrods, and ...

'IT'S A LONG WAY TO TIPPERARY,

IT'S A LONG WAY TO GO...'

My friends and I all look at each other and start to laugh with joy. On heading for the airport, I wrestled a strong desire to not return home but keep going into the unknown.

Naomi Duguid's Burmese Egg Curry

I am a huge fan of food writer Naomi Duguid, and especially her book *Burma: Rivers Of Flavour*, which features this exceptional recipe. It has become a staple in my kitchen – always cooked by my girlfriend.

Serves 4

4 large eggs

80 ml/3 fl oz/⅓ cup groundnut (peanut) oil

⅛ tsp turmeric

2 small shallots, minced

116

2 tsp minced garlic

¼ tsp chilli powder

2 medium tomatoes, rinsed and finely chopped

2 tsp fish sauce

½ tsp sea salt, or to taste

2 or 3 green cayenne chillies, seeded and sliced lengthways into strips

Place the eggs in a saucepan, add cold water to cover, bring to the boil and cook at a medium boil for 8 minutes. Drain the eggs and cool in cold water. When the eggs are cool enough to handle, peel them.

Heat the oil in a wide, heavy frying pan (skillet) over medium high heat. Add the turmeric and stir to dissolve it. When oil is hot enough to sizzle when a drop of water is dropped into it, add the peeled eggs and fry until golden and a little blistered all over: cook on each side in turn, then try to balance the eggs on their ends to cook the tips. Frying the eggs is a fun little task, quickly done, and it makes them very attractive.

With a slotted spoon, lift the eggs out of the hot oil and on to a plate. Cut them lengthways in half and set aside. Pour off all but 2–3 tablespoons of the oil (the oil can be used again for stir-frying).

Heat the oil remaining in the pan over medium heat, add the shallots and garlic and fry briefly, until translucent. Add the chilli powder and tomatoes and, stirring frequently to prevent sticking, cook at a strong simmer until the tomatoes have broken down into a softened mass, about 10 minutes.

Stir in the fish sauce and salt, then taste and adjust the seasoning if you wish. Raise the heat to medium high, add the chilli strips, and stir. Place the eggs cut side down in the sauce and cook until the oil sizzles, about 3 minutes.

Serve hot or at room temperature.

Auberge de la Mole

Every now and then in life, you come across a restaurant that gives infinite pleasure on every single level. The requirement for 'memorably good' doesn't necessarily have to be the very best food, as one's mood and the restaurant's location and ambience (ghastly word) come into it as well.

While I have eaten in some of the world's best, I rarely recall them with the same excitable fondness as those more provincial meals of greatness. With exceptions, however exquisite and pretty the food, and however beautiful their interiors, high-end establishments often leave me feeling as though I'm in church and I become oddly hushed.

This unceasing excellence somehow sucks me in as I find myself savouring the sincerity of the consommé, the single-minded pursuit of a celeriac's soul, the fragile delicacy of crunch and expressions of lamb. (Can you really cook a lamb's expressions?) I find it exhausting. And after years of restaurant chasing, I have returned to the food I love: a Greek mountain omelette made with clarified goat butter and buckwheat, a killer tomato salad, that rice with cinnamon in it, something grilled with the smell of charcoal about it.

Take me to San Sebastian to watch chacolí wine splash onto the waiter's shoes while sizzling turbot is rolled on to its white underside. Take me to my ravaged, dirtied tablecloth of stray noodles and crab shell in Vancouver's Chinatown. To that plate of pappardelle con cingale in a Tuscan trattoria, that bowl of curried salmon soup in Sweden, to that taco, that sauerkraut, those udon and so on.

Some fifteen years ago, my girlfriend Valentine (born on the same day of the same month of the same year, and with the same name) and I drove through the dry summer countryside between Nice and Cannes, looking for a roadside establishment called Auberge de la Mole, a fabled former truckers' stop she'd heard about, with a good reputation.

We walked into a tile-floored room, its tables laid with pink napkins and cloths of a colour that reminded me of silent elderly couples dining in restaurants around Cobham, where my grandmother lived. The food emerged from a green-tiled kitchen where an elderly lady and two men were working hard. They seemed to be family.

We sat, said we were happy with the house wine, which was promptly plonked in front of us, followed not two minutes later by two huge terrines, one coarse, one smooth, along with a two-litre jar of cornichons, and bread and butter. Not having the hang of the place, I took a small portion, only for the terrines to be whisked away and banged down on the table of a couple sitting just behind us.

The terrine was wonderful, a great brick, mottled like a drystone wall, of pork, white fat, offal and juniper. I wanted more but by now it was at the far end of the restaurant.

Knife down and ZOOOM! the plates were changed and a great, cherry-red mountain of crayfish, piled to a pleasing height, slid in between us, delicately cooked and dripping in hot butter. Hello. What's that taste? Nutmeg. Yum! French potted shrimp with added fiddling. It was amazingly good. I tore through the bread, mopping up the butter, spent shells falling off the edge of my plate like a penny-push arcade game.

'Slow down,' said Val, 'I've only had three!'

Shells whisked away, and THUMP! a crispy thing lands. And here is where it got really exciting. We have slices of overlapped potato. Crisped and opened to resemble something between a scorched artichoke and a sunburnt armadillo. The potato is salty and crispy with a soft umami fatgasm in its overlapped recesses. Val tells me to stop pulling off the petals, so I grab a knife and cut into it. Wake the mayor, it's delicious! Lined with apple, with a lobe of fresh foie gras at its centre like a grub in its cocoon, it is so good it shouldn't be allowed. We destroy it.

'The human body is a truly amazing thing,' says Val, looking at my expanding stomach. I tell her I have an excess fat outlet behind my kneecaps, and that it's all draining into my socks.

We think it's all over. That was brilliant, I think I need a vervain tea now. No such luck! The plates disappear, to be replaced by two more plates of crisp, pink duck breast with ceps.

I debate for a split second whether I have the strength to continue and then finish every last morsel.

And then chocolate mousse. I have no fondness for mousse as a rule, but in the mood to complete the job at hand, I scrape the last traces from the ramekin. Finally, unable to resist the thought of a digestif, fizzing and bubbling down through the system as it eats, erodes and dissolves, I order a 'drain cleaner', by which I mean a heady Armagnac to conclude a truly fabulous meal, if not the fattiest I have ever eaten.

I thank the family of cooks as I leave. Not looking up, she simply raises a wave over her shoulder while the two men smile briefly and nod. I like this. I sit in the passenger seat as we drive back, silent and smiling, window down, the warm smell of the mountains wafting in, and fall fast asleep.

That meal was just so. So completely just so that I will never return or attempt to repeat it. Well, not intentionally, anyway.

Advice on the Common Cold

If of any use to you at all, here's my tuppence on the common cold. The truth is, I don't really get colds and nor do I intend to. I don't have the time for them. I need to be getting on.

Perhaps once in every three years I succumb, reluctant and furious, to the sick bed. But I am convinced of the following:

First, I eat a lot of garlic. A serious amount. It makes its way in to gremolata, aioli, pomme purée, sauces, soups, stews. I relish it raw, roasted, grated, chopped or smushed. I swear it works!

Second – and not to be dismissed – I wear scarves. I rarely take them off. Even in hot weather, I will have something draped about my person. Natural thermostat comes in the type of material you wind around your neck. Silk for summer, wool for winter. I believe it to be even more effective than the garlic.

Third, you must say to yourself – and say it with conviction – to the sickly gathering in your ears and throat, 'There is no reason that I host or entertain you. Goodbye.'

If all else fails, drink ginger tea until it runs out from your under your eyeballs and go to bed in three jumpers. Bloody well sweat the brute out!

The Pig

This familiar pig.

I am scared of it.

I'm not man enough to climb the gate, shake the bucket and stand my ground.

This makes me feel fearful and weak.

My sister is woman enough for it.

We have finished a food shoot.

The weather is hot, too hot to want to be in a car.

And no place for a pavlova.

There is no home for the pavlova.

It doesn't fit in with anyone's onward plans.

However delicious looking.

Must we really throw it away?

I do not want to throw it away but I have no room, either in or out.

I carry it one-handed like a waiter with tray held high.

Under the evening sun across the orange field, smoking with pollen.

Pig trots forward in his menacing way as I reach the gate, the ticking wire seems a thin line of defence, little more than one drawn in pencil.

The gate shudders and drips with froth.

I'm not man enough to climb over the gate, as I have told you before.

I will throw it to this monstrous pig.

I throw badly, like an infant with a ball.

The pavlova lands on the pig's head, unbroken, slightly cocked to one side.

A French artist, actually more a Byzantine merchant, a Dutchman in Ottoman fashion.

Caught in the bristles the string of white currants makes a good pearl earring to finish the look.

Indignity aside, it suits him.

He turns and walks away looking almost elegant.

I walk off feeling foolish.

So much for being raised on a farm, as I'd once told the public weekly.

Black Pudding with Tomato Salad

This mixture is so delightful that I often find myself eating it for lunch. It's hard to find a good boudin noir in the UK. This French equivalent of black pudding is generally 'wetter' within as it tends to include more onion and often apple too, but less bulking from oats, rusk or whatever. But black pudding is just as tasty, be it generally considerably firmer. Go for one with a softer texture, closer to its French counterpart, if you can find such.

Serves 4

1 nice soft black pudding (I like Trealy Farm brand)

25 g/1 oz/2 tbsp butter

Splash of sunflower oil

1 good, ripe beef tomato or other large and interesting specimen, rinsed

1½ tsp red wine vinegar

1 tsp caster (superfine) sugar

1 heaped tsp Dijon mustard

1 small garlic clove, finely grated

3 tbsp extra virgin olive oil

1 apple

A few fresh basil leaves, torn

2 leaves of fresh lovage, finely chopped (optional)

Half a small red onion, very finely sliced

Sea salt

Take a good serving of black pudding and slice in thickish rounds, removing the skin if artificial. You can leave the skin on should it be a true skin.

In a small frying pan (skillet) heat the butter and sunflower oil and very gently sizzle the pudding, taking care not to burn it but nonetheless getting in crispy on both sides.

While the dark prince fries, slice the tomato and lay out on a plate. Season generously with salt.

In a tea cup or small bowl, mix together the vinegar, sugar and mustard with the grated garlic. Beat in the olive oil with a fork. The vinaigrette should become thick and creamy.

Peel and core the apple half and thinly slice, then cut the slices to matchsticks and sprinkle over the tomato. Spoon the vinaigrette over, then scatter the herb leaves and onion on top.

Take the cooked black pudding to the plate and enjoy with a cold glass of Normandy cider.

Tip Another suggestion would be to sauté some onions in butter until tender, then add apple pieces and continue to sauté until both the onion and apple are browned. Splash liberally with cognac or Armagnac and a dash of cider vinegar, then cook the alcohol away completely. Season with salt and pepper and eat with the black pudding.

Outside

Lying on the grass, the grass is not grass, the clouds are not clouds, the droning bees are not droning or bees and I am not me. All human labels have come loose and blown away.

It doesn't last long.

This happens rarely. I would like it to happen more and to be able to hang on to it longer.

It is exactly this 'want' that sees the end of it.

The Cake Story

So there I was smart jacket and shiny shoes, half cut but vibrant at some clustered drinks party in Notting Hill. My good humour has been somewhat worn away as I have been stuck with one of those meerkat types who constantly glance over your shoulder, scouting for the next 'mwoah' on their cocktail safari.

I didn't want to talk to this velveteen nitwit any longer when, looking for an exit, I suddenly felt a strong tugging on my arm.

It was Rita, famed authoritarian on living well, and soon I was steering her to give me the commission of a birthday cake for a Linley child, her godson. She wants a rocket, so I suggest that it should be modelled on Tintin's *Destination Moon* adventure: a red and white chequered rocket with meringue smoke.

Remembering an iced beehive cake I got for my third birthday, complete with little iced bees on angelica stems buzzing all about, I go on to suggest an angelica launch tower. Thankfully, I stop myself after this; it is clear the commission is mine and I'd be wise to curb my enthusiasm.

'Great,' she says. 'Bill me when it's done.' The cake's to be delivered in five days time to Kensington Palace at 3 pm.

My catering company, Green Pea, was hidden away off Ladbroke Grove in a knackered prefab building of two floors that also contained a working men's club, and certainly disguised any idea that lavish food preparation, sit-down dinners organized like military campaigns or thousands of fiddly fancies for celebrated fashion houses, might be prepared within. The common parts smelt of fag smoke and disinfectant, and every strip light outside our kitchen blinked or strobed. The floors were covered in panels of grey nylon knee-burn carpeting or goose shit-coloured lino, always wet with bad mop work. And our kitchen within it was the equivalent of a spotless, new white shoebox … just one that's placed within a large, damp cardboard box on the pavement.

Our rent was delightfully low, and the local vicar had suggested I occasionally buy a few rounds and a packet of stale pork scratchings for the chaps at the bar downstairs. Put some 50ps in the pool table and calmly face whatever gripe the grumpy maintenance manager would want to moan at me about. Show support in effect.

I bought a copy of *Destination Moon* and went to my head chef Debbs, a true 'Aussie battler', whose punctuality left a lot to be desired. But when there was work to be done she did it, and did it very well.

Debbie's particular talent was cakes. They were exceptional to the point that were she to make a squirrel cake, if it were put down next to a real squirrel, you'd be hard pushed to tell them apart until its whiskers twitched. Back home her cakes had won many competitions and been featured in magazines and we had delivered some 'real beauts' for many events. Her cakery was an additional string to our bow, as it's a discipline I had always shirked in the pursuit of savoury, lacking a single tooth that I'd describe as particularly sweet. My sponges on a bad day could dent car doors, while her sponges on a bad day were so light it was hard to keep them from floating off the stand. Where my iced cakes would resemble an adobe hut, hers resembled the ornate plasterwork of a palace ballroom.

I brief her on our rocket. 'No problem, girlfriend,' she replies in her thick accent, 'I can do this with my eyes closed.' She stuffs the copy of *Tintin* into her soft basket of cake magazines, yarns of wool and knitting needles.

I wish she'd never said that. I'm a superstitious man. A good job can only be expressed after a good job's been done.

Two days later I ask her if she'd started on the cake. 'Don't worry, girlfriend, plenty of time. I'll do it the day before.' I wasn't worried. She was a pro after all, having made hundreds of cakes far more complicated than a rocket.

The next day comes, and I can't find her either with my phone or with multiple anxious trips to the kitchen. 'Christ, the cake's for tomorrow,' I think.

... And then tomorrow comes.

Now, you may well ask why I couldn't have made the cake, given the situation. And the answer is I could have, but it would not have been able to command the price I'd charged. So I find myself on the day of delivery, no less, spare with worry. Despite my belief that you should not ring people before 9 o'clock in the morning, I've been hammering her number since 6.30 am after waking at 5 from restless Tintin-based anxiety dreams and broken sleep. Chain smoking isn't working, and I can't even fry myself an egg. Something's got to be very wrong when I won't make myself breakfast.

Finally, she calls. 'Now, girlfriend, you're not gonna loike what I hiv to say, but I got in two hours ago. Broke up the wagon and roasted the horses, if you know what I mean. I feel rough as a wombat's arse. I'll be at the kitchen in thirty ticks. Please don't be there yourself. You always striss me out when you're strissed.'

'So when should I come?' I ask.

'Come at one.'

'See you there.'

By midday, I can take the stress no longer and drive over.

Thank God I did. The kitchen is a bomb site of broken sponge, pink icing and knocked-over colouring. Smoke seeps from the oven.

'Meringue ...?' I murmur.

'Yis,' she whimpers.

I open the door and ... think of burnt villages.

'Right Debbs, for the record: I don't like you right now. Clear up this mess. Roll out some red icing and make some coffee. I'm going to Sainsbury's.'

126

My plan is as follows: buy two Swiss rolls, some chopsticks, a packet of ice-cream cones and pre-made meringues in a plastic box.

The supermarket is packed and the queue is horrendous. I'm fidgeting like a bank robber and I'm getting looks.

Back in the kitchen and Deborah is slouched in a chair, her mascara running. 'Val, I'm so sorr ...'

'No time for that. Cut some rocket fins out of that box and cover them in foil. Don't crinkle it.'

I stick the Swiss rolls on top of each other, fastening them together with two chopsticks. Another protruding chopstick at the top is fitted with an upside down ice-cream cone, now a mighty rocket nose cone. The fins made, we carefully roll the rocket in red icing, gluing it with apricot jam, the only jam to hand.

'Right,' I say. 'This will have to do.' I already know that to send a bill would be outrightly wrong. 'We'll stop of and get some white ribbon. Stripy rocket.'

'But we can't deliver this!' she says.

'What would you have me do, Debbs? Of course! Silly me! Why don't we pop down to the rocket cake shop! This is the cake, so let's just make the best of it!'

So we load this oversized red crayon into a box. We grab the bits and bobs and leave. Debbs probably shouldn't be driving but I'm leant over the back seat holding the rocket upright in the box in the boot.

We stop outside Temptation Alley haberdashers and she gets the ribbon. We turn down the entrance road for Kensington Palace and take the first speed bump too fast.

The rocket bends, a chopstick now pushing through the sponge and into the icing, which pushes the icing off the sponge while also detaching it from the iced section of the nose cone. The whole thing droops and tears, and now looks like some kind of a post-coital rhino's cock.

'Deborah, slow down!' I shout.

She brakes; it gets worse. I'm spare with stress as we park.

As we unload, Debbs looks at it. 'Chroist, it looks like a cock,' she says.

'Pass me my coat,' I say tightly. We cover the box with my black velvet jacket and carry it, one arm supporting the cake under the coat, one scooped under the box. I look like someone taking their cat to the vet.

We reach the security booth.

'Hello, sir.'

'I'm here to deliver a cake,' I say.

'Can we take a look please, sir?'

'It's a surprise!' I squeak.

'Maybe, sir, but we don't like surprises here, please remove the coat.'

So I do.

'Err what kind of cake is that then, sir?'

'A rocket cake,' I whisper, blushing and looking at the ground.

Professional to the end he tries to suppress giggles, but his eyes are beginning to well up. He nods for his colleague to take a look as another policeman strolls up to join him.

'Rocket cake,' he says, more that his mate gets the joke than anything else.

'Very good, sir, on you go.'

I can hear them sniggering as I walk on towards the entrance to the house. The Gates of Doom! At the door, I wish the ground would crack open and I'd slowly disappear underground like some character in a Tim Burton film, the empty smoking box and jacket burped out.

I haven't noticed until now but Debbs is still wearing her creased whites and pink-blotched apron. Her orange, wiry hair has largely crept out of its band. We look absolutely mad.

I recall one of the Linleys opens the door, I remember not who. 'Oh good, the cake,' they say warmly. 'Just leave it here.'

'Actually, I was wondering if we might be shown somewhere we can set it up and put on the finishing touches.'

I've stalled for time! Delayed mortification, if you prefer. We are shown into a drawing room and to a little table in the corner where we are invited to set it up.

We fudge the cake back to straightness. Turning the damage towards the bookshelf. The hopefully unseen side. I put the meringues down on the floor. 'Fins please,' I ask reaching out. Debbs rootles around in her bag and produces one. Just one. 'You're kidding,' I hiss.

'They musta fallen out or are still in the kitchen.'

My career is over, I think to myself, just as I move and kneel on the meringues. CRUNCH! We look at each other but say nothing.

We fix the lonely fin into the cake with the end of ribbon.

'Let me wind it. I'm better at this sort of thing' she says.

Around it goes. It looks more like a firework than a deep space penetrator. And, as we tighten the ribbon, we squeeze the top half of cake out through the side of the icing. It falls off the table into a fur rug.

I pick it up and stare at it. It has large hairs stuck to the jam and wears is little red pointy hat.

I now have two choices. Break down like Basil Fawlty, or fix it. Pluck off the hairs. Fix the top half back on. Secure the ribbon and stack the meringue crumbs in a truly unbillowing show of take-off smoke.

'Run,' I say. 'Just run.' And so we flee. Not looking back. I have never walked so fast across a car park, expecting to hear a 'Stop right there!'

'Bye, sir,' says the smiling policeman.

On High Street Kensington I explode in an eruption of expletives. And then something happens. I look at Debbs, who looks back at me, blinking serenely. And in seconds we are both crying with laughter. Stamping our feet and slapping the dashboard. I'm just short of wetting my trousers. 'I'm a rocket maaaan,' I attempt to sing, before we both collapse in hoots again.

I send Rita the equivalent fee for the job in tulips with a grovelling apology.

Foxes

My mother used to rent a holiday cottage on the edge of Loch Swilly in County Donegal, Ireland.

It was called the Ferry House and sat right at the lapping water's edge, the frontage more windows than brick, looking out on to more water than land. It was a haven of quiet and tranquillity. When there alone, my own thoughts were most likely the noisiest disturbance.

On summer evenings, as the lowering sun raised the moon, we'd sit outside looking over the flat, pink water. We'd sit there in silence just listening, separating the big squeak of the oyster catchers from the rising trill whistles of the curlews as they came down on to the shoreline. When the birds were quiet, I remember smiling at the sipping sound the grey mullet made as they fed among the floating fields of seaweed.

On the winter days, this silence was as quiet as the very native oysters strewn throughout the shallows. Strewn seems right, as there is something almost untidy in the way they lay willy-nilly, unlike their Pacific cousins.

It was not always quiet, though, as my sociable family had moved into a very social locale. Even when parties were not an intention, they seemed to happen anyway as 'pop in for a tea' turned into heavy drinking and cheese on toast at 4 am.

Beer, wine and whisky were usually fuel enough, but wild nights invariably involved poitín to keep the night fires burning and legs hopping. I'd buy it off some local lads who made a most fabulous poitín, very strong but a beautifully made potato-based spirit that encouraged dancing and declarations of love and friendship, loudly sworn.

In addition to the classic poitín, they also made a mint version. I had a particular fondness for it, and imagined it made from mint leaves, the tips picked with the morning dew upon them, and dried with a curlew's wing fan. Keen to know what this no doubt simple practice involved, I asked them one New Year's Eve. And they answered, word for word: 'Val! it is really quoit simple. If the Faxe's[2] Glacier Mint has not melted before it hits de bottom of da bottle, den it's not fockin strong enof!'

There are many things less dangerous to do with a potato.

---

[2] For which read Fox's, who've made this popular sweet in Leicester since 1918.

The Trouble
with Adulthood

Room Ten

I used to be a part owner of a wonderful, slate-stone pub in North Cornwall. Out of the way, it sat at the bottom of a dell over a small gurgling stream, in the middle of a tangly wood that resembled an Arthur Rackham illustration. I'm pretty sure fairies lived there, tucked into this damp crease of moss and brackens, as I heard them chattering more than once, and with not a drop of scrumpy involved. In the high wind, branches would clackety-clack outside the bedroom windows as torn rags of cloud moved across the moonlit sky. And a short walk down the hill lay Trebarwith Strand, a beautiful sandy beach, the surprising size of which was revealed every day by the receding tide.

I picture it now: those high black cliffs falling straight into the surf, low wind-combed hedges, herringbone drystone walls, and the wide golden sands below scattered with Lowry-esque human arrangements of colour. With dogs barking and children's laughter, the scent of seaweed snatched inland by the breeze, the seas sparkling all the way out to Gull Rock, it seemed a million miles from London at the best of times, and a truly magical place.

However pretty the scene I paint, this enclave of North Cornwall, which appeared quaint on first approach, was in fact nothing short of the lawless Wild West, the pub more a saloon, minus the swing doors, mezzanine floor and guns. Frequented by men in drag (aren't all coastal pubs, if you glance at the pinboards?), stoned surfers, brigands, wreckers, smugglers, call them what you will: nothing had changed here in years.

I can still remember the clicking of the latch on the door into the bar, the entry always met with a gush of warmth and the sound of someone laughing or placing an order. All there and a damned good soul, a wicked glint, and no intention of going to bed. Out-of-towners with maybe more pedestrian expectations of a 'quaint' West Country weekend would have no option but to enter the flow. And most did. Having travelled all that way, they had little choice and a million opportunities to strike up conversation or accept a drink from strangers. More conventional types would likely complain, and therefore benefit from a comped dinner or an adjusted bill.

Lock-ins were regular, it being far harder to get locked out. And the police didn't seem to mind, as long as it was contained.

On the whole, I spent happy days there. But it was not exactly plain sailing. We endured an aggressive Muscovy duck with a taste for the flesh of children; the dining room-cum-dance floor collapsed into the stream; and a stray firework went off under a car, to name just a few episodes in this logbook of misfortune. Worst of all was the visit of an unwanted stripper, arranged by a visiting stag weekend, that happened to coincide with a freak booking from four ex-Wing Commander types and their wives who wanted to celebrate their diamond wedding anniversaries that same night. You can only imagine. 'Yours, Outraged of Exeter.'

'Dinner's on us!'

And it was a hard place to staff. Even with the best intentions, 'escape from the city' managers and chefs soon fell prey to the remoteness or hard drinking.

So, one night, to offer support during a rocky patch, I drove down to cook for a week. The chef had gone AWOL ... again. I liked cooking there, as the fish was excellent and I could just cook rather than run the business.

It's a long journey. One that leaves you craving a pint on arrival. However on that particular trip, I parked up and went straight into service. I seem to remember that there was some cracking turbot that I put on the menu with peas and lettuce and bacon, some guinea fowl with roasted radicchio and peppers – I have a remarkable memory for what I've cooked and when. And, post-drive and service, my unwind and a pint of cider became pints, and a considerable session unfolded. Cornish Rattler comes with a clear warning: a pump handle of a snake wearing dark glasses. That night, glass after glass of adder juice saw me in a Cornish mess, the type that might see me naked with my head down a sett trying to commune with badgers.

Somewhere around three, I thought it wise to call it quits. Room Ten was my favourite, so I headed up to it without a second thought. Opening the door, I ran at the bed and leapt at it shouting something stupid like, 'Shiver me timbers!'

It might have been wise to check the visitors' book. I landed heavily on two obviously aged inhabitants, and heard a muffled yet arthritic crunch through the duvet. They had no idea what has hit them, and sat up to find me lying across them. Rather surprisingly, they said, 'Good morning' and stayed the next night, too.

So ... another weekend 'on the house'.

A few months later, I was on a beach in Costa Rica when I overheard two friends, sitting together on a towel, talking rather loudly about how much fun they'd had in the pub. Nevertheless, 'nuts' and 'bonkers' were among the words used. Back in the UK, I picked up the phone. I think we'd all come to the same conclusion. It could not continue. And we sold.

I made 50p on it.

Val's Temptation

This is a step closer to heaven if using the Swedish cured sprats and their sweet juice, but is nonetheless a pleasure without and using anchovies. Excellent companionship for a biting weather with a cruel nip in the air. As in a lot of Swedish food, the saltiness will leave you thirsty. Do not cut down on the salt, just drink more cold beer.

Serves 4

75 g/3 oz/6 tbsp butter

2 medium onions, halved and sliced thinly

4 large good, hard garlic cloves, very thickly sliced

250 g/9 oz celeriac, peeled and chopped into 5-cm/2-in matchsticks

250 g/9 oz Jerusalem artichokes, scrubbed and chopped into 5-cm/2-in matchsticks

250 g/9 oz waxy potatoes, scrubbed and chopped into 5-cm/2-in matchsticks

Heaped ¼ tsp ground nutmeg

Heaped ¼ tsp ground cinnamon

6 juniper berries, chopped

1 x 125-g/4½-oz can salted sprats (Abba brand), juice reserved. If using
   anchovies instead use 2 cans, drained of the oil
1 bay leaf
500 ml/17 fl oz/2 cups double (heavy) cream
80 g/3 oz/½ cup stale sourdough breadcrumbs, or Peter's Yard sourdough
   crispbread crumbs
1 tsp fennel seeds
½ tsp celery salt or sea salt
Freshly ground black pepper
Crispy onions (Top Taste brand), to serve

Preheat the oven to 200°C fan/220°C/425°F/gas mark 7.

In a heavy casserole or cast-iron pan (approximately 25 cm/10 in across) melt
two-thirds of the butter and add the onions. Cook them with the ¼ teaspoon
salt until golden and becoming well browned. Do not confuse this with
burning, as it's very important not to blacken the butter.

Add the garlic and cook for a further minute or so.

Put all the matchstick vegetables in a large bowl.

When the onions are done, add them to the bowl (keeping the pan to one
side) and mix everything together well for a nice even distribution with a
good grind of black pepper, the nutmeg, cinnamon and the juniper.

Return half the mix to the pan and spread it evenly across the base. Lay half
the sprats or anchovies in a clock formation, ends facing to the centre and
pan edge. Chop the bay leaf in half and put them among the veg.

Put the rest of the mix on top and repeat with the remaining sprats and bay
leaf. Pour the juice from the sprats all over. Glug the cream all over.

Dot with the remaining butter. Wrap in foil and put on a tray to catch the dribbles. Bake for an hour or until the veg are soft.

Meanwhile, in a saucepan, toast the breadcrumbs in the remaining butter with the fennel seeds and the celery or sea salt and a good grind of pepper until dry and crispy.

Once the vegetables are done, remove the foil (reserve to finger well or lick) and put back in the oven to colour the top of the temptation. Finally, scatter the breadcrumbs on top and give it another 5 minutes in the oven. Remove and scatter heavily with crispy onions.

Eat with lots of cold beer and aquavit, then retire for an evening of naked axe-throwing.

A View to a Kill

If God is a vegan, well that's me screwed ... but for a little of his fabled forgiveness. Purgatory, at best, and I'll have to pull a number from the customer ticket machine, and wait 20,000 years on an uncomfortable chair in this midway sorting house, the metaphysical equivalent of A&E on a rough Friday night.

Ushered into a room to face the parole board of Dinners Past, my chances are slim, for I face a gallery of a thousand stern rabbits, glaring pheasants, sombre woodcock, and pissed-off deer, cows, pigs and sheep. The snails in the front row are the hardest to read of all.

Gary Larson's cartoons come to mind.

No leg to stand on save my flexitarian outlook and a plea that 'I took great care to cook you with respect.'

But then, I have yet to face the fish ...

Sole with Sweet and Sour Onion Cream Sauce

Serves 1–2

1 large, fat lemon sole, head and tail snipped off if your pan is too small
   (alternatively use a small plump plaice or a fat flounder)

For the cream sauce

90 g/3¼ oz/1 stick butter, plus 50 g/1¾ oz/½ stick butter, for frying
1 large onion, halved and very finely sliced
1 tsp juniper berries
1 very small bay leaf
1 small sprig of fresh thyme
1 tbsp white wine vinegar
1½ tsp caster (superfine) sugar
½ tsp fresh Dijon mustard
100 ml/3½ fl oz/½ cup double (heavy) cream
Good chicken stock, if required (optional)
Sea salt and freshly ground black pepper

First make the sauce. In a saucepan, melt the 90 g/3¼ oz/1 stick butter over a medium heat and gently sauté the onion until tender with the juniper berries, bay and thyme. This never takes the so-often-advised 6–8 minutes, more likely 12–15 minutes. Stir often and DO NOT COLOUR the onion!

Add the vinegar and sugar, and then continue to rapidly simmer until all traces of liquid have evaporated. Stir in the mustard and pour in the cream, then simmer for no more than 2 minutes. The consistency should be only a little less thick than double cream. Please thin with milk if necessary. Season with salt and pepper, and leave to stand for at least 10 minutes.

Dry your fish very thoroughly with a tea towel or paper towels and season on the underside.

Melt the remaining butter in a non-stick, or proofed cast-iron frying pan (skillet) over a medium heat. Lower in the fish into the pan, brown side up, where it should sizzle immediately if the temperature is correct. Adjust heat if needs be, as there is a dial for a reason, and do not let the butter smoke! Cook the fish for approximately 4 minutes and then turn and cook for 3 on the underside.

Warm the sauce, thinning it with a dribble of extra stock if needs be. It should be the consistency of pouring double (heavy) cream.

Spoon sauce on to a plate and lay the sole on top. Eat with boiled potatoes tossed in butter, salt and chives. A glass of cold Sancerre white wine would be a damn fine idea.

How Did You Get Here?

I think there is a predisposition that anyone who decides to become a chef is born restless, born with whirring cogs that would rather keep the body on its feet than sitting down, always moving in an unending quest to see what happens if you mix this with that. The chef's job is to look to many outside sources for ideas – a location, an observation, an understanding of nature or historical research – then deliver them through the medium of ingredients. Life is one big tasty, stinky, textural experience!

Often chefs' personal lives are complicated; the clock commands strange hours to complicate it all further. I'd tentatively venture, with notable exceptions, that the more solemn the chef, the less I'm likely to enjoy the food. The 'cook' mentality, has seen this book very hard to write as the knots in my stomach display my sufference of the requirement to sit still and write. Multiple trips to the fridge were punctuated with very short bursts of writing.

Unsqueamish as a child I ate everything, snatching it without a second thought to gulp it down like a ravenous eagle chick. So it was very likely I would turn to food as career. Never born to count, become a linguist, academic, musician or deadly strategist; I loved eating, nature and art, and so here I am with food as my currency, my language, my second nature. It seems that I was born to understand the world by biting it.

My father was more an epicurean than a chef. It must be said that his repertoire for pork chops in Cinzano, fish curries, scrambled eggs and soufflés was excellent. My mother on the other hand is a genius in the kitchen, endlessly inventive, the undisputed reigning queen of new ideas and leftovers. She throws virtually nothing away and whether making tasty duck stock for soup or mushing up tinned mackerel for toast, it is that pinch of curry powder, scratch of orange zest, twinge of soy sauce or pastis that catapults all her food from greatness into excellence. Her collection of cookbooks is wide ranging but I rarely, if ever, recall her consulting them. She does, however, love the company of cooks and was always more likely to be found drinking wine with the late, great Marika Hanbury Tenison or discussing what makes a good tomato salad with Terence Conran.

But while my mother was the main cook of the house, it was my father who showed me the treats in the hedgerows. He showed me that green cobnuts were as nice as ripe ones and where the wild raspberries could be found. He encouraged inquisitiveness, boyish activity that once his sons had expressed an interest in fishing and hunting soon insisted that every life taken must be carried from the field to the pan.

As a family we travelled extensively across Europe on holidays where he was as delighted to find and enjoy a small trattoria as he was to take us to a grander restaurant. Taken to both such establishments my brother and I often fell asleep at the table, if not running around village back streets with new found friends while the grown-ups drank coffee or grappa. I remember him telling me of goats' cheese sprinkled with dried mountain herbs and eaten with wild honey as we walked a coastal goat track on Crete. I ate my first oysters with him in Paris while he talked of sea urchins. 78 years of life spent largely abroad – Japan, Russia, Italy, New York – his endlessly inquisitive nature meant that he embroidered, animated and illuminated food in a way that laid deep foundations, made my eyes wide, ears learn and mouth keen to move on to whatever tasty opportunity was next.

Travel, food, family meals around the table, a lot of weekend entertaining, home-cooking, restaurant-eating and growing up in the countryside on a farm, and soon I saw the world in divisions of what is edible or inedible.

Warners are notoriously greedy and I'd describe us as similar to a tribe of red faced hyennas squabbling and tearing at the flimsy carcass of a baby zebra. If any one of the three siblings successfully forked an extra chop or potato it would ensure the maneouvre was punctuated with a wink.

Away from the table, my brother and I were either violating the cheese board in the larder, pilfering cans of smoked oysters or raiding the fruit nets. Despite being amply fed we behaved like the most desperate of Victorian street urchins, hiding under tables or distant holly bushes to devour our thievery in sticky quiet. It drove mum mad.

Fast forward to summer 2018, when a man comes up to me and introduces himself. 'Hello, I'm Miles and you caused my business quite a lot of distress.' Spinning my rolodex of disaster in my head, I could not work out who this unfortunate man was.

'Put me out of my misery,' I said.

'Well, I own the trout farm next to your school, the farm you poached with enthusiasm. You had a fair few.'

'132, to be precise,' I replied. 'If you find the alder tree some 30 metres downstream it should say "VW – MP, 132 trout, 1988–1990" and there is a leaping trout carved in the bark above our tally.'

Thankfully, Miles saw the funny side while he was delighted on being informed that I'd been thrashed by his manager and received detention. I forgot to ask him how he found out it was me. Anyway, the point is that I hated school food and preferred to cook my own in the dormitory kitchens.

Following school, I went to art college. This was an unruly time. While attempting to find where I belonged, deep currents were perhaps bumping me towards my destination as I found myself, quite umprompted by books, cooking like a demon. Living on the Holloway Road above a saw mill that saw my bedsit daily covered by a shallow snowfall of MDF dust, I spent far more time excited for my results from the pan than results on canvas.

Not yet a cook, I left a painter. I know many chefs who are talented sketchers and painters and so too many painters who are excellent cooks.

One morning sitting in a café looking arty in brogues, painty jeans, wearing a scarf and cigarette, I thought, 'Right, today I will put down the brush and pick up the spoon.' And that was it, 'I want to be a cook.' I changed profession in a day.

I started work in a pub called The Cow where, thanks to its owner Tom Conran, I opened crowds of oysters, made boat-loads of moules marinière and cooked French sausages and beans. Happy times, it distracted me from the news of my dad's illness. Wild times too: happily, my picture is still in the photomontage on the wall to this day. I was 24 then.

Liking life as a cook and wanting to learn more I soon outgrew the pub.

Happening one day on Alistair Little's restaurant in Lancaster Road, I walked in with no idea who he was or how famous. A chat with Alistair and the reply, 'I'll give you a job, but go and work somewhere else first.' He sat me at a table and then sent me lunch: stuffed courgette flower, followed by a pork chop with sage and lentils – it was heavenly.

'See you soon,' I said to him on leaving. 'We'll see,' he replied.

So I went and got a job in the Halcyon Hotel where Nico Ladenis's sous chef Martin Hadden had taken up as head chef. I adored Martin. The brigade did not adore me, however. I had a posh voice and knew about food despite my lack of training. I learnt fast and was allowed to cook fish before those who'd been there longer. The pastry chef was forever pushing me aside and so one day I pushed him back. Unfortunately, he was carrying a tray of sugary fancies. Standing up daubed in cream he went for me and so we were both told to go home for two days. Excellent, I thought. He sobbed saying that if they won a star (we were expecting the inspector) while he was not there, he'd be gutted. I called him a cry-baby and we kicked off again.

I worked there for six months and the training was invaluable but I wanted to cook more provincial food. The rural food I had seen in Greece and France with my parents.

I returned to Alistair and got a job, and he blew my mind. In a small kitchen with no stations, my knowledge expanded very quickly. I was cooking foods I was a lot more comfortable with: bollito misto, squid and aïoli, squid ink risotto – I was in heaven. We were encouraged to eat heartily. But when the head chef left I was not prepared to work for the replacement. So I left.

I drifted from kitchen to kitchen for a few years, by which time I knew I needed new challenges and often. So I started a catering company. We worked mostly with the fashion and film industry: high-end clients. A sit down dinner for 1,000 was the scariest it got, and believe me it was scary.

I was too timid to open my own restaurant. I took the view that to be a good cook is not enough to permit opening a restaurant, a recipe for disaster given my dislike of spreadsheets, rotas, rates and all things that dull the creative mind. Dreams of a large wooden building with VAL'S in neon shining over the door, haunt me nevertheless. But practicality trumps fantasy, and while I would still love to have a restaurant, I know better.

It's why I call myself a cook, not a chef.

Later, I was contacted by Pat Llewellyn, of Optomen Productions. One of the great food TV producers of all time, she discovered Jamie Oliver, the Two Fat Ladies, created The F Word with Gordon Ramsay and The Great British Menu. She was a legend in food telly.

Finding myself in front of Pat, she said, 'I've been told you can cook and are quite chatty. Shall we do a screen test?' So we did a screen test, in fact we did three over two years. But, 'No luck, I'm afraid,' she said. 'You are odd, Val, and I don't know what to do with you, but don't go away.'

Some weeks later, I asked Pat and her husband Ben to dinner and, in a flash of good thinking and in need of a job, I said, 'Tell you what, Pat, why not let me work at Optomen researching ideas?' And that's what we did. After just two months we got a commission with 'What To Eat Now'.

I owe a lot to Pat and Ben. Working with them ushered in a time in my life that finally, finally after all the frustrated keenness to 'succeed' set me on a path that saw me travel, discover new ideas and slowly realize who I was.

I am now 48, and have moved from solids to liquids with a distillery business in Northumberland.

I believe cooking is absolutely key to my life in its understanding of nature, people and the world around me. I know in my heart that because I am able to make something from nothing wherever I am, then I am forever useful. Like my father, I am more likely to be talking octopus recipes with a

Greek widow than molecular gastronomy. I care for the fragile things in this fast-changing world.

I work in Norway a lot now at Holmen Lofoten with my friend Ingunn. Happy that my life is better spent in the deep nature I need and pine for.

But I know myself, I'm a changeable beast and am pleased that I've just finished turning my garage into a painter's studio.

A Taco via Rick aka Tortillas with Tomato and Pumpkin Seed Sauce and Eggs

This recipe was unearthed by Rick Stein on his television series *Rick Stein's Road to Mexico*. I loved it because, despite the easy-to-find ingredients, it was a far cry from the more 'accessible' recipe choices so often beloved by food telly commissioners. Its simplicity is its brilliance and the very reason I have fallen in love with the diverse food of Mexico on my own travels. Buy his book *The Road to Mexico* – it's fantastic. I've changed it ever so slightly as I don't roast the tomatoes, while I also like the zing of some fresh lime juice.

Serves 4

4 eggs

4 fleshy, juicy, ripe vine tomatoes, rinsed

140 g/5 oz/1 cup pumpkin seeds

Small handful of finely chopped fresh chives, about 1 tbsp

Larger handful of finely chopped fresh coriander (cilantro) leaf and stalks, about 2 tbsp

Dribble of lime juice (optional)

12 pure corn tortillas, *not* flour ones (see Tip)

Sea salt and freshly ground black pepper

Boil the eggs for 5½ minutes, so you get a nice soft middle, then plunge them straight into ice water to cool. Peel and set aside.

Cut the cores from the tomatoes and criss cross the bottoms with a knife. Steep in boiling water for a minute, then drain and peel. Set aside.

In a dry frying pan (skillet) over a medium heat, swirl the pumpkin seeds until they begin to crackle and pop, and darken in colour. Remove from the heat. Pound to a paste in a pestle and mortar.

Roughly chop the tomatoes and mix them gently through the bowl of pumpkin seed paste. Fold in the herbs and some salt to taste. Ever so slightly sharpen the mix with lime juice, if using, taking care not to let it dominate.

Warm the corn tortillas in a dry pan over a low heat, turning once until soft and floppy. Smear the tortilla thickly with the sauce and cut the eggs into quarters as you go, adding them to the tacos. Enjoy with an ice-cold beer, maybe with lime juice in it and a little salt on the rim of the glass.

Tip You can find pure corn tortillas online, try www.coolchile.co.uk.

Corn in a Mexican Style

It seems humiliating that a maize cob be derobed of its husk then put in a plastic box and pushed before the public. The indignity of this stripping! Not least because maize comes in nature's perfect packaging, and will spoil faster without it. (Moronic modern practice.) Come August and September I am upon corn on the cob with ravenous vigour. Please see the 'feeding machine' scene from Charlie Chaplin's *Modern Times* ...

Serves 2
2 tsp sunflower oil
1 small onion, chopped
2 tbsp finely chopped fresh coriander (cilantro) stalks

½ tsp dried oregano

¼ tsp ground cumin

1 garlic clove, chopped

2 cobs corn, kernels only

¾ tsp sea salt

Good dusting of hot smoked paprika

2 good dollops of crème fraîche

Enthusiastic fine grating of Wensleydale cheese

Freshly ground black pepper

2 quarters of a large juicy lime, to serve

Heat the oil in a saucepan and add the onion, coriander stalks, oregano, cumin and some black pepper. Sauté until totally tender. It should take 10–12 minutes and the onion should be pale golden.

Add the garlic and carefully cook for a further 2 minutes, or until tender.

Add the corn kernels and stir them into the onion mix, cooking them until just done – about 5 minutes.

Season with the salt and transfer the corn to two soup plates. Dust with smoked paprika and blob the crème fraîche on top. Scatter over with a heavy snowfall of the cheese, and place the lime wedges on the side.

Delicious lunch as it is, or with warmed corn tortillas.

Ox Cheek Tacos with Pink Pickled Onions

Serves 4–6

2 ancho chillies torn in half, seeds and stalk discarded

1 chipotle in adobo

330-ml/11-fl oz bottle Leffe Brun beer

Juice of 1 large tart and sweet orange

1½ tbsp Worcestershire sauce

1 tbsp apple, balsamic or cider vinegar

2 tbsp groundnut (peanut) oil, plus extra for warming the tortillas

4 ox cheeks, each cut into 4

1 tsp sea salt

1 tsp cracked black pepper

1 large red onion, very finely diced

Stems from 25 g/1 oz fresh coriander (cilantro), very finely chopped

1 tsp cumin seeds

3 cloves, heads pinched

1 cinnamon stick

1 star anise

4 garlic cloves, grated

1 tbsp tomato purée

2 tsp sweet smoked paprika

4–6 tbsp pumpkin seeds

Corn tortillas, to serve

For the Pink Pickled Onions

Juice of 2 limes

Juice of 1 large orange

2 tbsp cider vinegar

2 bay leaves

6 peppercorns

2 cloves

1 large red onion, halved from top to root end, peeled and thinly sliced

½ tsp sea salt

Heat a heavy casserole over a medium heat. Toast the ancho chillies, keeping them on the move so they don't burn and become bitter. When a nutty warm smell hits you, take them out.

Combine the chipotle in adobo, beer, orange juice, Worcestershire sauce and vinegar in measuring jug and put to one side. Add the oil to the casserole. Season the meat with the salt and pepper and fry until really scabbed and browned. Remove to a plate.

Fry the onions and coriander together with the oregano, cumin, bay, cloves, cinnamon and star anise, scratching the beef residue from the pan.

When the onions are very tender (this never takes any less than 8 minutes), stir in the garlic and tomato purée and reintroduce the anchos. Stir continuously until the tomato purée is starting to catch. Stir in the smoked paprika.

Return the meat to the pan and pour over the beer mixture. Put a lid on the pan. Cook gently at a wobble for about 2½ hours on the hob. Take care to check for sticking on the bottom of the casserole, as the end result will taste burnt; add a little more water along the way if need be.

When done, the meat should show barely any resistance at all to a probe with a knife, but should not be falling apart either. When getting near this point, remove the lid so that the sauce reduces until it is as thick as gravy and really intense-looking.

Before serving, if you want to go the whole hog, then refry the beef in a non-stick pan to give it semi-crisp and sticky texture with an even more intense flavour. Break the beef with a spoon into the sauce to become more taco-filler friendly.

For the pink pickled onions, take a bowl large enough to contain the onions once cooked, and add the citrus juices and vinegar. Nearly fill a medium-sized pan with water, add the bay, peppercorns and cloves and bring it to a lively boil. Add the onions and bring back to the boil. Cook for 30 seconds and then immediately drain. Tip the drained onions into the bowl of juice and vinegar, and mix well. Turn the onions every now and then. They will turn a garish pink that will only delight young daughters!

Into a small frying pan (skillet), tip more pumpkin seeds than you need as you will feverishly snack on them if they are there. Toast over a medium heat, stirring or swirling them. They will start to pop and change colour as their skins split. Cook until the majority have done this.

Warm your tortillas in a pan rubbed with but a drip of oil. Once each one is done, either hand out straight away or stack and keep warm under a cloth.

When ready, fill each taco with meat and a little sauce, then top with the onions and a good scattering of pumpkin seeds.

Short-term View

We live in the age of the shareholder and the avocado.
    Both are thirsty, while the healthy returns are questionable.

Clarissa

Skulking at the back of a singing class, part of a chef choir for a live Red Nose Day performance of Rick Astley's 'Never Gonna Give You Up'. God help me, as it's not only a song I detest, but I have also been chosen for the solo. Our teacher was the one and only choir master Gareth Malone. His was not an easy job as there seemed to be a collectively resistant attitude to his endeavours.
    'Must we take orders from a bossy little boy?' I hear hissed in my ear.

I was sitting at the back, next to Clarissa Dickson Wright. Rolling her eyes at every instruction and grimacing, she was now rummaging through her handbag looking for a pen. Rummage, rummage, pause, fidget. It went on for a remarkable length of time.

Head cocked to one side, almost as if listening, it was obvious that deep among those keys, a diary and old tissues, she had come across an opportunity and was trying to pin it down.

Rummage, pause – all this scuffling – I was now totally fascinated, imagining her hand in that bag was like a hedgehog coming across a worm among the leaves on a dark night.

A look of relief, a smile and finally she drew out her hand.

'Aha!' she exclaimed. Clutched in her plump paw was a lumpen cluster of tattered clingfilm (plastic wrap), bobbles of grey fluff and dust attached. She unwound the yellowing film. It had undoubtedly suffered a long residence within those dark confines.

'Dundee cake' she said unwrapping it. 'Unexpected teatime,' she went on triumphantly, loud enough to turn Worrall Thompson's head. She turned and in a hushed manner said ever so sweetly, 'Would you like to share it?'

How could I refuse? After all, when we've blown the world to bits, all that's left will be scorpions and Dundee cake.

Mustard

Quite the strangest funeral I've ever attended was Kisty Hesketh's, a close friend and a woman I enjoyed pretending was my grandmother, instead of accepting the one I had, a purse-lipped Christian Science fundamentalist.

I spent many wonderful times with Kisty, and would occasionally go and stay with her, just the two of us at weekends. In the months after her death, I often found myself dialling her, only to realize there could be no reply.

Many had gathered to see this truly exceptional woman off, and the service began as one would expect.

One of her sons, nicknamed Cappy, had been a student of mine on a weekly health cookery course agreed between his mother, himself and me. The objective was to combat his oversized appetite and gargantuan size with engaging salads, and that he learn to look after himself. This course changed shape within a fortnight, evolving into more of a salad and martini class with extra-curricular veal chops, at which point I threw in the kitchen towel.

While I enjoyed these subversive evenings pointing and laughing at the very greenery I'd arrived with, I'd quite simply failed. And, thanks to the subsequent heart problems his appetites had inflicted upon him, and given the additional stress of his mother's passing, it was recommended he not bear the coffin. Nevertheless, he did, and somewhere between the carrying of it and last rites, overcome by some arterial show stopper, he collapsed into the cemetery grass.

Frantic looks, scurrying chaplains and busy mobiles immediately addressed the emergency. Soon the air ambulance thumped into earshot, the crew quickly atop Cappy's body. Mayhem.

And calm. For, at the other end of the churchyard, to sombre words, Kisty was lowered below a fringe of daffodils into the ground.

Loaded and airborne once more, the helicopter turned on its axis and disappeared, leaving everyone shocked and confused. But despite reports that Cappy had already died, we were all herded towards the wake and a steadying glass of something.

Indoors and soon tired by the loud throng of voices, I went in search of the cloakroom and my cigarettes. All of a sudden, a woman, shaking, breathy and flustered, arrived at the bottom of a staircase reporting that, 'Lady Manton has collapsed upstairs.'

'Crikey,' I thought, 'that's the other grandmother down.'

The news spread fast, the collective guests now taking on a startled look as if Poirot had entered the room and announced that no one was to leave.

Another ambulance arrived.

Hungry now, I instead headed for the buffet. As I surveyed this pleasing landscape of potato salad, cold cuts and quiche, I heard the unmistakably vile tone of someone I have only ever less then liked.

'Good God! There is no mustard for the ham,' he declared.

Thinking him ridiculous, I offered, 'Then let me go and find you some. English or French?'

He turned to me with that well-known look of cruel excitement and replied, 'I knew you'd come in handy one day.'

It crossed my mind, thankfully with speed, that what this funeral really didn't need was a punch-up, broken tea cups and a squashed lemon drizzle cake. So, keeping the haymaker in my pocket, I went and found the mustard instead.

Outside, cigarette in hand, a huge smile beamed across my face. I have always believed that on 'moving through', all of us are released of earthly worries and concerns, to then look down with a sort of detached love, incomprehension and humour at those below still consumed by the nonsense and futility of their human worry and thrashing. I couldn't help picking up a sense, a cosmic radio wave from Kisty, sitting up there with her legs dangling over the rings of Jupiter, that she found the goings on of that day nothing short of comical.

And I'm happy to report that, high up above the fields and flowers, Cappy was prevented from joining her.

Fingerbobs

Midwinter, bitingly cold outside, and while frazzled in the nadir of my divorce, I couldn't wait to forget it all for just two days. A weekend in Devon with my friends. I'd counted down the days to this trip, not even going about my working week properly, instead simply waiting to leave London, with the full intention of surrounding myself with good company, laughter and fairly heavy drinking.

Arriving in the starry dark and a rushing gale, the last leg of the journey saw every silhouetted treetop, hedgerow and tussock rattling and bending. It was exhilarating.

The old oak door to the house is large, sturdy and studded, as much there to keep the elements out, as unwanted visitors. Yet on such a weekend as this, the twist of that iron ring and the loud 'clack' of it's latch were a starting pistol for good times.

Dry leaves scuttling around my feet, I pushed the door open to a beige glow from within, a warm rush of heat and the smell of a wood fire.

Unaware of our arrival, laughing voices, from somewhere out of sight, came to greet us. I felt happy but for a momentary glimpse of guilt that I should not be so. In the kitchen, pleased to see each other, I swiftly found a drink in my hand.

Half-cut and shown to my room just before dinner, I was told the sash window ropes were broken and on no account should I try and open it. A small Post-it-Note stuck on the glass said the same thing. DON'T OPEN.

'Sure, no problem,' I replied.

A fire had been lit in the grate opposite the bed. Everything was perfect.

Dinner was just as I'd hoped, hilarious and noisy, as other guests turned up in dribs and drabs to scraping chairs as we all got up to hug and throw our welcomes about each other.

Gin had turned into wine and then sloe gin and Armagnac. We'd feasted on mallard and pigeon burgers and shoved oven chips into our faces before starting on cheese and apple crumble with slow-moving West Country cream.

Near the end of dinner, my arch enemy, heartburn, took hold of my chest. I felt pale suddenly, pretty awful and very annoyed that, with such a likely outcome, I'd fallen on the food and drink with abandon. There was no hope for me. I understood this scenario well. I had to go to bed and deal with it as only I knew. I took my leave with an excuse.

The fire in my room had been stoked and was still crackling away. While this calmed and soothed me, I soon found the room was insufferably hot.

Undressed but for my boxer shorts, I climbed onto the raised box in the bay window and, somehow ignoring the note, unfastened the brass catch in the middle. Like a racing guillotine, I had no chance to react but only to gasp in surprise agony as down rushed the top half of the huge window 'SLAM' onto my finger joints, the last ones before the nails.

I uttered a 'Yowl!'

Startled into immediate anxiety, I realized I was held fast, with all my fingers caught between the two window frames. The night outside came racing into the room while the heat quickly bled out.

Shivering, both in shock and with the chill, I pulled, twisted, tugged and wriggled, but, like a poor fox in a gin trap, my contortions were agonizing and pointless. My fingers were feeling very strange, somewhere between thick and flat, with a throbbing pain of such excruciating depth it could only mean bad things – a frowning consultant and a tactful diagnosis.

I started to panic for my beloved fingers, jerking and pulling at them again, demented with pain and panic. I must've looked like some deranged synth player in the throes of his darkest frenzied solo.

Suddenly and surprisingly, I took stock and calmed down. I stayed still and listened.

Through the floor I could just about hear happy voices below. Aware not one of them would turn in before one or two in the morning, and with my fingers now turning blue, I decided I definitely needed to call for help.

Shouting out for some time, nobody heard.

So then I banged my foot on the bench repeatedly, somewhat gingerly at first. Nothing. I increased the volume to something I thought considerable. Still nothing.

I now had a further dilemma. The repeated banging with my feet coupled with the rather washed-out and exhausted elastic in my boxer shorts meant they had worked their down to below my hips, just short of the curls.

My fingers throbbed deeply, and had now taken on a peculiar lilac and white colouring. I had no choice but to ramp it up with a more violent stamping. I beat out a super-amplified SOS through the panelling.

Finally, finally! Voices on the stairs.

But ... oh God! My boxer shorts were now halfway over my cheeks and still slipping with the same fractional slow motion of a doomed car, front wheels over the cliff, teetering towards a bad outcome.

That terrible, dread slowness of the inevitable.

As help approached down the corridor with an 'Are you okay, Val?' I dared not move or reply. Too late. In a lightweight cotton flight, my pants kept on going. I could only now take on a bow-legged, ricket-like stance to try and stop them at my knees. For dignity.

My hosts arrived. Astonished, confronted with my ghost-white bottom and my trembling whimper of 'I've got a problem,' they burst into uproarious laughter, yet nonetheless showed due concern as they heaved the window off my wretched, indented fingers.

On surveying my poor hands, they restrained themselves to lesser outbursts of tightlipped, watery-eyed nose giggles. Despite fleeting moments of true concern, I shooed them out crossly on my release. Hands bound in frozen peas and tea towels, my heartburn retreated in the face of the greater distraction in my hands and I took to bed, miserable, embarrassed and sorry for myself.

My hours of torment had in fact lasted little more the six minutes.

As the story was obviously being recounted downstairs, a new muffled explosion of hysterics came up through the floorboards. I had to smile.

'At least I don't play piano,' I muttered to myself, and fell asleep grinning.

Heather

One London Fashion Week, I found myself working in conjunction with Mulberry fashion company (mulberry is my favourite fruit by the way) over a weekend at Spencer House, and delivering some talks about my distillery in Northumberland while dishing out cocktails into Spode chinaware.

At the end of my riveting talk, a woman asked me for a further understanding of the Northumberland moorland as an environment, and why the plant heather is so integral to it. She was not aware what this plant even looked like.

I reached for my phone and tapped 'heather' into the search bar. And what appeared on my screen was, at last, the perfect example of everything I've been trying to explain about my worry for the natural world: hundreds of pictures of sassy Heather Graham, and barely any pictures of bell heather in flower.

Were I ever to meet Heather Graham, I'm sure I'd like her. But I feel that heather, the plant, is infinitely more important.

Having said that, were Heather Graham to offer her support in protecting rain-lashed northern moorland, I'm sure she would do wonders.

Grouse with Corn and Plums

I love grouse. But, great as that love is, I do get tired of eating them cooked in the traditional way, which is so often the norm on menus. Grouse, corn and plums all are at their best come late August. Seasonal perfection.

Serves 2

2 large, juicy, sweet, tangy plums, halved and stoned

2 tbsp sunflower oil, plus extra for frying

2 fat grouse, breast and legs removed, carcasses retained and broken up

1 small onion, finely diced, skin set aside

Small sprig of fresh thyme

1 tsp tomato purée

150 ml/5 fl oz/⅔ cup Bordeaux red wine

600 ml/1 pint/2½ cups tasty brown or white chicken stock

110 g/4 oz/1 stick butter

2 large corn on the cobs, kernels cut from cob

100 ml/3½ fl oz/½ cup single (light) cream

1 tbsp apple cider vinegar

Handful of blackberries, to serve

Sea salt and freshly ground black pepper

Lay the plum halves on a tray and scatter ¼ teaspoon salt over their flesh side.

In a large saucepan, heat the sunflower oil and fry the broken up carcasses with the onion skins, garlic and fresh thyme. Fry until well browned before stirring in the tomato purée. When the tomato purée begins to catch, pour in the red wine and bring to the boil.

Add the chicken stock. Turn down the heat and let it wobble for an hour.

Strain, return the strained stock to the pan and reduce until there is little more than 4 tablespoons remaining. Season with salt.

While the stock cooks, fry the onion in 40 g/1½ oz of the butter until totally tender and nothing less. Do not colour the onion. Add the corn and continue to cook until it catches. Stir, and let this happen 2 or 3 times. Add the cream and simmer gently for 5 minutes. Remove from the heat and pass the mix through a fine sieve (strainer) into a fresh saucepan, and slowly reduce the mixture until wet but not too loose. Season with salt.

Season the grouse legs and breasts well with salt and pepper.

Lay the plums flat side down into a large frying (skillet) or sauté pan to sizzle in a further 40 g/1½ oz of the butter with a little sunflower oil added. Don't cook on too high a heat, but when thoroughly browned and beaten up, add the grouse legs and cook until browned on skin side. Turn over.

Add the breasts to the pan, skin side down, next to them. Turn the plums over. Cook the breasts until tender and pink, turning once.

Remove the meat from the pan to a board and allow to rest. Turn the plums back onto their flat side and deglaze the pan with apple cider vinegar.

Heat the corn and cream sauce. When bubbling, whisk in the remaining butter. Spoon the sauce onto a platter and place the grouse pieces on top. Spoon over the sauce, and place the plums and blackberries beside the meat. Serve with a watercress salad, if you like.

Only Five Things about Social Media

1. The other morning, I awoke and immediately reached for my phone for some Instagratification. I'd forgotten to reach for my girlfriend and say, 'Good morning.' I noticed this, and thought to myself ... 'Oh dear!'

2. Despite the inevitable – so it's a tenuous argument, really – I nonetheless laugh that, while trying to capture the interest of thousands of people I don't know, I couldn't make my marriage work out.

3. Moose are sneaky. In the most idyllic setting, a frozen white wood in which you could not hear a pin drop, with snow floating down, I saw two of them, but twenty feet away. They were huge. Side by side, they moved through the deep drifts with a nimble, stealthy silence that both surprised and touched me. Fumbling in my napsack for too long with mittens, Instagram and Twitter in mind, I raised my phone and ... they were gone. The guide smirked. Magic moment missed. Never again.

4. I once posted a picture of a label on some carrots, outraged at the use-by date on them. Despite being ten days past the throwaway date, they were pristine and immaculate. I've seen them kept for months and enjoyed the sweet results. In fact, I'd argue they improve with withering, but on this occasion that was not my point. My outrage was aimed at such waste and the idea that we rely on dates to determine freshness rather than touch, smell and sight ... only to get a reply from someone saying, 'Why did you buy Israeli carrots, you bastard?!'

5. We have enough to do, like cook and listen, so I try to resist stroking the glass hamster. I fail often. Did they like it? Are there any replies? Might I edit that ... again? It's a disease, an illness of the ego! I have contracted it, and I am seeking a cure. The symptoms are complicated.

Hold Fire

I think of this story often, as playing The Beatles and roasting pork are often done simultaneously in my house.

Should I be writing this? Well I guess I am. As an apology maybe.

I was rung up by a field-sports' magazine a long time ago, and asked whether I would be interested in doing an article for them on the return of the now considerable population of wild boar across southern England. The population was pushing 3,000 at that point, the bloodlines of individuals that had slipped the perimeter fence and run for their lives into parts of Kent, Sussex, Devon and Dorset.

I like the idea of boar returning into our woodland and forest rather than the loss of another species, an afternoon walk or jog once more containing a frisson of enjoyable danger.

I also, if not reluctantly, understand why a farmer does not want a rabble of wild pigs trashing his maize field, and while I celebrate the return of the boar, the ratio of arable land to forest is sure to result in confrontation over livelihood for both farmer and pig.

Left to their forest habits, I have seen the incredible movement of soil on the forest floor caused by boar rootling for bluebell bulbs. The damage is impressive. Yet I find it hard to call it 'damage', it's just a boar doing its thing.

To and fro I go, as I can't help wondering if the 'damage' in fact causes a positive effect in the long run. After all, boar have done this for millennia, and were once indigenous and so probably contribute rather than simply damage. When it comes to the minutiae of ecology and environment, we don't know half what a wild pig does.

But, taking the view of cook and the commission, I say yes. I would shoot and cook one. This would be *wild* boar not farmed wild boar, and meat I quite literally had a hand in. A rendezvous was arranged with a stalking guide and his small band of merry men, a jolly bunch.

A week later, I'm standing in a hazel and oak wood at the bottom of a rudimentary hide – actually more a ladder welded onto what looks like something salvaged from a children's playground. The ladder is tied to a tree with no more than a few rounds of orange twine. I settle into the top with my rifle, reliably informed that sugar beet and maize have been thrown about the area in front of me, and a good few pints of molasses daubed over logs and the tree bases in the view.

I'm left up there in the silence of the wood, but for the gusty wind and the creaking trees. I'm feeling a little nervous that, at some point, this swaying frame will give way to the rusty weak points and I'll fall on my head. As such a gun-toting brute, some might say rightfully deserved.

I've been told not to smoke. 'Pigs'll smell it. Bloody wily they are. Know we're after them. Ninja pigs.'

Two hours later and flexing my cold bitten fingers, I think I hear a rustle. There is movement. I sneak the gun slowly into position. It's a pheasant. I scrabble together a rollie and light it while trying unconvincingly to convince myself the smoke will travel high over the boars' heads and go undetected. The boars don't come. The pick-up returns. I get down, catch the train and return to London.

A week later the phone rings and I'm asked back for another try if I'd still like to. Of course I would; back I go. This time we are hunting them at night, a wise tactic as boar are primarily nocturnal, laying low in the woods by day.

It is a night-time safari and the verges and fields are hopping with rabbits, deer and foxes. There are badgers and owls, and some bats I'm surprised have not hibernated yet. I can smell the cold night air, the woods and cows. My nose feels as alive as a dog's.

Around we go, bumping, lurching, the lamp searching, concentrating its tunnel of light on the oak trunks that glow silver in the light.

There is something so very British, to me, about the sound of a diesel engine ticking over – that rattle – my breath in the air, the silhouettes of brambles in the red glow of the tail lights, and the squelching of mud as gates are squeaked open and clanged closed, however stealthy you try to be.

Scanning the woodland edge and open grass, we see every animal apart from the boar and decide that, once more, we have to call it a day. As we turn back I hear something.

'Shhhhhhh,' I command. We stay stock still and listen. Soon enough we hear a snapping stick followed by an oink and a grunt. The torch is switched onto red filter and I ready the rifle on the roof mat and stack my fists under the stock as the beam is pointed towards the noise.

I cannot believe it! There they are! A sounder of boars just within the woodland fence line. There are ten or so at about seventy metres. Looking at them through the rifle sight, it's beautiful. Here again, some 300 years after the last one was likely served in a room full of jeering and merriment. Close up through the rifle sight, it's amazing to see these creatures back in our woods – but it does not diminish the call of the cook.

I know I must not shoot the matriarch, and so I'm looking for a smaller pig, a tender pig, as the bigger boar will be tough and overly funky in taste.

My finger moves to the trigger.

'Don't shoo...'

CRACK!

It collapses, stone dead as the other boars flee, crashing cracking and scampering deep into the woodland.

'You bloody idiot,' he says and, before I can ask why, barks through gritted teeth, 'Get that fucking pig over here NOW!'

I'm confused. Having done my job efficiently, it's now marred by this apparent fury. Noticing all three of my companions now pelting down the field at breakneck speed, boots squelching and jackets rustling, I run down to help them heave it over the fence.

Whatever I've done has really put the wind up me. Just carrying a rifle scares me enough, let alone having shot something I should not have.

Reputable magazine, successful hunt. I'm anxious and baffled. 'What's wrong?' I ask.

'I'll tell you what's wrong!' he says. 'One, I did not tell you to shoot, and two you could've bloody shot a pig on Sir Paul McCartney's land.'

Happy thoughts of braising the neck and shoulder, ten minutes ago, maybe using some of the broth for a chestnut soup and making an escabeche from the head meat have lost their lustre and I'm now feeling embarrassed.

'Sorry lads,' I say and, in a moment of misplaced frivolity, 'Well, that's certainly the biggest carrot I've ever shot!' At which point two of them start laughing so hard we are given another furious 'Shhhhh!'

Thankfully, when we found the beast it was on the safe side of the fence. Boar rolled onto the back, our red tail lights slide away through the mud and into the night.

So, now, that's Roger Waters' plums (hanging over the footpath, two feet into the wrong side, I might add) and the wild pork (two feet on the right side). If I had the fruit and meat today, I'd make amends by cooking at a music charity fundraiser.

Taken Under

The other day as I sat on the banks of the River Test observing the hurry-scurry of nature around me, I noticed a water vole paddling, chin up, urgently towards the far bank. I was taken by a feeling that we had something in common. Where I was going through a very difficult patch in my life, he was negotiating treacherous waters, too. We were both trying to get to the 'other side', both paddling with concentration, both nervous, with an occasional glance over our shoulders.

I heartily wished him the best in life.

'Go little fellow,' I muttered.

As I did so, a huge surge of water rose in front of him, and in one splashy swirl, a vast hen pike snatched my acquaintance and took voley below, to munch on him in the reeds.

The waters became calm once more and the current of the river flowed on.

'Maybe we didn't have so much in common after all,' I thought, trying to quickly distance myself from any self-inflicted symbolism I'd imposed on the event. I picked up my rod and left the spot.

I went on to catch a few pike that afternoon, and killed a large one as they are easier to prepare for eating. Big pike are always females, and generally I don't like to kill them.

On arriving back in London at dusk I delivered her to the masterful chef Brett Graham of the Ledbury.

I went the following day to taste what he'd created, and while waiting for my dish of steamed pike with subtle sake sauce and caviar, I raised a glass of white Burgundy: a toast to the tiny departed vole in the hope that some justice had been served up.

A Buffet for My Lawyer, a Sandwich for Me

My lawyer is a Dickensian-looking man. Wiry, small, beaky nose and a trimmed ginger beard. His ties are loud and his suits shiny. He scurries about town, his hat and papers tight on head and underarm. He is a weedy-looking man, but don't be fooled by this. He is vicious, a professional fighter by trade.

His business is no frills, stripped down and functional. The shop front is dismal, the inside painted white. Scuffs and smudges mark the doors, edges and skirting.

His desk has dried bits on it that resemble fish food. These are of no matter to him, as the intensity of his work ethic places them low down the list of importance. The office is dark, almost a cell with its one high window.

He rightly expects everyone to get on with it, while I notice he enjoys displaying authority when summoning an underling to arrange coffee for me.

'Latte, Americano, flat white?' They are all awful.

He works hard, fights hard and goes home to rather too many other interests.

I want him to be just a lawyer not a poet, author, musician, athlete, barista and God knows what else.

He's weird. A sort of weapon's grade misfit.

I both like him and don't. Beady, argumentative and often objectionable, I have had to tell him to 'FUCK. OFF' a few times as these are tense times.

I often find myself playing a game though, a sort of collecting for my

Apocalypse Club. Defined as 'all those you'd need as counsel or ally should the lights go out and tribes return', I would want him close by.

On entering his office one morning, frazzled, gloomy and deeply sad with the goings on, he presented me with a glimmer of hope.

'I have some good news,' he said.

'Great,' I thought, 'Could this mean the beginning of reconciliation?'

No. His statement is like the beginning of a bad joke, continuing into 'I've just exchanged on another flat, it's in Southsea,' and then something about doing it up and renting it out.

Bewildered by the tactlessness, I congratulated him. Only on sitting down to matters of my own home, did I internally erupt in the knowledge that I did not give a shit about his property and also that my fees had probably paid for a considerable chunk of his new granny unit.

I couldn't hear, I was overcome with rage. He was no more than a muffled talking head across the desk.

I imagined myself, like a Mohican, tomahawk in one hand, knife clamped in mouth, leaping over the palisade wall to hear him shriek before felling him in the grass with wide-eyed glee.

But the desk is still between us and he has his biro in his hand, not embedded in his ear.

Leaving, £350 later, I took as many sweets from the jar in reception as I could carry.

Anchovies, Cold Butter and Onions

For this to be the simple pleasure it should be, ensure all the parts are A1 ace!

1 loaf of excellent, crusty sourdough with lovely moist, chewy, airy innards
Very good canned anchovies in oil (I heartily recommend Ortiz brand)
Really excellent unsalted butter, fridge cold
1 very good, hard, unsprouted red onion (thinly sliced as and when

needed. This cannot be pre-sliced and left in fridge as the onion will become limp and taste horrible.)

Put 2 slices of the sourdough bread and 6 of the anchovies, drained from their oil, on a plate. Next to it place a considerable portion of the butter, and next to that a small pile of the thinly sliced onion. Top the bread. While loading, be generous with the butter, estimate one anchovy per bite, and be gentle with the onion. Heaven. A chilled glass of a thin-bodied red wine would be a joy.

Lucky Seven – Some Advice about Lawyers

1. Don't go to a lawyer, unless you have no other option at all.

2. While surgeons like to cut, lawyers like to send letters. Keep this in mind.

3. Never talk to lawyers about your holiday or weekends. The more friendly you are, the more expensive the process will be.

4. Time the meetings. Know what you want to discuss before you arrive. Take a stopwatch.

5. Leave emotion at home – moaning costs money. Stick to the facts concisely. Say these facts once and clearly.

6. Be organized. Disorganization is expensive.

7. Eat baked beans and hot dogs and apples, and drink squash until you are done with your lawyer.

An Absolute

My decree absolute arrives in the post.

Am I happy? No. Do I want to pop Champagne and stay out all night? No. Do I jump in the air and shout 'YASSSS' and punch the sky? No. I do none of these things.

I recall great noise, distress and that something got out of control.

Too many opinions, a hurricane of outrage, regardless of the inevitability. I couldn't hear above the din.

I look blankly at my lunch feeling deeply annoyed with the current trend for avocados on toast.

So: this business is finished. That I am thankful for.

How do I feel? Exhausted is how I feel.

I imagine looking across a battlefield. The injured moan and call out, while their horses struggle and cannot right themselves. The cannons are all fired out, and smoke hangs low over the ground.

This neat decree is more a tattered standard.

Counsel has disbanded and gone back to their homes and families and it is strangely peaceful here.

I will stay a while longer.

Life indeed goes on but there is no hurry right now to run ahead and join it.

My Beautiful Launderette

While I was happy to leave the miniscule flat I lived in with my girlfriend – little bigger than my overcoat it seemed on frustrated days – I was very sad to say goodbye to Hamid, the Iranian dry cleaner I'd become extremely fond of.

Visiting his shop, if his parents weren't steaming garments or sewing in the window, it would often appear empty.

If they were there, on the tinkling of the pointless bell, his father would stamp loudly on the floorboards and yell 'HAAAAAAMIIIIID!' If his parents weren't there, I'd learnt to do the same.

'HAAAMMIIID!'

'Comiiiin,' would be the faint reply from the chemical belly of the room below, where the clothes tumbled around and around.

A lengthy minute or so later you'd hear 'clump, clump, clump' as he climbed the stairs. Finally Hamid's large, round, bald head and soft smiling face would appear through the floor like a little rising sun.

'Hello,' he'd say gently, his head wobbling in welcome.

Meeker customers could stand there for quite some time, pink tickets or bulging bags in hand, glancing at their watches and tutting.

Should I, on passing, notice a small queue but no Hamid I'd burst into the shop, stamp three times, yell 'HAAAAMIIIID!' and then immediately dash out.

I noticed that most customers found this behaviour somewhat surprising. While I'm happy to help, people really should take more initiative.

Always in thick white socks and flip-flops, Hamid was a hardworking and deeply kind man whom I would chat with often. The weather, work, food, the odd little man we both disliked, who was not only Hamid's landlord, but seemingly landlord of all the shops on the street.

Hamid was as close as I got to any idea of community over those three years in Brook Green.

One day I saluted him as I passed. It stuck. Whether me passing him or him sitting behind his sewing machine as I strode past, he'd stop work and I'd stop walking and we'd salute.

It got rather silly as I'd sometimes stand there, hand to forehead, for a ridiculous amount of time before he'd even notice and promptly return it.

At first I wasn't sure if he wanted to continue this, sometimes up to four or five times a day, but his face would light up every time. He'd even salute mid-conversation with other customers – his choice, as I wouldn't interrupt such an exchange. That is until I started to as well.

When in a hurry, if I ever caught him in full salute, having myself forgotten to, my hand would shoot up, only find my self saluting the hedge and railings having run out of window space to get one in. I got some very odd looks.

My children, when visiting, started saluting too, the three of us lined up outside his shop like a parade of air hostesses at the bottom of the Port-A-Steps.

His mother offered me some walnuts one day and soon after, in a gesture of exchange, whenever I went fishing I'd return with a fish.

Hamid liked trout, and was not fazed by a sizeable pike I offered him. I'd call him on my return and he'd dash from his house opposite the laundry and take the bag through the window to, no doubt, give to his mother. She was the cook. He was not married.

Next day, throwing my shirts on the counter, I'd be presented with a plastic box filled with a delicious mix of rice, lentils and crispy onions, or spiced greens, another with cold fried fish.

Salutes continuing, I'd drop off fish, pigeon and pheasant with regularity and no expectation of paying anything less than the going rate for my laundry. Which I did. I certainly got it back faster than other customers though.

Pretty handy that when I cut out the felt templates I'd made for my daughter's unicorn saddle, and Hamid stitched it together with such additional care and embroidery that I wondered if there was potentially a cottage-industry idea.

On one or two rainy days I found myself sitting behind the counter, sharing the most delicious dates, tiny green olives and tea with his parents. They didn't say much, just nodded and offered me more confections.

In the end my girlfriend and I moved. I said farewell with a final and lengthy salute. We hugged, then slapped our hands to our hearts in a gesture of goodwill so common to the Middle East.

His mother, as a farewell gift, produced a tin of rose-flavoured nougat containing the brightest green pistachios I have ever seen.

My new dry cleaner is an annoying little man who grumbles when I use my card rather than cash. He tried to charge me twenty quid to dry clean my woolly slippers, the brute.

So now I store up my shirts and go the extra three miles every two weeks to see Hamid. The salutes have begun again.

Special Tomatoes

16 fresh plum tomatoes, or medium-sized vine tomatoes, rinsed and
   halved
Caster (granulated) sugar, for dusting
2 tbsp sherry vinegar
1 tbsp coriander seeds, ground lightly
1 tbsp fennel seeds, ground lightly
2 generous tsp dried rosemary
1½ tsp dried oregano
Light dusting of smoked sweet paprika
Zest of 1 and rind of another small unwaxed lemon
15 g/½ oz fresh thyme sprigs
Handful of black grapes
Olive oil, for drizzling and storing (optional)
Sea salt and freshly ground black pepper

Preheat the oven to 90°C fan/110°C/225°F/gas mark ¼.

Line 1 large or 2 smaller baking trays with greaseproof paper. Regiment the
tomatoes side by side on the trays. Scatter with 3 teaspoons of salt and a
heavy aerial bombardment of black pepper. Sugar them and then pass over
with a good splash of vinegar.

Scatter the seeds and dried herbs over them, taking care not to waste too
much in the spaces between the tomatoes. Dust with the smoked paprika
and pass over with the lemon zest. Scatter the thyme so as to lie cross the
tomatoes. Scatter the black grapes here and there. Lastly, pass over with a
very enthusiastic sploshing of olive oil.

Cook for about 4 hours or until any obvious wateriness has departed. They
should be withered, but still juicy. The faintest browning is absolutely fine.

Either eat them immediately with grilled meat or fish, or put them in sterilized jars with 2 crumpled fresh bay leaves and a big strip of lemon peel per jar, then fill the jars to the top with good olive oil.

Tip Here are a couple of simple ways I like to use them. First, added to Fergus Bread (page 181), sandwiched between the fresh goat or sheep curd and the salsa. Second, I often reheat them and pop onto buttered toast, then pour over hot double (heavy) cream which has had an eye-watering dollop of Dijon mustard stirred in. Throw down fresh tarragon leaves that you haven't even bothered to chop on top. Blast with black pepper.

Not Ideal Home Show

I'm at the Ideal Home Show in Earl's Court. There to perform. It's packed. As the crowd are seated I enter the kitchen door to 'mic up'. Misjudging the makeshift MDF steps, I stumble. There is a terrible internal gristly, crunchy snap as my ankle explodes. I groan as a pain quite unlike any I have experienced shocks my every inch and corner. My fellow chefs turn to me as I go pale, then grey, then green and faint in the agony.

'Went down like a sack of potatoes,' apparently.

I come around on the floor.

There is a soft, pearly white light shining before me. Was my accident that bad? Is this heaven? No, it's Gino D'Acampo's immaculate teeth. He is looking down at me and cradling my head in his arms (I guess I'm every housewife's envy).

St John (not the restaurant) turn up and I'm hoiked into a wheelchair. Gregg thinks I'll be cheered by a cheeky joke. I want him to get away from me.

My trousers are warm. Oh God, it appears I've wet myself at the pain. Mumbling, unable to talk properly, I'm trying to ask for a blanket to cover me. I don't get one. I'm wheeled out into a packed show, a huge dark patch spreading from my crotch, with not so much as a packet of Bellota ham to disguise it.

You want entertainment, you got it ...

Oh, the indignity!

Clam Broth

So easy. So cleansing. Deny me shellfish, and I will fill the sea again with tears.

Serves 2

1 kg/2 lb 4 oz top-quality large Manila clams (buy them during the cold
   months before early spring)

50 ml/1⅔ fl oz/2¾ tbsp sake

1 tsp Japanese bonito dashi stock powder

5-cm/2-in strip of kombu

2 tsp Japanese soy sauce

2 nail-clipping-sized slices of lime rind

1 thumbnail-sized piece ginger, peeled and finely slivered

1 small stalk of fresh coriander (cilantro) with leaves

Rinse the clams well under a running tap. Discard any open clams. Tip them in to a large saucepan with just the water that clings to them.

Allow them to steam with the lid on over a medium heat until just opened. This should take 2–3 minutes with a jiggle of the pan here and there. Turn them over once. If they aren't opening just give them a little longer. They must be tender and giving. If overcooked, they are not the joy they should be.

Remove from the heat and tip into a colander set over a bowl to retain the juices. Remove and discard any clams that have not opened. Leave to one side.

Taking a medium-sized saucepan, pour in the sake and dissolve the dashi over a low heat. Add 550 ml/17½ fl oz/2¼ cups of water, the kombu and the soy sauce. Bring to the gentlest of simmers for barely more than 4 minutes.

If the clams are good, but for the minutest amount of grit, the juices from them should be a clear bluey grey.

Gently tip the clam juice into the broth stock, straining if you need to.

Pick through the clams, removing the majority from the shell but leaving 12 intact. Spoon the heated broth stock into 2 bowls and divide the shelled and unshelled clams between them. Garnish with the lime rind, ginger slivers and coriander stems. Sip in peace.

Termites

I am in Africa and we've driven through a field of termite mounds. We stop to take a look. I'm handed a stalk of grass and told to 'Fish ... Push it down the hole.' So, like a studious chimp, I dip my quill in the mound.

I pull it out while some cross termites, looking for a fight, march up and down its length. I pick one off and eat it as instructed. It tastes like passion fruit, so I have a few more. They taste similar to ants in sharpness, but ants are more lemony. Far better than any centre of a Quality Street.

In the campsite we make a fire and I get a pot of oxtail and ginger on. We cook some guinea fowl that have been caught. I make a peanut sauce, a kind of 'afro-romesco' as we have some hot peppers and tomatoes to use. While I'm tending to the gourds, roasting gently in piled-up hot ash, a giraffe walks past and blinks at me. A log for a chopping board, a bucket for a sink, hot stones for a stove. A cook without a kitchen, I have everything I need.

The Best Compliment Ever!

'You cooked my knickers off!'

The Backgammon Board

I'm looking at a single lentil in the bottom of a cast-iron casserole. The lentil is me, a dot on the gaming board, a figurine in the model arena of the gods.

Circumstances change and I, for one, am not seemingly someone the Fates ever allow to settle for too long. And so, with my marriage went my house and with my house went my kitchen. My spacious kitchen with its marble slab to encourage smooth-skinned strokes with pastry, an oven into which hopped goats, double ducks, toothy hake and other such things I hoped to honour into the gastronomic afterlife.

Opening the flush wooden panel of my fridge door revealed a bright winter palace, while ample work space rolled out to the right of it, allowing the spread of an expansive cook.

It also rejoiced in the very machine I'd long denied myself (that manual work keep a fit and modest mind), a dishwasher.

My favourite pots and pans were arranged across long open shelves, my troops, there to salute every morning, while the top shelf was more an altar adorned with kitchen obscurities and favourites. Crocodile nutcrackers, bottles, rabbit plates, a Japanese toad-shaped clay mug, jelly moulds were arranged toward the centrepiece, Alan Davidson's very own fish kettle. This is the only possession I've ever bid for in an auction, glad the gavel fell at £70, that I did not win to further bloody-minded extravagance.

At the far end of this most favourite of rooms sat my long Eames table, next to doors unfolding into a small garden of roses. Whether summer or winter, over the clickety click of salad tongs or an unctuous stew, the happy volume of friends would increase for ever-joyful suppers of eating and drinking in the pleasure of company.

But, as you know, the cook lost his kitchen, and I moved into the flat of my girlfriend. She calls it 'the barnacle' and I, more generously, 'the backgammon board'. It is a flat suited to one immaculate person.

That you really understand the barnacle, it has no permanent table, only a worktop with breakfasting lip. There is a folding card table when needed, although baize is not ideal for escaped soup. It lives behind the mirror in a community of other hidden things.

The kitchen cupboards double up as a medicine chest, with vitamins roaming among various tins of beans. Cabinet reshuffles and careless moves will often see a bag of flour powder-bomb the worktop, a box of tea plop into the sink or see sheets of *nori* inadvertently dealt out across the hob.

These cupboards hang so low, washing up is taken on blind, hands operating in dark and out of eyesight. I am now expert in feeling when a plate is clean.

It is a better suited space for ready-meal regulars with conventional tastes. Curry nights can become curry weeks – the close proximity of soft furnishings is most welcoming of cooking smells, especially with little competition from the extractor, more a wall-mounted wheeze box with a curious lack of any extraction to the outside world.

Freako, as I know it, most hated of fridges. The oversized freezer compartment wrongly sits on the shoulders of its infinitely more visited twin, meaning that to see what's within I have to stoop so low I feel like Luke Skywalker entering Yoda's hut.

The freezer knows my hatred, either firing cascades of peas at me, on tugging the handle from its insanely stubborn vacuum, or slipping a frozen trout onto my bare toes.

Cooking is regularly interrupted by the washing machine that, on spin, shakes the whole kitchen so violently, knives take on a millipede grace as they scuttle towards the counter's edge. The ferocity of these ill-timed tremors has been known to vibrate credit cards and car keys into unknown recesses, if they are not replaced to wallet or hook pre-washing.

This kitchen no more affords me space than a mussel confined in its shell. There is barely room to swing an anchovy, certainly not a cat, so pans will often find themselves cooling among the flower pots of herbs on the lintel. As the kitchen is three floors up, its really quite amazing no one sunning below has been met with death from above, their brains dashed to mayonnaise by a misplaced three kilos of cast iron and ratatouille.

My nemesis is, surprisingly, none of the above but more what's below. The floor is black, jet black marble, and illuminates any washing powder or crumbs as the Milky Way across the backdrop of night.

In this tiny dictator state everything must, I repeat, must have its place lest anarchy or screaming frustration flare. However ... we must change and adapt. I can be brattish and spoilt, so I must remind myself that there are those with even less space and families maybe even forced to leave their smashed home for food and into streets where snipers watch.

So while my tea towels quietly ignite in close confines to the hob, it's best to also remind myself that in all this hugga-mugga a new way of cooking has evolved, less contrived, simpler, maybe even more imaginative, certainly effective and built for its very own environment.

Porridge Oat and Salmon Cakes

I cannot bear throwing away cold porridge. On Vancouver island, with a glut of salmon in my fridge, this struck me as a good idea one morning.

Serves 2
1 medium sweet onion
50 g/1¾ oz/½ stick butter
150 g/5½ oz cooked cold jumbo oat porridge
125 g/4½ oz cold leftover flaked salmon pieces

15–20 g/½–¾ oz parsley, finely chopped
Good grinding of black pepper
Pinch of sea salt
Squeeze of lemon, to serve

In a small frying pan (skillet), fry the onion in half the butter until totally tender and soft. This will take 7–8 minutes or so if the onion is diced as finely as suggested.

Meanwhile, place the porridge together with the fish, parsley and seasoning.

When the onion is cooked, add it in. While it's good to have some chunky bits of fish, the majority of the salmon needs smushing so that the cakes don't break up when frying.

Melt the remaining butter in the frying pan and then fry the cakes on a low-medium heat until crispy on both sides, turning once carefully. (Note: they will take longer than you think, partly because it's better to not fry them too fast, and secondly because of the water content, even in stiff porridge.)

Take to a plate and pass over with a squeeze of lemon. Avoid mayonnaise, as they are so simply delectable and giving without it.

Blue Hubbard Squash Stuffed with Cheese, Ceps and Walnuts

Serves 2–4
2 kg/4 lb 8 oz blue hubbard squash
50 g/1¾ oz/½ stick butter, plus extra for frying (optional)
70 g/2½ oz/¾ cup Tomme de Savoie cheese, grated
50 g/1¾ oz/½ cup raclette cheese, grated
Pinch of nutmeg
100 ml/3½ oz/½ cup double (heavy) cream

3 garlic cloves, grated

Large handful of shelled walnut halves

4 medium-sized fresh ceps (otherwise use an extra packet of dried porcini, pre-soak them and drain them of water)

1 small packet of rehydrated porcini or, better still, fresh ones

Olive oil, for frying (optional)

Fresh parsley, finely chopped

Sea salt and freshly ground black pepper

Preheat the oven to 170°C fan/190°C/375°F/gas mark 5.

Cut a 'lid' from the top of the squash and set to one side. Scoop the seeds from the centre of the squash and retain them for roasting and enjoying later.

Smear the inside of the squash with the butter, season generously with salt and pepper, then smear the salt and pepper around the inside, too. Replace the lid on the squash.

Place the squash on a baking tray and bake for 1 hour or until it appears to have withered and burnt a little at the edges of the lid and sides. Remove from the oven and remove the lid from the top. The flesh within should be very soft.

Mix the cheeses with the nutmeg and add to the squash.

Mix the cream with the grated garlic and nutmeg and then pour it into the squash. Replace the lid and put the squash back in the oven for a further 10 minutes.

Put the walnuts on a small baking tray and slip them into the oven next to the squash for 5–7 minutes or until toasted and slightly darker.

Meanwhile, slice and fry the ceps in a little butter or olive oil until nicely browned. Season with salt and add the parsley. If using dried, soaked porcini, add to a frying pan (skillet) with the soaking liquid and a large knob of butter. Rapidly simmer until all the liquid has evaporated. The mushrooms will then start to fry in the butter – cook until nicely browned and season with salt.

Remove the squash and walnuts from the oven. Toss the walnuts together with the mushrooms and parsley. Remove the lid of the squash and tip in the nut and mushroom mix. Replace the lid and serve.

Steer Clear ... or ... On PR and Marketing

I used to have a rule that, if I stock something in my fridge or kitchen cupboards, then should that company ring me up with a job offer, I can work for them.

I'm not so sure I adhere to this now. I've seen more of the world, and so I am perhaps more discerning in my choices, despite the barely navigable minefield of good intent and contradiction that is modern life.

There are some brilliant PR and marketing companies that really understand what they're doing and who it is they represent or, if a client's new to them, make sure that they learn everything there is to learn about the client. And there are others where I cannot comprehend a) how they get any work at all, and b) how they manage to dupe the client into parting with so much cash.

Suffice to say, I was rung up by a PR company who represented a massive dairy brand and asked if I'd like to work for their creamy spread. 'Yeah, sure,' I said. It was in my fridge, and my kids like it. And the idea was that happy cows with more grazing space produce better milk and cheese. Welfare for all involved. Hooray!

So I drove to Kent on a very cold day and pulled into the farm, to be greeted by the usual fleet of cars and a camera crew and photographer screwing things together from flight cases strewn all over the yard while the PR kids, a baffling number of them, paced around on their phones, all wearing brand-new, brightly coloured wellingtons with absurd external fur rims at their tops. Mud and bramble magnets, I thought. And some minutes later, I found myself standing in a field with a table of ingredients in front of me, as someone brushed my hair.

At the photographer's command, four cows were steered through a daffodil-dotted gateway into the field. And the girl with the clipboard said, 'Amazeballs, everyone! We've got Val, we've got cows, the table looks good. So let's go, shall we?'

'We've got a bit of a problem,' I replied.

'Not from where I'm standing, Val. Is something wrong?' Her pursed smile suggesting that there'd better not be.

'You tell me,' I said.

'I'm not with you.'

'Well, this is about creamy milk and happy, dribbling teats. And there's not a pink swinging udder in sight! They're heifers.'

'They're cows, Val,' she said. 'A cow's a cow. So shall we get on with it?'

'If we do, you'll be in a big heap of cowpat!'

It took a while to talk them out of continuing, followed by lots of phone calls, glances at me and exasperated hands on heads. The farmer looked pissed off. I was not Mr Popular.

So I went in search of some stunt cows, and a few hours later two farmhands from a different farm produced a pair of Friesians on halters, initially desperate-looking things, plastered in muck, until they had their hair and make-up.

Our second attempt at filming fared little better because the cameraman ran away shrieking every time a cow came within ten feet of him, and ended up filming everything from the other side of the fence.

Never have I been so glad to get home. And never has the opening of a lid reminded me of something so much.

Fergus Bread (Sourdough, Soft, White, Fresh Cheese and Green Sauce)

This genius recipe was first offered to me (a hand-sized island of unctuous excellence) by Margot Henderson, Fergus's wife. This is my own interpretation of the green sauce.

Serves 6

Good-quality sourdough bread

2 x 150-g/5-oz tubs of very tangy fresh goats' or sheep's curd or, failing that, cream cheese

For the green sauce

50 g/1¾ oz fresh parsley leaves (I prefer young, tender curly parsley)

25 g/1 oz fresh tarragon leaves

15 g/½ oz fresh sweet marjoram (optional)

10 g/¼ oz fresh dill

10 g/¼ oz fresh coriander (cilantro)

4 salted anchovies, washed of salt, or from oil (preferably Ortiz)

3 tbsp capers, rinsed and drained

2 heaped tsp Dijon mustard

1 tbsp shallot very finely chopped, rinsed and patted dry

1 good, hard garlic clove with no shoots, finely grated

Just under 1 tsp sea salt

6 tbsp extra virgin olive oil

Enough red wine vinegar to sharpen the mix but not overpower it

Combine everything for the green sauce, adding the oil and vinegar last of all. Remember that, while its fine to make the sauce a little ahead of time, it might be worth keeping the vinegar back as, left to sit, it will discolour the herbs.

Slice and toast the bread and smear very thickly with the cheese. Spoon a hefty dollop of the green sauce over the top.

The Cost of Food

I respect my peers hugely, but sometimes when I'm talking things come
out the wrong way, like a high-pressure fart. Were I a royal courtier in
some bygone age, I would likely early on have been imaginatively executed,
doubtless because of an unwise aside. It pays to be polite, I know. But I also
feel a 'reputation' does not mean that one must always kneel before it instead
of speaking freely.

Years of hindsight and regret have taught me it pays to play the game,
even if playing said game only flatters questionable systems and myths into
continuation. Better to keep shtum, as a quote from a Russian hermit in one
of my favourite books, *Consolations of the Forest* by Sylvain Tesson, reminds us:

'The less you talk the longer you live.'

I agree with this most definitely … despite my inclinations. But sometimes
I simply cannot help myself.

I'm filming in Donostia (also called San Sebastián), an insert for the
show *Market Kitchen*, or *Market Carnage*, as it was lovingly then called by all
involved. It's been a good trip; we have greatly enjoyed the Bar Txepetxa
(temple of the anchovy), the private dining clubs, the annual ritual of *txotx*
(pronounced 'choch') – tasting the new cider.

This town is indeed one of the greatest in the world to eat in, and I'd
learnt a lot. Most particularly that chacolí wine, poured from a great height
as is the custom, seems more intended for the inside of the waiter's shoes
than the customers' glass.

We end up filming at Restaurante Arzak, and visiting the great man himself.

Arzak, a good name for a magician, was an original innovator of
molecular gastronomy and modern Basque cuisine. An inspiration to Ferran
Adrià and Heston the Great, Arzak can transform olive oil into snow-white
rocks that dissolve on the tongue, or make strawberries turn into peas. You
know the sort of thing.

At first, he strikes me as a somewhat grumpy, impatient man, but on
realizing that I know my onions and take my food seriously, he mellows

and invites me to cook in the kitchen with him, where rows of chefs in icing-white, pressed uniforms meticulously go about their duties. We have a lovely time and he presents me with a lobster and corn dish that's pretty as a picture and almost resembles a piece of coral reef transferred from ocean to plate. It's very delicious!

So I'm trusted enough to be taken to his cabinet of curiosity.

Producing a small key, I'd like to say from a small chain around his neck (but maybe this is wishful thinking), he fiddles it in the lock and we enter a dark room. Low lighting flicks on to reveal rows and rows of shelves on which are stacked, seemingly hundreds high, lots of little plastic boxes, the type that you'd leave a takeaway with.

'When my chefs are tired or, how you say, need ideas they come here to find inspiration and fire their senses,' he exclaims, raising his fingers to the ceiling like an Asterix caricature. Reaching for a tub, he pulls back the lid and invites me to sniff inside.

'Iranian dried lemons,' he says. The next is a beautiful pastel green rice that has a smell I do not expect. Spices, powders, many oddities are put under by nose and I sniff away. Delighted with his treasure cave, he turns to me and says, 'Are your senses amazed? What do you think? It's wonderful, no?'

'Senor Arzak,' I reply, 'It is indeed wonderful, but it reminds me of my grandmother's store cupboard. Like her spice collection in a shoebox, everything smells of everything else. Although, unlike her, you do put the lids on properly. I think sealed glass might be better than porous plastic tubs.'

It is translated by Elena, his daughter.

He looks at me, and I feel he's on the verge of doing a Rumpelstiltskin, about to hold his breath until he turns red, and then stamp until the floor collapses. He's furious with me. In effect, I've just told Napoleon that his military campaign is no more strategic than a brawl in the coach park.

We are marched out. He's livid and, handing us over for his daughter to finish the tour, stomps off.

The director shoots me a glance.

'He did ask me,' I feebly offer.

I apologize to Arzak's daughter. She looks back at me with a kind of, 'Uh oh, that won't have gone down well' sort of look. It's all somewhat frosty after that. We finish the tour, and it seems he still intends to serve us lunch. So the crew and I are all seated. Napkins pulled open, and Arzak enters through the kitchen door with four waiters carrying his 'chicken and egg' dish. At this very point the director places his scrumpled napkin on the table and says to me, 'Right, change of plan. I need GVs [general views], everyone outside. Not you, Val, you and Sarah can eat.'

'You can't be serious,' I say. 'I've already pissed him off. Are you actually going to leave the room as this food arrives?'

'Val, I have a programme to make, a flight in four hours, and I want to make sure I've covered everything. You do your job and eat it, and I'll do mine.'

So, as the food is being set before us, everyone but me and Sarah the runner gets up and leaves. Adding insult to injury, Richard the 'I hate wanky pretentious food' cameraman turns and, in broken Spanish-English, asks 'Can you bung it in the oven and keep it warm for us?'

While Arzak can do many things, he thankfully cannot magic us into frogs, catch us up and remove our legs or indeed turn us into seven walnuts. His face is puce. He's definitely going to Rumpelstiltskin this time. He tells us we are rude. I heartily agree, as I verbally disassociate myself from the crew and set about trying to wrestle a second 'chicken and egg' dish from the waiter, now trying to remove it from an empty placing. The egg slips from the bowl and, with its disk of reduced-stock 'chicken paper', lands 'plop' on top of my own egg in front of me.

Too much for him, Arzak marches off again.

He does a lot of marching off, it strikes me.

I have a nice lunch with Sarah while I simultaneously can't wait to leave. And when we do, Arzak stands at the door, I think to make sure we've definitely gone. He's silent, so we thank Elena. She is wonderful.

Two years later, outside the Observer Food Monthly Awards, and wizard Arzak steps from a cab with his daughter. I walk up to him and say, 'I don't know if you remember me but ...'

'Remember you?' he says, 'I forgive you only yesterday!'

Islands of the Gods

Where the fresh wind blows white horses towards sharp black mountains that fall steeply to the sea, where giant cod swim deep below the sharp eyes of circling sea eagles, the moss-carpeted Lofoten islands sit in the far northerly west of Norway below Tromsø, ninety-five miles north of the Arctic Circle.

I have long felt an inexplicable connection with Scandinavia. As a boy, I sat wide eyed, listening to tales of Viking ravages and splintering monastery doors, the chronicles of the violent Norse gods and stories of trolls. And this interest only grew, alongside my love for nature, the forest and all things made of wood. I longed to see this cold-climate wilderness of pines, lichen-covered granite, lakes, huts and axes, and silently asked that I might one day visit.

My father had always said to me, in one way or another, 'Quietly send your desires towards the stars, as true intention will be answered.'

It appears the astral clockwork answered this desire; in 2012 I ended up filming *Valentine Warner Eats Scandinavia*. This ten-part series, across Denmark, Sweden and Norway, fishing, hunting, drinking birch sap and cooking reindeer heart in -40°C/-40°F, was aired on UKTV, most particularly to an audience of Ingunn Rassmussen and her husband Trond Melhus, far away in Korea.

A year later, Ingunn sent me an email saying she had watched this series and others I'd made, and thought it right I should come and see her hotel, Holmen Lofoten, to get a sense of the place and have a chat. She wanted the hotel to be something more out of the ordinary.

Time poor, I could ill afford a jolly, but on ringing her up, liked her bright voice and understood her to be an interesting, inquisitive and humorous woman. And so, acting on a hunch, I said yes.

A few months later, after a staggeringly beautiful drive through the fjords, I arrived in a town called Å at a collection of wooden fishermen's huts or *rorbuer*, '*ro*' (row) and '*bu*' (live), sitting higgledy-piggledy at the water's edge. It was love at first sight.

But for a roaring waterfall tipping foam into deep space, this was a hotel on the edge of the world. In this clean air, the overwhelming and invigorating elements chased urban worries from out my head and across the sea.

'I belong here,' I felt.

I have yet to swab my lineage but, as a lover of log piles and the cold, were I to find Nordic blood flowing within, it would come as little surprise.

Cooking in Lofoten is a joy; the islands are rich in ingredients which, at the same time, require you to think on your feet every day.

Nature and the weather here dictate a more immediate menu, as does what may be bought in from the mainland ... or not.

Under the constant light show of the midnight sun, or the inky short days of winter with the aurora trembling overhead, I have spent many happy hours in the kitchen at Holmen, braising the mountain hares, smoking the white-trousered ptarmigan brought in by hunters, or preparing cod the size of Labradors. The seas are rich with muscular carpets of halibut, coley, haddock, pollack and summer mackerel.

As the growth of yellow, scarlet and purple berries erupts in summertime, the islands turn a bright emerald green. The lakes provide the most beautiful species of trout, the delicate-tasting char with its green and orange colouring. From surrounding small plots and gardens, astonishing strawberries, the colour of blood, and vegetables ripened under the unceasing gaze of a midnight sun will bring a smile with their flavour.

Before pre-ordering any anchovies, Dijon mustard or spices, it is best to stand still and look at what is already here. Soon all manner of possibilities arrive, whether it means picking the green juniper in the car park, pulling yellow-footed mushrooms from under a nearby cluster of spruce, collecting seaweed from the shoreline or local goats' cheese from the shop.

With an eye towards more conventional ingredients, the Lofoten lamb, dare I say it, is the best I've ever eaten. They are more feral than domesticated, spending their lives in the high mountains nibbling all manner of herbs and plants. Although delicious, their very pale and tender meat is minimal, kept to size by the elements in the same way the dwarf birches are stunted by the cold ocean gales. Their shoulders are barely larger than a turkey leg, but oh! the taste. Oof!

Cockles, their meat the size of sweetbreads, litter certain shallow bays, while the bottom of the sea clicks with crawling brown crabs.

But Lofoten is most famous for its cod. Around April the skrei, or 'snow cod' as I prefer to call them, turn up in these rich waters to feed and spawn until May. Testament to this important industry is a small railtrack that runs from the jetty at Holmen. So great were the catches that the fishing boats, laden low and slow in the water from the weight of their haul, would unload the cod into a trolley that could be pushed on the rails with ease up to the cleaning area.

The skrei is seemingly identical to our own cod, but these migratory fish reach remarkable sizes when compared. The largest Lofoten specimen in 2017 was 52 kg/115 lb. A good UK fish would be only 15 kg/33 lb.

Fishing for them is a thrill, especially in a considerable sea swell with Odin shouting wind and hail coming down like Thor's hammer. Exhausting reel-cranking and colossal fish was warmly rewarded with dinner and aquavit ... a lot of aquavit. Cleaning the skrei in the harbour with sharp knives, amid a lot of blood, there is something extremely visceral about remote Norway. That people lived on these shores so long ago, ravaged by the weather, hardship and the seas, with so many different ways to die, you can see why their gods were so fearsome, why the Norwegians are so open and practical. It's hard to shock a Norwegian.

Cooked by Ingunn's extended family, my first Skrei dinner was memorable. The roes were wrapped in greaseproof paper with bay leaves and black pepper, bound in string, and poached. The fresh liver was rendered with onion, then poured over waxy, yellow boiled potatoes, seasoned with salt – not to be associated with the cod liver oil from a bottle that I twisted and writhed to avoid as a child.

The meat was steamed, and all parts served together with needless to say ... more aquavit. The warmth of the fire, the timber-framed room, candles, the friendly volume of company, and it was a dinner I will never forget. Many guests came, including a Mexican blacksmith from Oaxaca doubling as professional bongo player. Many intriguing folk seem to accumulate in the Lofotens, and no one does a single job but likely two or three.

Due to a history of trade and exchange with the Portuguese, it nonetheless surprised me to find myself eating this rehydrated cod in a thick sauce of tomato and olives bought north from Portugal.

But it's not all cod and aquavit. Coming to work here often, I cannot stop cooking when at Holmen, even when not required too.

Liquorice bread and cured fish, hare soup, pickled mushrooms, curried cods' heads, Nordic-inspired pizzas, toastlets of wood grouse, razor clam rice, smoked king crab and salted Jerusalem artichokes, it's an incredible place to bring other like-minded cooks. So I have.

Washed down with the most astonishing cocktails we had from Monica Berg and Nick Strangeway that included such ingredients as fir, butter-washed gin, sea urchins, lingon and cloudberries, the bartenders have as much to discover along the shoreline and behind the bar.

You see, it has now become a second home, as everything I love in food and nature lives here, plus rewarding company, solitude, community, warmth, something visceral and elemental and essential.

Knowing many chefs would give their eye teeth to cook here, I bought Mark Hix to this raw frontier. He, like me, understood immediately that this is a very special place, that nature here is the true luxury.

Mark has continued to help Ingunn and I offer something wonderful for those seeking to escape their phone screens, digital pollution and the hectic day to day, and to swap them for wilderness, rebalance and relaxation.

Typical Mark, a dish he made summed up the comfortable simplicity of Holmen Lofoten. The Lofoten Breakfast Scallop (see page 194) has now become a breakfast essential.

Who knows how the future will unravel, as maybe these words will find you here while I cook for you?

Cods' Roe with Horseradish Cream

I love this.

Serves 3–4
100 ml/3½ fl oz/½ cup whipping cream
2 heaped tsp Dijon mustard
Quarter of a fresh hot horseradish, peeled and finely grated
270 g/9½ oz smoked cods' roe
6–8 slices German-style dark rye bread, toasted or not (it's up to you as
   both are good)
Good butter, for spreading
Sea salt and freshly ground black pepper

In a bowl, whip the cream with the mustard until fluffy and fairly stiff. Stir
through the horseradish and add a pinch of salt. Put to one side.

Slit the skin of the smoked cods' roe and scoop the flesh out with a teaspoon.

Butter the bread or toast and thickly smear the roe on top. Blob with a little
fluffy cloud of horseradish cream and pass over with a grind of pepper.

Serve with very cold vodka from the freezer.

Salt Cod in a Norwegian Style

Hanging around the fish counter in Waitrose, I occasionally find that older fish is bagged and placed on the countertop, bargain sticker slapped on. I strike like a heron at such value. In this case, cod.

Often unaware of how trade and travel have affected different nations' cuisines, I love such stories when they arise. Here is a very favourite salt cod recipe, or my version of it, from Norway, heavily influenced by the Portuguese, who are so dependent on Norway as a supply of cod. Of course, it would normally be made with the leather-hard salted *Klippfisk*, which has an intense flavour not to everyone's taste. For this, you need to salt the cod the night before for the following evening's pleasure.

Serves 4

350 g/12 oz cod loin, from the thick end (pollock or coley work too)

2½ tbsp sea salt

4 tbsp olive oil

2 medium onions, halved and finely sliced

2 fresh bay leaves

3 cloves, heads pinched when adding

6 whole peppercorns

4 garlic cloves, finely sliced

3 tbsp tomato purée

Pinch of hot chilli powder (optional)

2 x 400-g/14-oz cans whole plum tomatoes, juice drained

2 large carrots, peeled and sliced into rounds

600 g/1 lb 5 oz waxy potatoes, scrubbed and cut into large dice

20 pitted black olives (not horrible green ones dyed black)

2 tbsp capers

15–20 g/½– ¾ oz fresh parsley, finely chopped

Place the cod loin in a tray skin side down and scatter the salt evenly all over the flesh. Cover with clingfilm (plastic wrap) and place in the fridge for a minimum of 12 hours.

Pour the olive oil into a large casserole and, over a medium heat, gently sauté the onions with the bay leaves and spices for 10–15 minutes, until tender but not coloured.

Add the garlic and cook for a minute, then stir in the tomato purée and continue to cook for 3–4 minutes until the tomato purée begins to catch on the bottom of the pan. Add a smidgen of chilli powder here, if desired. A warm glow on the back of the throat is desired, not violence. Add the drained canned tomatoes, carrots, potatoes and olives. Top up with water, until the carrots and potatoes are just covered. Cook for about 45 minutes until vegetables are tender. Do not season!

Wipe any excess salt off the cod but do not rinse. Divide it into large chunks. Stir the capers into the stew and then nestle the fish into the stew base.

Bring to a simmer and cook for 4–5 minutes, until the fish is just cooked through. Be careful not to overcook. Break up the fish in the stew tenderly with a spoon.

Scatter over the chopped parsley and eat with bread and cold beer.

Lamb with Seaweed

If you stand in nature and simply observe, more often than not cooking ideas come to you. Ingredients that exist side by side outdoors do well at home side by side on a plate. How many times have I observed the tiny Lofoten sheep standing on the shoreline below the junipers? That's the inspiration for this alternative lamb shoulder dish, which is very pleasing. My memory was jogged by a recipe I found in an old cookbook for mutton stewed in laverbread with capers and oranges. Who knows how I got there, but this is now a staple dish at the Holmen Lofoten table.

Juniper wood, with its heady incense notes, coupled with the salty umami seasoning from the seaweed, really makes this special. Please do make an effort to order juniper chips if there is no bush nearby. It's very useful for cooking fish, too.

A proper charcoal barbecue is essential for the final stage as a gas barbecue – a truly pointless concept, little more than a stove wheeled into the garden – just won't do. Boo.

Serves 4

2 kg/4 lb 8 oz shoulder of lamb

1 tsp fennel seeds

1 tsp dried thyme

1 tsp finely chopped or pounded juniper berries

3 huge armfuls of fresh bladderwrack seaweed, washed

8 large 'long' shallots, whole, unpeeled, with a deep slash cut down the length of each

400 ml/14 fl oz/1¾ cups dry white wine

1 tbsp Japanese soy sauce

Juice of 1 orange

Sea salt and freshly ground black pepper

Charcoal for the outdoor grill

6 juniper berries, chopped

Preheat the oven to 170°C fan/190°C/375°F/gas mark 5.

Score the shoulder lamb fat in close, uniform lines. Do the same on the exposed meat of the underside.

Using a pestle and mortar, finely grind the fennel seeds, thyme, juniper berries and an industrial blast of black pepper. Rub well into the lamb.

Line the bottom of a large roasting tray with a third of the seaweed. Place the lamb on top, pale side facing up. Scatter the shallots over the top. Pour the wine into the tray around the lamb, but not over it as that will wash off the seasoning. Cover the lamb with the rest of the seaweed. Seal the tray tightly with double-layered foil.

Bake the lamb for 1 hour and 20 minutes. Half an hour before the lamb comes out, light the charcoal for the barbecue and let it burn down to a nice white colour with a warm orange glimmer.

Once cooked, remove the lamb and shallots to a clean roasting tray. Carefully remove the seaweed and strain the cooking juices through a sieve (strainer) into a small saucepan. Add the seaweed and then the orange juice and soy sauce to the juices. Bring to a simmer and reduce to about two-thirds, skimming as you go. The jus will have a somewhat milky appearance. This is normal. It shouldn't need seasoning due to the seaweed, but do taste. Remove from the heat and set aside.

Season the lamb with salt and, keeping the lid of the barbecue down, grill on both sides until golden brown and crispy. The meat should be just pink.

As it cooks, occasionally remove the lid to force some manageable lengths of juniper branch onto the charcoal where it will crackle, pop and smoke. Immediately replace the lid so that the meat takes up the juniper smoke. (Alternatively, you can soak juniper chips before cooking, drain them thoroughly and add them to the coals at the beginning of cooking.)

Rest the meat for 10 minutes on a tray so that you can collect any juices. Add the juices to the sauce, then gently reheat.

Delicious with celery salad and boiled potatoes tossed with butter and dill.

Favourite Nordic Breakfast

Hardly a recipe but a very good start to the day.

Serves 1

1–2 heaped tbsp full-fat cottage cheese
4 thick slices of peeled cucumber
6 pieces of Elsinore herrings in sweet spicy marinade, drained
Pinch of mild curry powder
1 hard-boiled egg
2 round sourdough crispbreads (I like Peter's Yard)
Sea salt and freshly ground black pepper

Blob cottage cheese on to a plate and grind over some pepper. Arrange the cucumber nearby and season with salt. Arrange the herrings nearby and pinch over with curry powder. Peel the egg, slice in half, season and add to other residents. Eat with the sourdough crispbreads and strong coffee.

Lofoten Breakfast Scallop

Mark Hix is a wonderful cook! Were you to watch him in the kitchen, his movements seem minimal while the subsequent delicious mouthfuls are many. This magic has never been more apparent than at a ten-course 'tail to barbule' cod dinner; he seemed to make everything effortless.

I remember taking him to the harbour on our first trip to Norway, and pushing towards him a box of scallops the size of dinner plates. This is what he made us all for breakfast. I thought it perhaps preferable to the nonetheless equally delightful sautéed cod sperm on toast. Anyone?

Serves 2

½ tbsp butter or olive oil

2 rashers streaky bacon, cut into 5-mm/¼-in dice, or about 50 g/1¾ oz
  smoked lardons

4 very fresh large scallops, cleaned (with the cupped half-shell and orange
  coral kept for later)

4 free-range eggs

Flaked sea salt and freshly ground black pepper

Preheat the oven to 180°C fan/200°C/400°F/gas mark 6.

Heat the butter or oil in a small frying pan (skillet) and gently cook the
bacon on a low heat for 2–3 minutes, then remove from the heat.

Meanwhile, detach the roes from the scallops, cut them into 3–4 pieces each,
add to the bacon and continue to cook for a couple more minutes.

Meanwhile, divide the scallop meat between the 4 scallop shells, placing it
on one side of the shell and season. Crack an egg into each shell beside the
scallop meat and place the shells on a baking tray in the oven for about 10
minutes, or until the eggs white is just set.

To serve, scatter the bacon and roes over the scallops.

Tip Should you want a variation on the theme, sauté a small piece of fresh
cod – making sure you get a crispy skin – and dish it up with a fried egg
and bacon, scattered with chives. Another favourite of our Lofoten island
breakfasts.

Growing Up

Remercier Harry Mathews

Harry Mathews was my godfather, a flamboyant American writer and poet who lived between France and the USA. He died in 2017. While I never fully understood what friendship meant to my father, Harry was certainly one of his closest friends, theirs a deep bond growing from strong foundations – an initial dislike of each other.

Harry was extraordinarily intelligent, very funny and, although I saw him little (seemingly a prerequisite for all my godparents), I remember every time I did so.

He was crazy about food and while seemingly not expanding his waist, it certainly did his mind. He drank and ate with Epicurean enthusiasm, becoming excited and intricately descriptive as mouthfuls were converted to words. A man of appetites and acrobatic thought, food and drink were super-connectors, the glue between ideas, emotions, spirituality, sex and everything it is to be human.

He was married to the sculptor Niki de Saint Phalle, and then the author Marie Chaix. He was the first American member of the curious Oulipo group, working closely alongside Georges Perec, a man famous for writing a novel without using the letter 'e' and, perhaps more relevant, an inventory of one whole year's eating.

As in everything Harry and my father turned their minds to, to be inquisitive led the way. A perfect soufflé, like a perfect sentence. Food was a subject never to be gotten to the bottom of, as life is fleeting. Further learning, no doubt, to be continued across the next plain.

I wrote the below as a contribution to his funeral. I have included it in this book as my love of food was made more excitable and curious for his brief involvement.

Harry. I always remember Harry, tall, stripped to the waist, wood
    chips and leaves stuck to his sweating skin. Smiling with my father
    as they surveyed an afternoon's work among the trees.
I remember reading *Singular Pleasures* as a teenager with wide eyes.

The flourish of bright scarves and embroidered conversation that
planted an early excitement in me of what it might be to talk freely.

I remember the cold of Grenoble, patches of snow, mountain flowers
and the glasses of wine that followed the adults.

I remember wanting so much to show Harry my own books, while
more immediate words felt clumsy in his presence.

I remember Harry jumping in darkness for the security light to come on
while we smoked and chatted in the shock of my own father's death.

I remember *My Life in CIA* and how I laughed and laughed.

I remember the stiff little coffees in London and the cow's muzzle
vinaigrette in Paris.

He never forgot to call me on our shared birthday.

I remember the emotional gaze of a fine man, a one off. Truth and
fantasy. Now a gap, but one filled with multi colours and the faintest
smell of cigar.

Alpine Macaroni

Smash in case of emergency on a very cold day.

Serves 4
250 g/9 oz aged Gruyère cheese, but normal will suffice
25 g/1 oz/2 tbsp butter
1 tbsp plain (all-purpose) flour
150 ml/5 fl oz/⅔ cup Riesling or Mâcon white wine
2 tsp Dijon mustard
Approximately 200 ml/7 fl oz/scant 1 cup double (heavy) cream
250 g/9 oz dried macaroni
100 g/3½ oz smoked bacon or pancetta lardons
2 good, hard garlic cloves, finely grated
Large sea salt flakes

For the apple sauce

3 Cox, Russet or Braeburn apples, peeled, cored and chopped into small
   pieces

125 ml/4 fl oz/½ cup water

1 tsp caster (superfine) sugar

White wine vinegar

A little sea salt

For the crisp onions

2 medium onions, halved and very finely sliced

A little flour (no more than a dessertspoon)

250 ml/8½ fl oz/1 cup sunflower oil (or enough to cover the bottom of
   your pan with 1 cm/½ in of oil)

Grate all the cheese and leave to one side.

Take a large non-stick saucepan and melt the butter, not allowing it to burn.
Add the flour to the pan and, using a whisk, thoroughly blend the two. After
the flour has foamed for about 20 seconds (do not let it brown), start adding
the wine bit by bit. At first it will clag up, but keep on dribbling in the wine
and whisking, and soon it will become a velvety emulsion. Introduce the
cheese to the sauce and whisk it in until melted, followed by the mustard and
cream. Season with salt and put to one side.

For the apple sauce, peel the apples, put the apples in a pan with the water,
sugar and a splash of white wine vinegar. Simmer, partially covered with a
lid, until the apples have completely collapsed. Blend or mash to a fine purée,
season with the salt and leave to one side.

While the apples are cooking, chop the onions and toss in the flour.

In a frying pan (skillet), heat the oil until it's hot enough to immediately
frizzle one of your onion slices on entry. Add half the onion slices, making
sure they are not piled up but spread evenly over the pan. Regulate the heat

if they start colouring too fast, and continually move them around the pan to ensure even cooking. Watch them intently. Remove to drain on paper towels when dark golden brown and crisp. Cook the remaining onions in the same way. Leave to cool then season well with salt.

Put water on to boil for the macaroni.

Put the cheese sauce over a low heat and slowly bring it to heat, not letting it catch. It should be a lovely consistency, only a fraction thicker than pouring double cream. Loosen with a little extra cream if needs be.

Return the apple sauce to a saucepan and heat gently over a low heat.

Put the macaroni into the boiling water with a big pinch of salt and cook following the packet instructions. *Al dente* is nothing to do with this dish. The macaroni wants to be cooked through, but not so that it's mushy.

While the pasta cooks, sauté the lardons in a small frying pan until nicely, but not too deeply, coloured.

Remove the cheese sauce from the heat and stir in the lardons and grated garlic. Drain the macaroni thoroughly, return to the pan, stir in the cheese sauce mixture and mix well. Turn the whole lot into an appropriate large serving bowl and scatter the crisp onions all over the top.

Serve it with the apple sauce to dollop on top.

Bacon and Lentils

One of my favourite dishes. It is however dependent on going to a butcher that stocks, or is able to pre-order, smoked streaky bacon that has not been sliced. A smoked pancetta would be a good replacement.

Serves 4

150 g/5½ oz/¾ cup Puy lentils

1 bay leaf

2 garlic cloves

600 g/1 lb 5 oz uncut smoked streaky bacon

2 medium 'long' shallots

4 medium carrots, peeled

½ tsp peppercorns

2 tbsp Dijon mustard (optional)

Red wine vinegar

2 tbsp capers, drained and rinsed

3 tbsp extra virgin olive oil

50 g/1¾ oz parsley, very finely chopped

Place the lentils, bay leaf and garlic in a saucepan. Cover with water and bring to the boil. Remove from the heat. Strain the lentils, return them to the saucepan and put to one side.

Place the bacon, shallots and carrots in a heavy casserole (that owns a lid and will snugly fit the bacon and vegetables) and cover with water to 2.5 cm/1 in above the meat. Drop in the peppercorns. Cook for 90 minutes, or until it is easy to slide a knife into the bacon, but it's not collapsing. Take off the heat. Remove the carrots and shallots and set aside. When they are cool enough, cut the carrots in to a medium dice and roughly chop the shallots. Reserve the cooking liquid.

Pour 400 ml/14 fl oz/1¾ cups of the cooking liquid over the lentils. Bring them to the boil, and cook until tender but not collapsed, about 20 minutes. Drain. While still warm, stir the chopped poached veg through the lentils, followed by the mustard, vinegar, capers and olive oil. Allow to cool to tepid before adding the parsley.

Slice the bacon. Spoon some lentils on to each plate and lay the sliced bacon on top. Normandy cider and wine are good accompaniments.

The Hut

From the minute we wake, noise, radio waves and branding come at us like a shower of arrows. The breakfast tabloids pour out tragedy and shame, shelled cities to shelled prawns in the rustle of a page turn.

I have pretty much stopped reading newspapers, instead preferring to zone out to the spitting of fried eggs, or wonder if tits and finches actually teleport rather than fly to the window. Zip zip.

Ten days in the city is about as much as I can bear in any one stretch.

Bad manners, never-ending emails, impatience, Samsung's walking dead and I've had enough. London, I love you, but I never pine for you in the way I do for those green places.

I'm bursting out of my skin. We are not meant to have to process all of this. I'm sure of it.

Nature is our default setting. I need resetting.

So, a sea trout-fishing weekend in deep Devon with my close friend Andy couldn't come quick enough.

Obligation-free weekends are as rare as corncrakes, and adventure will be found stumbling through black woods and tearing jeans on barbed wire.

I feel lucky that the very things I enjoy mean that I need to be in places such as these.

Headlights pointed to the gate, I tussle with the padlock in the drizzle and we creep the car down a mile of muddy track through forestry some might find scary.

The hut appears – a blacker square than the surrounding darkness. Climbing from the car, the River Lynher jostles, rushes and gurgles. The air is full of water, wet moss and owl hoots.

Candles lit, and giant moths immediately started to bump about their vast shadows, strobing across the chipboard walls in the low orange light. A noisy cockchafer joins us, bringing joy with its noise. I have not seen one for far too long. It's been a worry.

Sleeping bags are unrolled onto squeaky bunks, whisky nipped, sardine cans curled open and forked over oily chins. Tackle is hurriedly put up in the dark with the speed only those well versed in the art can feel their way through. Pockets are filled with worms.

We fished for sea trout from the inky dripping woods, flicking those writhing worms into the warm night drizzle towards the gurgling, popping water, or better still, the occasional slaps of restless peel[1].

Tired we trudged hut-wards at 4 am, guided by the little green lights from glow worms marking the edge of the bank.

Sleep came fast, uninterrupted by dreams.

Daytime. We spat toothpaste into the grass and ignored soap, a wash in the river, more for cleaning the soul and quickening the heart.

Black coffee was drunk from enamel cups, the one sea trout fried in a small, dented frying pan with lazy tongues of bacon lolling around it. Bread was buttered with a spoon, the fish and bacon eaten with fingers.

Sea trout, better chased at night, we lay in the sunny grass, smoking rollies, then took our tobacco to the pub, where cider-fuelled chats with irreverent strangers restored my faith in kindness and making do.

Another night on the river only explains that the fish have not yet arrived in any numbers, but there is no disappointment. Come the return trip home, the bag is only two small fish.

My jeans are two-tone, wet below the knee, my trainers squelchy and warm. My hair is thick with fire smoke and bacon fat.

I arrive back in London with mud under my nails, happy.

Mother nature is a wonderful mother if you remember her.

Summer Trout with Tea and Toast

Preferably, use a wild brown trout caught with a worm while camping ... but a fishmonger's specimen will do, as long as it's fresh.

---

[1] A West Country term for sea trout.

Serves 1

1 small fresh trout, cleaned

70 g/2½ oz/¾ stick butter

1 head of elderflower in full blossom plucked from a bush (not after rain
as it will have much reduced perfume, the pollen having been knocked
away by the raindrops)

Squeeze of lemon (optional)

Salt and freshly ground white pepper (black will do)

Dry the trout thoroughly with paper towels and season very generously with
salt and pepper on both sides.

In a frying pan (skillet), melt the butter over a medium heat and when
foaming place in the trout. Fry gently for about 4 minutes on each side taking
care *not* to burn the butter.

To check whether the fish is done, prod a knife into the thickest meat behind
the head. There should only be the faintest resistance where you imagine the
point touches the spine. The trout should look browned and crisped on both
sides. If the butter is nut brown by this stage – that's perfect.

Put the trout on a plate. Place the elderflower head in the butter and cook
until all popping sounds have stopped. Remove the elderflower head from
the pan and jiggle it over the pan to return any butter on the flower to the
pan. Discard.

Squeeze in but half a tablespoon of lemon juice, if using, then swirl and pour
the elder butter over the trout.

Eat with hot buttered toast and a cup of Yorkshire tea.

Tip Lobster is wonderful treated like this and drizzled with meadowsweet
butter.

Growing Up to Goat Bells

The sun is up above the Pyrenees.

Outside my children's home on top of the hill, in a village of six houses, I can see far across the valley of stony fields, strips of oak woodland and the dry river of rubble. The scale in front of me, looking out towards France, is wide and open. October, and it's still hot, the sky blue and cloudless. It's a clear, glorious day.

So still are my surroundings, the only thing that can be heard is the chirruping of a small flock of finches swooping from tree to tree. Nothing else. Not even a car.

José-Antonio and his friends have gathered in the yard. Standing together, they all clutch their caps in one fist and a ten-foot pole in the other. Five rotund septuagenarians in faded boiler suits, the sixth thin and tall. They are having a confab, muttering occasionally, lifting the hatted fists to their heads in thought. There is obviously no hurry on this chosen day for harvesting almonds, all will be done.

They have eaten a breakfast of bread and ham and polished off two bottles of red wine and some brandy.

They walk into the almond orchard, my children beckoned by them to follow. A tractor is reversed from the garage where it attaches to a huge hydraulic net on small wheels that opens like a garden laundry-drying carousel. In the middle there is a low fixed seat.

The tractor bumps and lurches into the field, the lifting gear jangling over the judder of the ancient engine. The finches flee far down into the valley. Reversing, the slit in the net is backed onto a tree trunk so that it surrounds the base of the tree.

The friends set to work, gently 'tappety, tap, tapping' their poles against the baize-skinned almonds.

Knocked from among their peach-like leaves, they fall to the net.

I close my eyes and standing still in this mountain air, the scent of pines and dry mountain herbs in the lightest breeze, the click of the sticks in the branches, occasional distant words among the men, and all my fears and worries gently float away. I feel free and light, for a while enjoying the softness of all that's around me. Nothing else matters, nothing else matters at all.

My daughter tugs my arm and points at the net operator sitting in the centre of the net.

'Look Daddy,' she says. 'They've caught an elf.'

I can't stop laughing. But my laughter then ushers in a great sadness that I do not live here with her in this Eden.

She joins her brother, and crouched beneath a tree, they are happily bashing the stray almonds they have collected, picking the kernels from the smithereens of shell. Silhouetted, they look like two happy little macaques. José-Antonio is encouraging them to eat as many as they can, occasionally hobbling over to give them one himself from his tanned arthritic claws. Every almond they receive is as much a delight as the previous.

Apart from lunch, we stay with the almond gathering, and when the day is done, they're are tipped out onto a huge tarpaulin in the yard. They make for a most beautiful mixture of colours – copper, brown, yellowing and still green. Shovelled into another rattling machine that has been wheeled out, it sorts them from the wrinkled leaves and sticks. Out the other side they spill, into 25-kilogram (55-pound) sacks propped up in rows against a warm wall next to the wigwam of poles that will do no more tapping until the following year.

Caps back in fists, the old men wipe their sweaty heads, puff and start to head back to José-Antonio's house for more wine and almonds, I imagine. My children are still relentlessly collecting up more of their own stash, bashing and nibbling them.

I speak in pathetic, overly gestural broken Spanish and English to José-Antonio.

'Where will this harvest go now'? I ask.

My ex-wife translates.

'I give them to friends and sell a few. I cannot sell them as I used to. No one wants them.'

'I do not understand,' and tell him, 'I've been eating almonds with my sherry nightly in Aínsa. The region is famous for them.'

'Those you eat are Chinese almonds,' he says and, rubbing imaginary cash between his thumb and forefinger, grimacing as the Spanish are so prone to do, he says, 'Cheap, they are cheap.'

'World's gone nuts,' I think to myself.

The children don't want tea. They are stuffed and tired and want to watch *Sponge Bob Square Pants* (my favourite as well).

As the sun dips, it's been a most perfect day. We collected the last tomatoes at lunch and shooed the chickens from their eggs. It's really, in fact, been one of the most peaceful days I can ever remember. I've had a play at the simple life I hope to find when my ambition has died.

Strange how history repeats itself. Tomorrow I must leave my kids, and a terrible, immediate dread sets in, that same anxious gloom I felt when I was returned to boarding school by my parents. Family (in a more conventional sense) seems beyond my reach.

But this is not how my life has played out and I must not let it show. I have snapped that bit of my heart off and must keep it tucked away elsewhere so that my children do not notice.

The plus side? Well, they're surrounded by nature and community. With forests to adventure in and rivers to swim in, they are already bilingual. I just hate the distance between us. The next morning I leave for London, social media and selfishness. With a bag full of clothes and almonds, I leave my children, once more, growing up to the sound of goat bells.

Mountain Beans Astrurias Style

This is delicious: a pig blanket of warmth that will give you gluey lips, and is so welcome when the Pyrenean cold is biting your fingers like wolf's teeth. Proper village food. The vegans will whimper. All I would say is that please, please buy good pork as Spanish pig farms break my heart.

Nothing I appear to have written above sounds tempting. I ASSURE YOU IT'S DELICIOUS! And whatever the nutritionists say, eaten after a hard day's labour, this will do you a world of good.

Serves a hungry 4, but really 6

2 tbsp olive oil

200 g/7 oz fatty pork belly, skin left on and cut into double-sugar-lump-sized chunks

2 large bay leaves

150 g/5½ oz good-quality cooking chorizo, sliced

75–100 g/2½–3½ oz unsliced smoked bacon or pancetta, sliced into sugar-lump-sized cubes

2 medium onions, finely diced

2 cloves, heads pinched

6 whole peppercorns

½ tsp dried oregano

4 garlic cloves, thinly sliced

1 tbsp tomato purée

2 tsp smoked sweet paprika

Pinch of saffron threads

500 ml/17 fl oz/2 cups medium (hard) cider

1.5 litres/2½ pints/6 cups water

1 red (bell) pepper, halved, deseeded and medium diced

400 g/14 oz/2¼ cups dried beans (cannellini, white flageolet, butter/lima or pinto) soaked in enough water to cover them by 5 cm/2 in overnight, then drained

1 large pig's trotter – ask the butcher to chop it in 2 so it fits in the pan (I had to walk back to the butcher as I only had a hacksaw for balsawood modelling and my girlfriend refused to let me use the garden bow saw)

2 tsp sea salt

2 tsp sherry vinegar

Pickled green chillies, to serve

In a large cast-iron or heavy casserole, heat the oil and fry the diced pork belly with the bay leaves until the meat is well browned.

Add the chorizo and bacon or pancetta and the onions, along with the cloves, peppercorns and oregano and cook until the onion is softened – 12 minutes or so.

Add the garlic with the tomato purée and cook until the tomato purée appears to catch. Add the smoked paprika and saffron. Pour in the cider and water, and add the chopped red pepper. Pour in the drained beans and stir all together.

Lower in the trotter. Bring to a simmer, then turn the heat right down and put the lid on. It must just simmer and no more. Remember the heat will rise once the lid is on. Simmer for 3 hours, stirring occasionally to prevent catching. Stir in the sherry vinegar with about 20 minutes to go.

Remove the lid. Reduce more rapidly until wet but with a loose, thickish and creamy consistency ... say like pea and ham soup.

Season with the salt and eat with the pickled chillies, cheap white crusty bread and good, affordable Spanish red.

The Edge of Reason

Knives are very personal things. I could bore you about each of the ones I own, but I'll just write the following instead.

Were you to see Alex Pole and Ed Hunt standing side by side on a battlefield, they would be best avoided. An obvious unit, one is immediately struck with a simple understanding that they have each other's backs. Alex is a thick-wristed Titan, and, were he to hold an axe in one hand and a shield in the other, most would simply turn and run. Those gingerly marching forward, weeing in their breeks and sobbing on to their breastplate, would be promptly battered into the ground. In the fray and clatter, Ed, wiry, wild haired and slight, would be the one you never saw coming, a few fleet steps, a glint and a grin, a knife through your armpit.

Absurdity and violence aside, I am lucky to say that I now stand beside them.

They are not such fearsome folk, but a rather charming blacksmith and knife maker. Alex describes himself as having the 'body of a mountain with the heart of a starling' while Ed is of gentle soul and mind, constantly searching for truth. Between them, brilliant engineers of wood, metal and leather, you would certainly pick them for 'the team' most likely to head a post-apocalyptic tribe.

There is little these two cannot turn their hands to, the work finished with immaculate care and a mentality that would rather see them start again, should things not go according to plan. With Ed's words in my mind as I write this, I can hear him say, 'You can always do better than that'll do.'

Endlessly searching for a better way, nonetheless, they are experts and, always wanting to know more myself, they are cider-drinking company I want to keep.

I met them at a festival in 2017. At that very same event, I soon found myself cooking field mushrooms and côte de boeuf at one end of the forge, while Alex heated metal at the other. Ed puffed on his crumpled rollie and winked as he sharpened blades. It seemed so obvious that the three of us, joined by the element of fire, should come together.

I now carry their blades, and work with Alex and Ed whenever possible. Sometimes at the forge, where my workbench doubles up as the kitchen table, which has a vice attached. My spoons hang with the hammers.

The deeply personal collection of knives I have received from them represent hours and hours of painstaking work. Knives, I like to think, that would fail in any hands other than my own. My own personal Excaliburs – if you can indeed have more than one.

To see a handle, uncut, a growing limb of apple tree, to watch a squidgy but obstinate square of hot metal pastry be beaten into beauty, its form eked out, is truly astonishing.

In a gesture of exchange, their knives in hand, I cut things from the hedges or dismantle beasts and cook for them. Respite from their hot, intricate work.

My question, though, is when is a knife not a knife?

Ed said, 'Hey, I know what you'll like, Val: what about this piece of wood? It's from a sixteenth-century oak strut taken from a bed at Cricket St Thomas.' A house I knew from growing up in Dorset. Wow. This was not just because of the location – but that a knife handle suddenly becomes more than simply a knife handle. What struck me was that some 500 years ago, characters in different night dress, with different fears, talking a significantly different English, slept on this knife handle, part of their place of rest. What frolics, giggles or nightmares were had upon such a piece of wood?

The potential to fuse histories from wood and metal into a knife is certainly far different from all the 'factory' knives I've ever held before. It seems to guide a deeper consideration in every stage of my own cooking. To hold such a thing is no less than to hold a cook's wand. My knife is part bed frame, part Landrover leaf spring.

More to the point: life's too short for bad kit.

Squid Braised in Pomona

A favourite of mine, squid must be cooked one of two ways,: fast or slow, that tenderness be achieved. Anything in between is a rubbery place. Here it is the latter. Take the time to make the good, punchy, condensed base before the final braise. Super-sweet and tasty, I have no idea why fishmongers scrape off the reddish-purple outer skin of the squid. It makes a deep-flavoured 'sea caramel' in the bottom of the pan, only intensifying the joy of a dish such as this.

Serves 2
2 medium–large squid, cleaned but with red outer skin left on and sliced
   in large squares, the legs divided into 2 pieces
A little sunflower oil
50 g/1¾ oz/½ stick butter
1 medium onion, finely diced

1 bay leaf

4 whole peppercorns

1 small sprig of fresh thyme

1 star anise

Tiny pinch of ground clove

1 strip of orange rind

½ tsp sweet smoked paprika

4 good, hard garlic cloves, grated

1 tbsp tomato purée

1 x 400-g/14-oz can whole plum tomatoes, drained of horrible juice

1 tsp sherry or cider vinegar

125 ml/4 fl oz/½ cup Somerset Pomona (from The Somerset Cider Brandy
  Company) or Madeira

1 tbsp very finely chopped fresh parsley

Get the frying pan (skillet) hot, hot.

Toss the squid in just enough sunflower oil to grease it. Fry the squid hard
until utterly browned with caramel-like deposits on the bottom of the pan.
Do in batches to prevent close proximity in the pan from making it watery.

Remove the squid to a plate and add the butter to the pan.

Once the butter is melted, add the onions, stirring them so that the squid
caramel from the bottom of the pan releases and is then stirred in. Add the
bay leaf, peppercorns, star anise, thyme, clove, orange rind and paprika, and
then cook gently until the onions are totally soft, 12 minutes or so.

Stir in the garlic and continue to cook until that too is soft. Add the tomato
purée and cook into the onions until it starts to catch. Add the tomatoes and
vinegar, then bash and stir them in. Cook until fairly thick.

Replace the squid in the pan and glug in the Pomona or Madeira. Top up
with water to cover the squid and bring to a gentle simmer. Cook for 70–90

minutes or until the squid is tender. Top up with water when needed during this braising time.

When happy with the tenderness of the squid, reduce the sauce to a consistency that is silky and creamy in thickness. Not thin and watery.

Adjust seasoning and add one final tiny splash of Pomona or Madeira.

Scatter with chopped parsley and serve in the pan alongside boiled, drained and heavily buttered pudding rice, pressed into bowls then upended out onto the plates.

Visitor

A hawker dragonfly has just crashed my kitchen. I'm not sure which type it is. Not the thin, blue, coatpin-sized, damsel dragonfly you usually see flitting over the pond; this battle helicopter is the length of a sparrow, its body a military green khaki and black. So powerful are its frustrated wing movements it has knocked over a tiny eau de vie glass on the draining board.

The frantic high-speed flapping is not exactly deafening but remarkably loud nonetheless, and there is a frustrated, ferocious urgency that fills the kitchen and makes me nervous. Its movements impinged by the window frame, its agitation is increasing every second.

I throw my apron over it, taking huge care to lightly clamp it without damaging it.

I flick the apron open in the garden and she climbs high over the rooftops, to hunt I imagine. I say 'she' because, from the picture I post, someone immediately replies to tell me that the fused markings at the end of the abdomen indicate it's a female Southern Hawker.

Imagining myself shrunken and tiny, I would hate to be hunted by such a thing, this less fantastical encounter has seen me mesmerized. By design, colour, intent, 'ugliness' or 'beauty', it's infinitely more interesting than anything I've written this morning. Am I working on the right things?

Sámi

I'm with journalist William Sitwell, and Ollie and Suzi, wildlife artists. It's -30°C/-22°F outside. All on sleds, we are sliding through whiteness but for the black sticks and scabs of the birch trees.

Our little dogs are straining in eagerness to pull us ever forward. All about is a blanket of quiet but for my cold, sharp breathing, the 'schhhhhh' of the sled, scampering feet and the occasional bark.

The dogs pooing as they run, I'm hit with little warm pockets of pong. Out they come, nasty smell, smush and gone.

That morning William has made me laugh so hard about the poops, I've fallen off my sled and been dragged along until I manage to rest myself on the brake mat. By the time we arrive at the cabin, the sun has broken out, and is so bright that, without goggles, I cannot look either into the blue sky or at the polished silver snow. Squinting, I put my goggles back on.

We unpack and are soon gathered again outside.

A small group of Sámi reindeer herders has arrived. All wear soft leather mitts, embroidered rimless hats that cover the ears, and spotted seal-skin boots. Two knives dangle from beneath branded outdoor gear.

They have with them a young reindeer on a red rope, held near the muzzle. I have a strong sense these are its last moments. Head drooped, I think it does too.

'It's most unusual for them to kill such a young animal,' I'm told by our guide. 'They are doing this for your visit.'

I understand a weightier animal, grown on, would mean more pelt, more horn, more meat for them. But it's not important. I'm sure the animal has been paid for.

An elderly woman appears carrying a bucket and branch end of silver birch. Two men gather around the reindeer, the animal not so much restrained as securely comforted. There is a tenderness. Mitts are removed and a small knife is drawn. Very pointed with a bone handle. A Sámi knife, I'm sure, is squeamishly sharp. Swiftly, it's placed at the back of the reindeer's head and pushed in with quick, forceful and precise intention. There is a brief gristly crunch. Supported gently, the reindeer collapses instantly. Its throat is cut and much of the blood collected into the bucket. I'm given the birch branch and told to stir continuously to stop the blood coagulating and freezing.

The crimson splash in the snow under the sun. The steam from the bucket. I will never forget it.

Working fast, as you must in -30 with no gloves, the animal is gutted, the legs broken and cut at the knee. The calf is hauled away for skinning. Snow tumbles down through the branches of a nearby tree and I look up. Two ravens have landed in a nearby spruce.

'Gaaark,' says one.

So the great cook-up begins. In the kitchen, I'm gestured at and prodded to add flour to the blood. The mixture is thick, shiny red gloop. I'm astonished that the meat has already been portioned and is being dropped into a great vat of almost boiling, wobbling water. Most is being poached on the bone, while some of the larger bones have been kept whole and set aside for later.

Plopping great dobs of blood dumpling mix into the stock pot with two spoons, I watch them sink and settle on the meat and turn dark grey. There is a delicious smell from some golden onions, chopped straight through in rings, browning in a lot of butter.

The days are short and soon its black outside.

They do not cook the meat as long as I expect, and soon we are sitting at dinner. The meat is dished onto enamel plates. A great pile of sweet onions flopped on top. The dumplings are offered around; they are a dense, bloody fudge, yet enjoyable for their simplicity. The meat is delicious, with a slight taste of moss, and surprisingly tender.

There is a crack as a claw hammer is brought down to the whole bones. The pink raw marrow is removed, chopped and thrown onto salty potatoes to slide between them and melt like butter. The bowl is pushed into the centre of the table. It's a feast. I'm handed a plastic mug. The broth, just salt, meat and water, has been armed with invigorating amounts of vodka. Relatively unchatty, we are all so happy, no effort for conversation is really needed.

I pull a long reindeer hair from my mouth. One man points at it with his knife and says, 'Vegetables.'

We eat the whole animal and are soon slumped against the walls, sitting on the benches, legs outstretched. Drunk on reindeer and vodka tea, I haul on my gear and go outside. It's my birthday.

Under a canopy of stars I would only feel clumsy in attempting to explain – it's spectacular! – I wonder where I feel I am in my life. And as I do, a great star drops across the sky. Not fast, but slow and fizzing.

I return inside where Olly and Suzi give me a folded piece of A2 paper with 'Happy Birthday' written on it. I unfold it to find a drawing in purple and orange pencil of a polar bear. I am looking at it while I write this.

Yukon Gold

There is a STOP sign on a junction outside Dawson City. City maybe once, this is two cabins bigger than a town. Underneath STOP, someone has sprayed in black dribbled paint 'THE DRIPPING'.

STOP THE DRIPPING, it reads.

Christ, I think, what is it exactly that's dripping? Is this what happens to men's minds in the ravaged outlands?

First impression of Dawson is one of dilapidation, but with the questionable charm of a spaghetti Western set. This place feels forgotten. The gigantic mole hills of earth and rubble piled for miles outside town are a testament to its long-gone boom town days.

There is a chewable air of hardship, desperation and disappointment, to be spat out like a brown squirt of tobacco. I can only guess that any of those who escaped with their life and a bucket of golden nuggets bought faraway farms in green, rolling hills, and the few who prospered and stayed ended up no better off.

The dirt roads through town are potholed and splashy as rust-eaten SUVs plough through them. One truck that passes looks so rotted away it appears little more than a pile of autumn leaves with glass and wheels, growling and farting blue smoke.

Me and the crew are tired, and head straight for a diner. We eat pancakes and bacon with coffee. I go outside for a cigarette and, while looking at my phone, hear the stamp and jingle of spurs. I turn to see a wild-looking man in a battered waxed long coat, smashed-in hat and cowboy boots. His face is smudgy with dirt. He is tanned, with a close beard and an earring. I wonder if he has a sawn-off shotgun under his coat

'My name is Charlie Brown and I fuck dogs,' are his first words. I'm so flat tired this doesn't have the desired effect, if there was indeed meant to be one.

'Good for you,' I reply. 'Plenty of action,' I continue, nodding toward some scrawny mongrel that trots past with its lipstick pizzle sticking out.

'You're not from here,' he says.

'No,' I reply, 'which is why I'm hoping you could tell me if that's the sun or the moon up there.'

He laughs hard and then coughs (I couldn't make this up if I tried) and asks if I might be around for a drink in Diamond Tooth Gertie's later on.

'Perhaps,' I reply, while thinking to myself that, although an establishment with such a name needs to be investigated, would I get gunned off the mezzanine or exit through the window in a burst of glass? Mind you, perfect chaperone I think, continuing to weigh up the odds.

'Suit yerself,' he says, 'ask for Charlie Brown,' with a wave over his shoulder as he disappears.

I head for the Ravens Nook outfitters and buy a pair of Redwing boots that in London would cost four times the price. The attendant sees I'm proud of them and says, 'Steel toecaps, you could kick a bear with those.'

'Is it likely?' I inquire, getting the impression chances are high.

It's difficult to leave such a shop, the kind of shop that only Canada and the US can boast. Coats, caps, boots, plaid shirts, with likely a candy-coloured display of fishing lures and other outdoor essentials. Thick socks and a musky[2] spoon[3], my kinda place.

It's bitterly cold and grey outside, and my fingers feel like they would smash like china. I buy some mittens at the counter.

Back on the street I see 'WE BUY GOLD' or 'GOLD FOR SALE' signs in many shops. I'm surprised to see a few considerable lumps on display, but most of the gold is tiny and pebble sized, dust in plastic bags, or otherwise locked away. I'm not interested in buying any as I can't help associating it with the cuts and gashes made by the brutal excavation of the surrounding territory. Gold fever.

Despite the oppressive foggy weather, I decide I'm enjoying Dawson in a gloomy sort of way, while also cheered to find James, our sound man, wandering about. He shows me the barber's shop called Hair Cabaret, and I dare him to get his hair cut and to ask for the local special. 'Only if you give me all your per diems,' he says.

Why am I here though? To become a member of the Dawson City Sour Toe Club.

This club grew out of frostbite, amputation (by axe) to prevent gangrene and some continued bravado that became tradition, a cult.

So a cook walks into a bar (this is not a joke) called the Sourdough Saloon. Inside the dim environs, two guys are playing pool. Despite my inclination to start up conversation, I decide quickly that it would be wise to avoid them. They look like they could take anything the wrong way. Bearded mercury switches. They are shouting, falling over and laughing. They have savage eyes and are the worse for whiskey, beer and I suspect whatever they've smoked off silver foil in exchange for gold. They look fucking dangerous.

---

[2] Muskelunge, a species of pike that grow to a huge size and can be found in the lakes of North America and Canada.

[3] A type of fishing lure.

The music plays, the outbursts continue, the pool balls click and we are seated. A hunched and exhausted-looking Chinese man appears in an oversized pea coat and white skipper's hat, the type with the blue peak. He is the Master of Rites for the Sour Toe Challenge. He looks tired of it all and rattles through the pledge, mumbling it quickly, like it's an inconvenience.

I recall the bit: 'You can drink it fast. You can drink it slow.

But your lips must touch that horrible, hideous, gnarly toe.'

And so the toe is bought in on a small mountain of rock salt (presumably for hygiene and preservation purposes). At first, it looks like a well-chewed cigar stump. Closer inspection reveals the yellowing big toenail, the splintered bone two inches away at the other end of this grotesque, medjool-date-sized digit. It's hideous! Hell's buffalo wing!

'By the way, do not swallow the toe! You will be fined!'

'Why would I want to do that?' I ask.

'Last week some joker swallowed it. Became a YouToob sensation. It's the last toe we have. Don't swallow it.'

'Where do you get 'em all??'

'From all over.'

I don't want to know any more. Has this been posted by a bent surgeon? Hacked off by disturbed and sympathetic super-fans? Dug up by French grave diggers?

I'm so tired, so desperately unimpressed and travel-weary. The minute the toe is plopped in the glass and the whiskey glugged on top (or maybe the other way around, who cares?), I swipe it from the table, tilt my head and upend the glass. The whisky shoots down. Do I detect savoury? There is however no bump on the lips from the toe. Keeping the glass upturned above my head I squint into it, only to see the toe lodged across its base.

'It must touch the lips!' comes a hoot from an expectant crowd that's suddenly gathered from nowhere.

'Yeah, alright, don't get all hairiated,' I grumble. Two good taps with my left hand and it falls to rest on my lips. Lowering my head and the glass, it falls back in.

A Dutchman with a rat's tail and crimped hair (God only knows) whoops and makes a fist.

I receive a piece of yellow paper, and am incredulous to learn I'm somewhere around the fifty thousandth and three hundredth member of the club. Are there really 49,000 or so folk living in Dawson?

It turns out that the Sour Toe Club is very popular ... international, and now has well over 100,000 members. I learn why. A young man bounces up and thumps me on the back with an over-the-top declaration of camaraderie.

'Isn't this great?' he says.

'Are you asking me or telling me?' I wonder, before asking, 'Where are you from anyway?'

'We've driven up from Miami to do this.'

'Couldn't you have spent the money on a nice holiday in the Caribbean?' I ask, baffled.

'You English!' he laughs, with the shake of his head.

'Personally I'd rather eat a pig's vagina taco,' I reply (see page oo).

Yukon Silver

I'm in the middle of a small wood on a little island in the middle of the 'great, grey-green, greasy'[4] Yukon River. I am with Sam, a fisherman, his wife and the film crew. Sam is First Nations. Short, strong, beady-eyed, wearing a bashed-in peaked cap and puffer coat. He's an odd mix of sulky and cordial. It's confusing. Since meeting him at 6 am, he's also been doing his terrible impersonation of a cockney accent and then chortling heartily to himself.

'Oi mate!' he says, 'Put the kettle on and let's have a cuppa char, shall we?' A perfect impersonation of Dick Van Dyke mixed with Boer Afrikaans. It's

---

[4] Taken directly from one of my favourite Kipling descriptions ever – he was referring, of course, to the Limpopo River.

getting irritating, wearing in fact, but with his constantly changing mood, I think it best to pretend it's funny. I need him.

There are no rabbits in the snares. Having checked our empty traps, we walk back to the hut. Sam stops and reaches up on his tip toes and pulls a squidgy amber blob of resin from the crack in the bark of a tall spruce. He rolls it between his fingers and passes it to me with a twinkle in his eye. He tells me that it was and still is important sustenance for his people, 'the first chewing gum' from which he believes the international chew grew.

Eagerly I pinch it from his finger tips and give it a thorough and committed chomping. Too hasty. This resinous glue is too much. It's bitter, overwhelmingly piney to the point I feel I've chewed on the bow resin of a whole string section. 'Gah, euch, ptt, ptt!' I spit and spit, my hand in my mouth trying to pick out this sticky, tacky mastic that's broken into tiny threads and is attached to each and every tooth.

Sam is leaning against a tree with one arm and slapping his leg with the other, he's howling and crying with laughter. 'Ancient chewing gum, ancient chewing gum, ha ha ha ha ha, ancient chewing gum, yeah right!' He can hardly get the words out.

I'm wiping my mouth on my arm of my jacket. Euch!

'Oi mate, shall we put the kettle on and brew uppa cuppa.' Hysterics again. Grrrrrr.

We come out of the woods and head to the boat to 'look see' what's in the fish wheel.

Two miles downriver and it's one of the most ingenious contraptions I have seen in my life. Belonging to his family, he recalls working on it with his father as a boy 'when the river was thick with fish'.

'It needs repairing every year,' he sighs, and it doesn't surprise me that the elements here take their toll.

The idea couldn't be simpler. Built into a platform of gangplanks with a mooring, it resembles a small mill wheel, one built by Robinson Crusoe. Maybe ten feet in diameter, it is primarily constructed of timber, but where the paddles would be there are instead taut orange twine nets stretched across frames. These nets are strung at an angle towards a slipway that falls to a holding box. Appearing some what flimsy, the structure is in fact very sound.

The fish wheel is positioned and anchored just off the bank across a run where the salmon are relied on to pass yearly. Operated by the flow of the current, the wheel turns almost silently but for a faint 'wheeze, creak, splosh', 'wheeze, creak, splosh'. The salmon, as they swim through, are scooped into the rotating nets and lifted up. Sliding across the angled netting, they then tip down the chute into the holding box.

I peer in and it's heaving with bewildered salmon, all swaying from side to side as they tread water, but for an occasional frustrated thrashing.

We net them from the box. The females are thrown back into this wide, silty river, the males clocked on the head and laid in a polystyrene box, their stripy silver, maroon and black sides twitching and shivering in the spasm of death. Their camouflage is immaculate for the seaweeds they have left far behind. I can smell the slime on the fish and the river, autumn damp and forest. It's wonderful.

The arrival of the salmon in the autumn, the turning of the wheel, the clockwork of it all is remarkable, simple, effective and so very distant from the big boats and winches I associate with the fishing industry back home.

Sam is shaking his head and looking agitated. 'We have to go,' he says looking to the sky. 'We have to go right now.'

A mass of purple and flint-blue cloud, gathered a mile or so down river, is now approaching at speed, as if flying out like a cape from behind the neck of some invisible, giant, native god, running over the water to catch us up.

The whole sultry silence of the river, the now brooding sky, and it's the second time that day I've wondered if we would have been wise to do a smudging ritual that other guides have insisted on during this trip.

Motor running at full throttle, we pelt back but this time on the opposite side of the river. Dead whale? Dropped piano? Exploded saloon? We whizz past what is in fact the wreckage of an old paddle steamer, its smashed carcass strangely resting among the trees of another small island. This land is beautiful, but no place for the faint-hearted. Racing the storm, hats pulled tight on our heads, we are all looking forward in thoughtful silence.

I cannot help thinking of this once abundant land before the trappers, prospectors and settlers turned up. Perhaps Sam's moods are intertwined with my questions about the history of this river system and his people.

For all the wealth of the land that was snatched away from Sam's ancestors, these times are not long gone, and I've seen enough on this trip to witness an inspiring, proud people left with remnants of a culture and little means to sew it back together. I feel an inherited grudge still lies raw and just below the surface.

The river is dying, the salmon are fewer and the piles of earth, the scars of gold fever are now, willy-nilly, left all over.

We cannot outrun the startling pace of the storm, and beach the boat just as a deluge collapses upon us. I have seen few such memorable downpours in my life, the glass rods of rain so solid they obscure my vision of the hut, beach and company.

And then the sun comes out and everything glows in a bright yellow light, a shimmering world of golden droplets. The river is now covered in the last of the autumn leaves that the squall has shaken from the trees.

Sam's wife heads to the hut.

Having peeled of my wet clothes and changed, I am warm again and now cooking a pre-secured TV production stunt rabbit while Sam's wife fries up some greasy bannock. We eat in a row, on a log, from enamel cups, rabbit legs sticking out, a great doughnut of ungainly bannock plonked on top. It's delicious.

Sam finishes cleaning his fish. We load up and head back as the sky charges up with thunder. No one talks on the way home. The river is wide, wide, wide and the forests look lonely and fearsome and I miss my children with an ache I cannot describe.

Two Good Folk

I've become very fond of a man called Peter Hannan. A tall, gregarious and extremely funny butcher, warm in a way I find so particular to the Northern

Irish, he also has the most enviable manners. His operation is demanding but never, I imagine, to the loss of elegance. He is one of life's 'goodies', his generosity and humility simply that.

Astonishing beef aside, if I can be so dismissive of such triumph, what I particularly like about Peter is his turn of phrase. I attempt never to have tea to my lips when I ring him, as his first comment will inevitably be something like, 'Well hello, Val. Now what will you be sending down mi poipe this morning?' The effect is always the same. I start laughing.

One snowy day, after working in his test kitchen above the butchery, we took a break and huddled in the yard, puffing away and discussing life. Explaining someone he knew to me, someone he obviously cared for, he went on to say that, 'Da man was like pepper on a goose.'

'What does pepper on a goose mean?' I asked.

'Fockin chaotic!' came the reply. I burst out in hysterics and the tea came out. *****.

Is having your hands in the soil every day what makes someone so grounded and gentle? I imagine it might be, as Mark Diacono is one such person. While calm is a word I'd use for him, there's a rebel monkey that swings through the orchard of his mind, its speedy approach often given away by a glint and a smirk.

Picking herbs at a festival one day, wearing our aprons, seated upon two slightly in-turned chairs, our knees touching, we looked somewhat like two Mediterranean widows plucking chickens in the yard. Pulling at the tarragon, he suddenly turned to me and said, 'Trifle ... it should only ever be eaten in boxer shorts, bathed in the light of an open fridge door.'

I love the company I keep.

Short Ribs of Beef with Tomatoes, Basil and Anchovies (and pasta re-incarnation with leftovers)

I like the idea of a long cook that allows concentration on other things while the cooking is done. I like the idea that, during this cooking time, my energy will be expended in other ways to be then replenished by the steaming pot that has served its time. But it never quite turns out like this.

Cooking times are guidelines that only a fool would implicitly trust. And so, too, temperature, one woman's oven is another man's incinerator. So regular checking is needed to avoid dismay at finding a burnt bottom.

What's more, I am a cook so it is my currency to check and to fidget, as I was born to stand and move.

I like to understand metamorphosis, from raw to finished, and the subsequent knowledge of how long the wait for gratification. But nerves demand a taste, so the action to taste is really no different from another Marlboro Light.

Born a fidget (handy as a cook), I subsequently visit the contents of the pot during their metamorphosis. Slightly defeating both full concentration on that other thing. No, the long slow cook for me is constant visitation.

Serves 4
50 ml/1⅔ fl oz/2¾ tbsp olive oil
½ head of garlic, separated into cloves and peeled
1 large onion, very finely diced
1 can anchovies in oil (preferably Ortiz)
1 tsp fennel seeds
1 tsp dried thyme
140 g/5 oz tomato purée
2 x 40-g/14-oz cans whole plum tomatoes, juice rinsed off
4 short ribs of beef
1 bottle good Montepulciano red
25 g/1 oz fresh basil leaves with stalks, roughly chopped
A lot of patience

For the gremolata
4 tbsp finely chopped fresh parsley
Finely grated zest from 1 small unwaxed lemon
2 garlic cloves, very finely chopped

Pour the olive oil into a heavy-bottomed pan and bring to a medium heat. Lightly colour the garlic, flat side down, until golden, then stir in the onion, anchovies and fennel seeds and thyme. Stir all together until the anchovies have collapsed and then flop in the tomato purée, stir constantly until beginning to colour. Plop in the tomatoes. Lower in the meat with a thought for the animal.

Glug in the wine, add enough water so that the meat is covered. Twist the basil in half and drop in, give it a stir and bring to a simmer. Turn the heat down so that the liquid just trembles and put the lid on. Cook for 5 hours, topping up with water if necessary so that the meat is always covered, and stirring the bottom of the pan to check nothing is catching.

Towards the end of cooking, get the gremolata ready – mix the three ingredients together in a bowl.

When the meat is tender and only just clinging to the bone, remove the lid and rapidly reduce the liquid at a fast boil. Cook to the same consistency as of passata, adjust the seasoning accordingly. Serve the ribs in a large serving bowl with the sauce with a healthy passing over of gremolata and extra virgin olive oil. Eat alongside wet polenta, potatoes roasted in olive oil with rosemary and garlic or toasted sourdough bread rubbed with garlic.

Tip For leftovers, strip any remaining meat from the bones, mix with the remainder of the sauce and toss through some cooked penne pasta. Sleet with Parmesan and any remaining gremolata.

Burrata with Roasted Endive and Salmoriglio

Serves 4
1 large *Treviso* (red endive) or endive, root end intact, divided lengthways

into 8

70 ml/2 fl oz/¼ cup melted butter

Good splash of balsamic vinegar

2 tsp caster (superfine) sugar

4 tbsp fresh oregano leaves, very, very finely chopped

90 ml/3 fl oz/⅓ cup extra virgin olive oil

Pinch of dried chilli

Juice of half a large lemon

2 burrata

2 tbsp pine nuts, toasted

Sea salt and freshly ground black pepper

Preheat the oven to 170°C fan/190°C/375°F/gas mark 5.

Line a baking tray with greaseproof paper. Lay out two rows of the endive segments, each slightly splayed out. Paint with half the melted butter and then vigorously splash about with the vinegar. Sprinkle enthusiastically with salt and less so with 1 teaspoon of the sugar.

Roast until the white of the endive is turning golden and the leaf a golden crispy brown. Turn the endive segments over and paint with the remaining melted butter, splash with vinegar and season with salt and the remaining teaspoon of sugar.

Return to the oven to roast while keeping a close eye on it. When done, the leaf part should look dark, almost appearing burnt. It should be very crispy and the stalk a lovely golden colour.

Meanwhile, make the salmoriglio. Mix the oregano with the oil, and chilli. Only add the lemon juice at this stage if the salad is immediately going to the table as it will discolour the oregano if made too far ahead of time. If serving later, add the lemon juice at the last minute.

To serve, put half a burrata in the centre of each plate. Take 4 warm lengths of endive and drape them over and around the burrata. Spoon the salmoriglio here and there. Scatter with the toasted pine nuts and go over with pepper.

Lamb Chops with Black Pudding and Butter Beans

Serves 2–3

Olive oil, for rubbing

6 lamb chops, seasoned with dried oregano, salt and pepper

6 deep slices of juicy, 'wetter' style of black pudding or boudin noir (consider Macsween or Trealy Farm)

For the chimichurri sauce

6 finger-length long Dutch red chillies, stalks and seeds removed, then minutely chopped

6 large garlic cloves, minutely chopped

¼ tsp smoked paprika

¼ tsp cumin seeds, toasted and pounded

1 tbsp dried rosemary

2 tbsp dried oregano

3 tbsp red wine vinegar

4 tbsp olive oil

50 ml/1⅔ fl oz/2¾ tbsp warm water

1 tbsp tomato purée, cooked in a dry pan and stirred continuously until beginning to catch and colour

1½ tsp sea salt

1 tsp black pepper

15 g/½ oz fresh parsley, finely chopped

10 g/¼ oz fresh coriander (cilantro), finely chopped

Patience (it will need to sit for a good hour before serving)

For the beans

2 medium onions

30 g/1 oz/2 tbsp butter

2 tbsp olive oil

2 x 400-g/14-oz cans butter beans (lima beans), undrained

50 ml/1⅔ fl oz/2¾ tbsp whole milk or, better still, single (light) cream

50 g/1¾ oz/½ cup blue cheese, such as gorgonzola

Sea salt and freshly ground black pepper

Prepare all the ingredients for the chimichurri sauce (as instructed ... you brutes... minute is the key... not garlic pieces the size of rabbit's teeth), adding them to a bowl as you go. Stir together and leave to sit for at least an hour. It will happily keep in the fridge for a week and is as good on fish such as barbecued halibut and turbot as it is on red meats.

For the beans, sweat the onions in the butter and olive oil and cook them until completely tender, stirring often, 12–15 minutes or so. They should not brown, so cook over a sensible heat. Add the beans and their juice and let them simmer with the onions for 5 minutes or so. Add the milk or cream and bring back to a simmer before adding the cheese. The consistency should be creamy. Season with salt and pepper to taste and put to one side.

Generously oil the chops with olive oil.

Get a large frying pan (skillet) nice and hot before cooking the meat. (Alternatively, and better still, the meat could be cooked over charcoal.) It should be hot enough that the chops sizzle on entry. Fry the chops over a medium heat on both sides until nice and crispy brown on the outside and pink within.

Remove the chops to a board and let them rest while you set about cooking the black pudding. If using slices, fry in a little butter over low heat. If using boudin noir, you may wish to warm the links through in the oven.

Rewarm the beans if needs be. Spoon the beans onto plates and rest the chops and black pudding on top. Throw the chimichurri about as wished.

Seeds of Change

2018 saw a summer of radical weather, with early rainstorms that could hammer metal and sun that would see you crawl under its ferocity. Our foxgloves were smashed and now the grass was tan brown.

We evacuated our seed trays to shelter in the kitchen and bathroom.

Brushing my teeth one morning, my dressing gown undone, flip-flops on and a silver chain around my neck, I burst out laughing into the mirror. I look like an East End gangster residing in the Algarve. I've since given up the chain.

But then I notice the tray of seedlings on the window ledge, and I am suddenly moved beyond belief. I'm staggered. The world fades away but for these infant shoots five inches from my nose.

The seeds I poked into the tray but three days ago have sprouted, their tiny green points protruding, delicate and determined. I feel instantly connected to them in a way I have never before noticed. I want them to do well with the very same tenderness I have for my children.

Excuse the pun, but I'm rooting for them.

A seed, a miniscule dry parcel, a dot that, when poked in a hole and watered, erupts into food, wood, materials, medicine, life, with so little required. Why has this magic never struck me before? How lucky I am to be so graced with such a simple action and exchange! We've got it good.

I suddenly understand the obsession of gardeners and why it's become my girlfriend's new passion. I want to take a week off with a magnifying glass and squint intently in the hope of witnessing visible growth.

One week later, and I'm talking on a panel for The Goldsmith Foundation about Teddy Goldsmith's book *The Way*. I'm telling the audience about my simple revelation in the bathroom, and all of a sudden there is a lump in my throat, my voice cracks, I'm welling up. I really have to prevent myself from crying. I feel angry with the world, I feel stupid and frustrated. I see nothing but our destruction.

I pull myself together, no one has noticed, maybe other than to put it down to passion.

Am I moved to tears solely by those shoots in the seed tray, or by our disregard for the natural wealth around us? Could it be, having also told the audience of my children growing up in the Pyrenees, that I grieve that I cannot nurture my own two Warner seedlings as much as I'd like? I can't tell, but feel that perhaps nature, young life, nurture and my frustration are likely all intertwined.

I leave the tent once finished, and head for the sea with a towel. I squelch towards the water, the silt between my toes, the samphire and arrow grass trembling in the strong coastal breeze. When the water's deep enough I launch towards the Isle of Wight. In the sea I feel instantly better.

Spinnakers out, a hundred coloured sails are on the water and the island looks beautiful in the sun. I have to go back to London after my swim but I don't want to leave. I sit on a memorial bench surrounded by flapping plastic bags caught in the tangle of brambles, and look out to sea.

Big changes are afoot and I must pay attention.

Cantaloupe Melon and Yuzu Granita

Serves 10–12
3 large cantaloupe melons, peeled, deseeded and cut into chunks
70 ml/2 fl oz/¼ cup yuzu juice
Sugar, to taste

Blitz the melon in a food processor and then push it through a very fine sieve (strainer) into a bowl.

Add 200 ml/7 fl oz/scant 1 cup of water to the bowl. Mix in the yuzu juice and add sugar, to taste. Aim to slightly oversweeten with the sugar, as the freezing process will affect how sweet the granita tastes.

Pour into a freezerproof container and affix a lid or cover with foil. Pop in the freezer.

Check the mix after 2 hours, and distress it thoroughly with a fork. Continue to do this every hour until you have the equivalent of a snowy texture.

Serve on a hot day.

The Mulberry Tree

There is a large mulberry tree in my local park. Like most mulberry trees I've encountered, over time, it has fallen. Unlike others, though, this one has no support from crutch posts. It reclines completely in the grass, as relaxed as a nude on a picnic.

It is festooned with fruit, kilos and kilos of it, and I visit every day to nibble the few that have ripened, the main crop to be ready in a couple of weeks. As its name implies, the fruit of the black mulberry is better left to ripen to its deep, deep red appearance before picking.

Because they are stubborn to pull yet delicate in body, the berries spurt blood easily. To come out from under a mulberry tree is to look like a vampire exiting an alleyway. I dress tactically for the mulberry, in a tattered Eat British Trout T-shirt, disliked oversized shorts that fall down (in Sainsbury's) if an iPhone is placed in pocket, Birkenstock troll sandals that I couldn't care less about if dripped on.

While picking, as people pass, should they show any interest, I am delighted to introduce them to my absolute favourite fruit. That is part of my job, after all. Soon though, what is ripe has gone, and I'm happy in the knowledge a huge stealth harvest is imminent. But I should probably stop telling people what it is.

Happy, that is, until checking the tree one day with my daughter, we bump into a small bald Indian man squeezing the fruit on the branch while chewing some, his cheeks stuffed like a hamster's.

'Mmmmm,' he mumbles, mouth full, 'Do you know what this tree is?'

'Yes, I do,' I reply somewhat stiffly. He's picking fruit I'd still be inclined to let ripen.

'We have many in India,' he says.

This man is a serious threat to my mulberrying, becoming even more so when, with the stroke of a hand down his T-shirt, he informs me that he too dresses for the job.

'Messy business,' he says.

More absurd than my outfit, but not because of the trashed green flash or stripy T-shirt, is his sky-blue pair of shorts. Shorts of such shorty, shortness and tightness that they more resemble budgie smugglers.

'They are ready,' he opines.

I want to suggest that they are far from ready, but don't.

'Why is he picking them from your tree, Daddy?' asks my daughter. I like this. He's called away by his family and so moves off. 'Cheerio,' he waves over his shoulder. And I am left with a choice. Pick now, add sugar and make ice cream. Or wait.

I'll take a chance. I'll wait a week and leave them until I get back from Port Eliot Festival. I take my daughter for a glass of pop. One week later, back from Cornwall, I race to the tree with my basket. It is stripped bare.

I see my opponent a week later and he smiles warmly as I pass. 'The brute!' I think to myself. Next year, I'll be ready for him.

Vanilla Pomegranate Ripple Ice Cream

A cheat. But a delicious one.

Serves 4–6

Buy a tub or two of good-quality vanilla ice cream. And a bottle of pomegranate molasses. You may even have one lurking in the cupboard.

Remove the ice cream from the freezer and allow it to soften a little.

Spread a third of the ice cream in an uneven layer over the bottom of a freezerproof container and then blob about generously with the pomegranate molasses to mimic what you'd expect from a good raspberry ripple ice cream.

Repeat until all the tub is all used up.

Stir a little but not so that it all turns pink. Put a lid on the container and place in the freezer to firm up again.

Tip Simpler version – scoop ice cream into a bowl, then blob pomegranate molasses on top. Either way, you can't stop going back.

Brave New Weird

I worry for the world, where soon the sky will be so filled with drones that the swallows will not dare return.

When I was a boy, I thrilled to the comic *2000AD*. It scared me too, as I lay on the floor of my room, turning the pages, wide-eyed at its crowded view of the future. Mega-City One. And now I fear its dystopic vision is in fact not as far away a reality as I perhaps then thought.

Like clouds of midges, the drones will sometime come, silhouettes of whirring fuzz bearing takeaway bags in all directions through the dusk, to arrive through the crack in the curtains just as you step naked from the bath.

But not to worry: at least your buffalo quinoa wings with avocado spirulina dip will hang straight and still beneath a blur of propellers, carrying your dinner with such economical movement and airborne grace the sauce will barely ripple.

The complete opposite will it be to the moped hordes who, with a screech of rubber, nightly ride out from restaurants nationwide, like bats swarming from a twilight cave. Arriving at the door, they hand you a bag, the equivalent to one bearing a severed head, dripping bloody sauce on your shoes.

Why do I care? Why do I write this? Because I care about food. It is my currency, and I cannot stand to witness delivery scooters making 45 mph airborne leaps off road humps and taking 45-degree corners, for I know the cooks' endeavours they carry will be smeared about and battered in the inside of the bag. And because I think that if you can't cook, you ain't a grown up.

Distillery Ceps ... and the Martini

I am about to plug my gin. Our gin, for there are five of us behind it, made in the wilds of Northumberland, distilled in the cold breath from the mountain, Hepple. It has become something of a tradition for me to visit the distillery some time between September and October, excited by the knowledge that, for a few hours, I will ignore all things work and botanical and go in search of boletus mushrooms, namely ceps and bay boletes.

Every year, however, the same dismay unfolds. For a stone's throw from the kitchen, in the long grass under the rope swing, lies a plentiful gift of ceps that have already come on and been ignored by my beloved friend and distillery partner, Walter, the owner of this mushroom-buttoned fiefdom.

'Why didn't you pick them?' I ask, exasperated, when I find these once prime specimens now turned to maggoty sponges or mouse-distressed fragments.

'Well, I'm still not sure if they're the right ones,' he replies. (Dear reader, never pick and cook a wild mushroom if you're not sure it's the right one.)

'But I must've told you five times by now!' I say. But Walter looks defiant, with an air of 'you appear to have mistaken me for someone who's as interested as you'd like me to be'. Fair dos, I guess.

So I head into the woods with Nick, the other partner, Tweed and Tattoos, as we've been called, to scan between the bracken, pine needles and fir cones for those mushrooms more hidden away.

I look up. And there is Nick, twenty feet away, curled hands to his eyes, giggling. He's not holding binoculars but two enormous ceps, and the next hour is spent filling our basket. We are in the zone.

'There really is no need for that initial exchange with Walter,' I think to myself. 'It always plays out the same.' And we feast on ceps that evening with lamb. And again for breakfast the following morning with eggs. And again in a hurried lunch (we're always rushing for the train) with cod.

In two days, I've had my fill of fresh porcini. And thus I return to London with no nagging urge to find Ceps in the City...

TA DAAA! Sorry, all that for a dodgy joke.

I do, however, return with an urge to mix a martini. I think the martini is probably the most sophisticated and grown up of all cocktails, precisely because it is one of the simplest to make and yet hardest to perfect. Which is one of the reasons why we make our own gin.

I have long wondered how to explain the martini. I think I'm happy with this: a martini is a silver brick thrown through the front window of your evening. It delivers a direct hit – a sensational and elegant explosion within.

These acute levels, while meeting the requirements of the orderer's preference for wet or dry or dirty, must be executed by a very skilled bartender. He is the conduit for the exquisite outcome, and he has ample opportunity for failure.

I, for one, do not like straight, frozen gin poured on to a non-existence of vermouth. No. I find it a closed fist of alcohol that must instead be enchanted upon. Dilution is essential, but shaking a no-no for it blindly chips the ice. A calm stir in a glass beaker, that gentle rattling turning to a tinkling as round and round it goes in this carousel of joy, is the ONLY way to reveal its complexities, those very voices of the botanicals us gin makers talk so much about.

Olive or lemon, it is up to you. Or perhaps try four tiny, pearl-sized pickled silver skin onions with a few drops of their juice poured in for something of a Dirty Gibson. I highly advise it.

One is excellent. Two is perfect. Please never drink three. God forbid four. Once the bomb bay door is open and the release lever pulled, you cannot grab the words back as they whistle away. Martinis have often been known to produce apologies the following morning ...

Eggs and Ceps

Amazing for breakfast, lunch or dinner.

Serves 2

2–4 large or medium ceps or bay bolete (preferably very firm and new; wipe clean and cut away any mouse nibbling)

2 tbsp unsalted butter or olive oil, plus extra for frying

1 large garlic clove, sliced paper thin (optional)

Squeeze of lemon juice (optional)

4 eggs

Small handful of fresh chives, finely chopped

Sea salt and freshly ground black pepper

Slice the ceps or bay bolete 5 mm/¼ in thick, giving whole cross-sections of the mushroom.

Heat the butter or oil in a frying pan (skillet) and cook the mushrooms, turning, until they have lost a lot of their water content and are well coloured on both sides. Add the garlic, if using, and stir through, cooking lightly. Add a squeeze of lemon juice, if using, and season with salt and pepper.

Spoon from the pan onto plates.

Wipe out the frying pan. Add a little more butter or olive oil. Crack the eggs and fry to your liking. Place on top of the ceps and serve garnished with the chopped chives.

On Shooting

With torn orange streaks of dawn appearing through the silhouetted oaks, I have awaited the barely audible 'whoosh' of descending teal as they quietly drop into their dark pond, 'plop, plop, plop'.

I've shot deer in the heather and woodland and, with rolled sleeves and red arms, dragged them off that ground. I have squelched through Irish bogs for the hope of a darting snipe and, at day's end, returned home sodden but happy with just three in my pocket and toast in my thoughts.

I have spent lazy evenings sitting behind hay bales, mesmerized by the dust in the evening rays as the pigeons arc and clap above, no inclination to pull the trigger as those already in my rucksack mean I will quietly sit out the end of day with a rollie.

I've hunted feral goats through the mists and on to the shoreline of Jura, and pheasants in the wooded creases and steep hills of North Cornwall. These wonderful times, chasing game, are the memories that will be with me forever.

It is hard to argue a love of hunting. It divides people, to say the least, for what more could my 'love of hunting' mean other than a 'love of killing'?

I will try to explain, so that you do not put the Magic Finger[5] on me.

The UK is a scribble of roads with a supermarket in all the gaps between those random lines, so were you to ask me if I needed to hunt then I guess the answer would be no. Fact is, I spent a lot of my life growing up and living in the countryside. That food and cooking were of growing interest from an early age meant I began to view the outdoor world as quite simply 'edible or inedible.'

We lived on a dairy farm with a small amount of Charolais beef production in rural West Dorset and, while a farmer and passionate gardener, my father was forever emptying his pockets of rose hips for syrup

---

[5] Please read Roald Dahl's *The Magic Finger*.

or delivering puffballs and field mushrooms from his giant hands. He cooked us the rockling we pulled from among the huge stones of the sea wall, and taught us to extract the invisible sweet nectar drop of sweetness from a honeysuckle flower. The coconut smell of gorse, an abundance of wild strawberries, blackberries, sorrel and hedgerow crab apples, he showed us many things.

From an early age, growing in up in nature's larder, I was learning a love of both wild and cultivated flavours. All food, I soon began to understand, was the outdoors brought indoors, and in the rural West Country of the seventies this was perhaps far more obvious than it would appear today. So I cannot separate nature and food. And nor should anyone.

My field guides are as useful as my cookbooks and, as you already may know, I'd rather decide on a menu dictated by the immediate terrain I stand upon whenever possible. I am a provincial cook of this land, and so I want to understand its capabilities and comforts at table, both of flora and fauna.

I had an air rifle from the age of twelve and, when my father came across his old non-ejecting twelve-bore, I was fifteen, and with it my first wood pigeon fell crashing through the elder branches with my first cartridge. It was then taken home, cooked and eaten. Shooting was instantly a pursuit I knew I would continue.

I have a deep love of fishing too, and this meant both my gun and fishing rods became essential to my understanding of food, as important to my own cooking as the spoon, whisk, knife or mixing bowl. To me they were simply extensions of what may be classed as kitchen utensils.

Long before I ever concerned myself with the provenance of husbanded animals, my rod and gun were already providing fish and meat of infinite deliciousness, that simultaneously taught me valuable lessons in field craft and responsibility. I never enjoyed the gruesome eviscerating of dead animals; it was simply part of the ground rules. 'You shoot it or catch it, then you clean it and eat it.'

This instilled care, and also valuable lessons learnt from carelessness, those moments when 'I'll clean those ducks tomorrow' meant a hot day or flies would be sure to take advantage of my laziness, and see them thrown away uneaten.

Quite literally, I had my hand in all parts of my quarry – its pursuit, death, preparation and cooking – and it taught me much of which I feel would be beneficial to many young minds today. Blood on my hands taught me ideas of self-sufficiency and cooking, and taught me that, to take a life, you must respect that life afterwards.

While I killed those fish and animals (left gaps in nature), the very pursuit of them also taught me a lot of their habits (there is much pleasure in quiet observation with no wish to pull the trigger, and bringing my own children into the world has perhaps mellowed me, too, as today my inclination to not pull the trigger only grows). I knew which branches the wood pigeons preferred, and which bush was my last point of advantage before they'd see me, break cover and clatter from the leaves.

I knew the banks and nettle beds where the rabbit cities were, the rotting haystack where I'd watch the French partridge play king of the castle. I knew where everything went but for the deer (which I started stalking much later), and I could hunt fairly specifically for the recipes I planned to cook, likely chosen from Florence White, Marika Hanbury-Tenison, Mrs Beeton, just some of the hundred or so cookbooks in my mother's collection.

Out with my gun, I saw many wonderful sights: a group of long-eared owls oddly searching the grass, or barn owls starting into their evening hunts. I'd stop under the cascading whistle streams of starlings in the beeches and listen. I saw hares box, weasels scampering up into the oak branches and, once, on the riverbank witnessed a pike come up to snatch a swimming grass snake while I waited for mallards. I spent hours watching the roe deer step out from the verges of hawthorn at dusk. I saw many things that stopped me in my tracks. Setting out in early morning or returning at dusk, my thoughts and reflections changing with the light, the weather and the landscape.

I was, however, out hunting and so, when presented with an opportunity, I did pull the trigger and shatter the spell. Yet I think it possible to both hunt and love wildlife. To have a feathered body in hand, its warmth dissipating, its head lolling, brings with it an inevitable sadness. I am often perplexed by my destruction and the guilt I experience. Why do it, if such feelings arise?

Perhaps perversely, I feel these emotions of sadness and guilt are both essential and important, far more valuable than *just choosing*, as in just choosing a chicken from behind glass, or lifting a chop from the chill shelf. However 'responsible' the purchase of such items, it nonetheless comes with a blankness, and few feelings, if any. My sadness, my awareness that I have snuffed out a life for my own purpose, ensures good usage of that which I had decided to kill.

I have stopped describing game animals as having 'a good life with one bad day'. There is no humour in such death. But I would argue that to die instantly in a field with a blade of grass in the mouth is better for both the animal and myself. Better that than eat a poorly raised animal whose life is hidden behind a label depicting a smiling farmer or a sticker for quasi 'good practice'.

No doubt though there are those who would say they'd prefer to see me dead in a field with a blade of grass in my mouth. But as I've already said, with blood on my hands, hunting and fishing nonetheless taught me about death and ultimately about respect and self-sufficiency.

In fact, sitting in the warm log cabin restaurant of Fäviken in the snowbound spruce forest of Sweden's Jämtland, my chef friend Magnus Nillson says to me over a plate of roasted capercaillie (an enormous, black, woodland-dwelling grouse), 'What do you think about a meat licence? I think people should have to get one if they want to eat it. They need to learn about nature, welfare, husbandry and slaughter. They need to pass practical and written exams to get one. Maybe a crazy idea though, huh?'

'No, Magnus, I don't think it's a crazy idea at all, I like it,' I reply. 'But good luck with getting that passed!'

Ultimately, we are all hunters. It lies deep in our marrow, the passed-on baton in the relay race of evolution. For who we are today is the sum part of everything that went before. An ancient coding for survival, we are hardwired to forage, hunt, gather, take, collect, whatever you want to call it.

This hunter-gatherer nature is so intrinsic to our survival it has never gone away. When food comes to us easily we turn our attention away from it. But when food is scarce, it's the first thing we turn back to.

Whether hunting for the latest sunglasses, fashion, restaurants, Instagram followers, money, it is nonetheless the hunter-gathering for his or her own prosperity, or for the wider group of family and friends.

Because of my love of cooking and the natural world, my very manual and analogue needs are perhaps more visibly primal, very much in the blood as well as the marrow. Indeed, where I have spent time with the Sámi people of Lapland, with the First Nations of Canada, in rural parts of Africa, Italy, France and Spain, I'd suggest that the remoter the population, the more I find myself among older ways, where there is a greater understanding of food in relation to the surrounding landscape.

No waste and with a strong gastronomic culture, such communities almost certainly will have hunting very much at their centre. There are practices there I do not like, but I am writing about myself and, suffice to say, would decline participation in such things if the opportunity arose. But, believing in this ancient coding, I'd like to try to introduce you to what I would describe as the 'pleasure' in hunting, or the actual feelings that result from doing it.

To hunt a deer, for instance, requires guile, stealth and patience. Your heart is in your throat and bumping in your eardrums, your body rinsed with adrenalin. Watch a human and dog hunting together side by side and they both behave in an almost identical way, the human no less animalistic than the dog. Blood is up, their state altered to super-alert, all senses switched on.

Both will be as cunning as they know how, pausing, advancing, waiting, crouching, alert to moves of that prey they intend to catch.

I'm certainly aware of my own super-heightened senses when out shooting, how my breathing changes, my agility and alertness enhanced until the kill has been achieved.

When the animal lies at my feet, my body feels released from this consuming tension, patience and concentration. Like leaving the gym, there are undeniable feelings of exhilaration and gain. Flooded by endorphins, my legs sometimes shivering, there are also the ancient, handed-down feelings of happiness, exhilaration and relief in the knowledge you have extended your own survival and that of those whom you will share the meat with.

It's impossible not to feel this, it is old and deep in the core. It is possible, however, not to understand this when turning to the subject of reared and driven game. 'What of pheasants and partridges?' you say, 'shot in their hundreds.' Well, you have a point, and a timely one. And the heightened senses of hunting alone over wide ground that I speak of above are barely there.

Two years ago, in a wooded glade, gun smoke hanging over the rusty bracken, I was on a sizable driven shoot. We'd shot a lot when, suddenly, it came at me hard but not exactly out of the blue that I simply didn't enjoy this type of hunting any longer. And I had not for some time.

I realized that I preferred my lonely excursions into the hills with a bag over my shoulder or the friendship of only a handful if shooting in company. Quite simply, from now on, if was I to intentionally set out to kill, then it seemed only fair that my intended prey had every means to avoid me.

So I've now decided that, with very few exceptions, I'll not lift a gun to an animal that has no other option than to cross my path. This will mean I shoot far less, but I'd rather return home with a headful of dusk, evening smells and observation than a scorecard of shots fired and numbers dead. This is what they call 'field sports'. It is the word 'sport' here that I've always struggled with.

I will hunt what I can eat. And there are some species, such as the brown hare and golden plover, I no longer shoot at all.

To be clear: I 'largely' support hunting, although I'm sure this piece of writing will annoy many, both those against and indeed for, given the last part. But, tough: I cannot be liked by all.

I believe for shooting to survive it must be humane and respectful, and that it is seen as a provider of food which is eaten not wasted.

I eat meat and, like Magnus Nillson, feel that whenever possible it should therefore be my hand that kills it. I'm eating venison tonight on toast with fresh goats' cheese and green sauce. There are two million wild deer in the UK, and growing. So all I ask is this: consider your options before buying that piece of pig.

Very Simple Rose Hip Cough Mixture

Last time I made this was after my son and I had filled every available pocket from an abundant little rose hip bush next to a beautiful little chapel in the Spanish Pyrenees. With no vinegar to hand, I pulled an unripe pomegranate from the village tree. They worked very well together.

500 g/1 lb 2 oz rose hips, rinsed, stalks removed

200 g/7 oz/1 cup caster (superfine) sugar

3 whole peppercorns (optional)

Strip of unwaxed lemon rind

1 tbsp cider or red wine vinegar

If your rose hips are young and hard, they will still be delicious, but I'd probably make a cut down one side of each with a paring knife while watching telly. If soft specimens, just bash them up a bit with a spoon. There is no need to chop them in a food processor. Just more washing up.

Place them into a saucepan. Pour the caster sugar over the rose hips and mix well. Leave in the pan in a cool place (I do not mean the local disco) with a cloth over the top for 2 hours.

Pour over enough water to cover them by 2.5 cm/1 in. Set over the heat and bring to the boil. Slowly reduce to a simmer, but not so low that the mixture catches on the side of the pan and goes brown. Cook until the recognizable consistency of cough mixture.

Add the vinegar and bring back to the boil for 30 seconds.

Strain into a glass bowl through two layers of clean muslin, or some very expensive, clean tights. Transfer to a sterilized glass bottle or jar.

This will keep for 2 weeks in the fridge, and isn't half bad mixed into a dressing for cold duck. Also great in a Rose Hip Collins made with Hepple Gin.

Tip When picking in the lanes and hedgerows, do choose those rose hips in late autumn that are 'bletted' (wrinkly and with a squidge) as these will be sweeter and have better flavour.

Pigeon and Blue Cheese Bun

Wood pigeon is delicious. The clatter of grey wings from the wheat stubble or woodland floor means that, from September and onwards through the autumn, many will grace my plate.

If using the whole birds, once the breasts have been removed, wash the blood from the carcass and use them to make stock. Simmered with the water from rehydrating dried mushrooms and the mushrooms themselves, they make a truly wonderful dark, clear broth.

If you don't like eating them rare or a least pink, do not bother.

Serves 1
40 g/1½ oz/⅓ cup blue cheese
1 tbsp double (heavy) cream
1 small garlic clove, finely grated
½ tbsp Dijon mustard
1 tsp fennel seeds
Small handful of baby kale or adult kale stripped from the stringy stalk
Half a small uncooked yellow, white or red beetroot (beet), sliced
1 tsp muscovado sugar
2 tsp cider vinegar
Drizzle of rapeseed (canola) or sunflower oil
30 g/1 oz/2 tbsp butter
2 skinless pigeon breasts
1 brioche burger bun, halved
Sea salt and freshly ground black pepper

Take a small saucepan, and over a low heat melt the cheese into the cream. Stir in the garlic and mustard and put to one side.

In a dry frying pan (skillet) over a low heat, toast the fennel seeds, swirling them a bit. They should be crunchy after about 4 minutes.

Put them in a bowl with the kale and beetroot slices, and toss in the sugar, vinegar and a drizzle of oil. Season with salt and leave to stand.

Add the butter to a frying pan with a splash of oil, and place over a medium heat. Season the breasts on both sides with salt and pepper and pop them in the pan. They should sizzle on entry. Cook for 1½–2 minutes per side, then remove them from the heat and allow to rest for 2 minutes or so.

Pour any excess oil from the pan and gently toast the cut side of the bun halves in the pan.

Lay the pigeon meat on the bottom half of the bun and spoon over a good amount of the blue cheese sauce. Top with some of the beetroot and kale salad. Enjoy with a glass of cider.

Monkey Puzzle

Our houses are filled with nature at every turn. I only have to look around as I write this to see a life-size concrete porcini on the bookshelf and cut flowers in the kitchen window. My son's socks sit on the table. They have gibbons on them. My daughter's tights, cats. I'm drinking tea from a mug with a moth printed on it, chosen over the zebra one. Christmas cards display trees, deer, a bear in a hat, geese and tigers. My sofa cushions have prawns embroidered on them.

Many prints and drawings of animals, birds' eggs, bats and landscapes may be found throughout. Walking from room to room is no less than a safari. A trip to the fridge finds a stale chocolate bunny inside and a magnet fish on the door.

My ringtone is chirruping crickets.

While my house has perhaps more nature in it than other people's, I'd suggest that to stop and look at the majority of homes, one would quickly find nature on curtain or duvet, phone case or spirit bottle.

In our nests we keep pets and outside we keep gardens. The books we read our children are 99.9 per cent about animals, Winnie-the-Pooh, Ant and Bee, *Just So Stories, The Wind in the Willows*, Beatrix Potter ... We need to be in close proximity to nature and run to it when the buildings, work and emotions lean inwards.

Blue Planet comes on and families come together, while animals on Instagram have enough followers to get a telly show.

An author called Miriam has written a book on owls. She is weekly gifted with owl towels, key rings, mugs, stickers ... 'We thought you'd like this,' say the accompanying letters. 'I prefer the real ones,' she informs the audience at her talk.

Nature is our default setting. We do not exist without it. The same cannot be said the other way around!

Does anyone have the answer as to why we are so keen to exploit the natural world? I do not. But I wonder: is it all playing out as it should? Are we, the *homo sapiens* animal, simply making developments as intended, with the brain that allows us to. Directed by choice, is it all going to plan as the Kardashians shop?

We cannot fall back on something once it's gone. Let us not be so keen to leave our mark on the world that we scratch her to death, our houses turned into a million little museums or shrines to the departed.

Long in the Tooth

My mum keeps on suggesting I should investigate Replant hair invigorator (or whatever it's called). Alternatively, she says, 'I do wish you'd stop touching your head, you're not exactly helping hair loss.'

This is raised consistently, so much so that I stood in a mirrored lift the other day trying to position myself so that I could gauge exactly what is going on behind my back. It's not exactly monk-like. But really, in truth, maybe grateful for the advantage of height, I couldn't care less. And anyway, what may wander down on to my computer keys as I write this is certainly being re-wilded on my back and shoulders, a new kind of thin down that gives a lovely, wispy, breezy sensation as I move from bed to bathroom.

In this new Victorian era, I now have a beard too.

My chalky knees have been worn down by disco. I wear glasses now, my last pair found outside Sainsbury's, freshly crushed under their delivery van. I was so hip once that I will probably need a new one soon.

I'm reminded of one of my favourite films, *Brazil* by Terry Gilliam. Mrs Terrain, who having had extensive cosmetic surgery, is seen bandaged like a mummy in a wheelchair with a drip. When asked what's wrong by Mr Tuttle, she says, 'My complication has had a little complication.' Later on, when unwrapped, she simply dissolves into a viscous pool of cosmetic slurry.

This is not my way.

What I've learnt has replaced how I've looked. Worn down and heavier, but still strong, I like this position, and I'll tell you why. To those hushed, tender narrations of David Attenborough, I have many times observed the hierarchy of lions, buffalo, bears and baboons. So I conclude that I am happy to be an elder, a bull of the Masai Mara. Until challenged and completely chased into solitude, I wear my flatter teeth, bigger belly and patchy fur with authoritative pride.

Let the white hairs come. I like my new suit.

Gooseberry Mess

I don't make puddings, as you can probably tell. But here's one I don't mind throwing together if pushed. I normally head for the cheeseboard. Less of a recipe, more of a DIY delight.

1 punnet of gooseberries or canned gooseberries reduced down in a pan
Caster (superfine) sugar
Elderflower cordial
Whipping cream
1 unwaxed lemon
Icing (confectioners') sugar
Ready-made meringues

Rinse the gooseberries well under a running tap. Drain and tip into a small saucepan with the water that clings to them. Add the caster sugar and cook past collapsed, reducing them so that the consistency of the fruit is not watery, but more compote-like. Finish the sweetening with enough cordial that the taste of elderflower is faint but recognizable. Allow to cool.

Pour the cream into a mixing bowl and finely grate in the zest of half the lemon. Sweeten the cream with a touch of icing sugar and beat until just-stiff peaks are formed. (Overly stiff, semi-split cream makes for a bad mess.)

Sharpen the cooled gooseberry mixture with a little grated zest of the other half of the lemon.

Take a meringue or two, break them into a bowl and add the cream and the gooseberry mix. Turn gently together into a disorganized state, and then eat it.

The Hart of the Woods

I am in a wood, stalking deer. I approach a thicket of dense bramble and elder between some dead pines. All of a sudden the bush explodes as a white hart leaps out from within. It jumps across my head. I can see its throat, its curled front legs passing, its wide stomach, the fine detail of hair on its belly, its pizzle, its hind legs and hooves, the upturned tail. My head is back, my mouth open in amazement.

I turn to watch it land and run off through the trees: but it doesn't. It doesn't land at all. It simply dissolves into the trunk of a thick oak tree.

I unload my rifle immediately. Hunting is finished for today. With a bearable shiver of fear in my spine I walk the path home and out of the woods, hyper-alert to I know not what.

I tell my friend. He does not challenge me.

We open a bottle of wine and finish it quietly.

Out of Stock

When I check out, preferably keeling over into the hedgerows under a fruiting blackthorn on a post-lunch stroll, it is my wish that I be buried in a prize-winning giant pumpkin, one that grew large enough to house me, bent into a croissant shape, before the rigors of death set me.

Then, if you'd be so good, please pop a seed in my mouth that it may sprout through my head and give juicy apples[6] in time to come.

Please make good use of the pumpkin flesh. A soup, something to keep your hands warm in church, before the continuing celebration that, I insist, should go on until late and include a roasted ox and oysters.

While I'm on the subject, I'd like J S Bach – The Well-tempered Clavier Book 1: Prelude No.1 in C Major BWV 846 – and then 'The Ghetto' by Donny Hathaway. After that play what you like. And have a drink on me.

THE END ... of this book as well.

---

[6] Egremont Russet

Val's Restaurant

'Two Dots' Lusine

'There's More To Life Than This – Live At The Milk Bar Toilets' Björk

'The Shape You're In' Art Feynman

'Expansions' Lonnie Liston Smith

'Fallen' One Dove

'Cavatina' Stanley Myers, Craig Ogden

'Bill Is Dead' The Fall

'Java Jive' Inkspots

'See-line Woman' Nina Simone

'Lost In Music' The Fall

'I Feel Love' Donna Summer

'Where's Me Jumper?' Sultans Of Ping F.C.

'Runnin' Away' Sly & The Family Stone

'Strange Little Girl' The Stranglers

'Walk on By' The Stranglers

'Skin Deep' The Stranglers

'Train in Vain' The Clash

'Controller' Hercules & Love Affair (feat. Faris Badwan)

'It's My Life' Talk Talk

'Imperfect List – Part 1' Big Hard Excellent Fish

'Have a Good Time' Paul Simon

'Longer Boats' Cat Stevens

'We Are the Music Makers' Aphex Twin

'Fresh Feeling' Eels

'The Ballad Of Lucy Jordan' Marianne Faithfull

'Bette Davis Eyes' Kim Carnes

'Her Fantasy' Matthew Dear

'Bones' Brandi Ifgray (Vibe Mix)

'1979' The Smashing Pumpkins

'Anemone' The Brian Jonestown Massacre

'Let Me Do It To You' JJ Cale

'Little Boxes' Pete Seeger

'Use Me' Bill Withers

'Cycle Eyes' Cosmonauts (Psychemagik Lagoon Nebula Mix)

'The Rifle' Alela Diane

'Roscoe' Midlake (Beyond the Wizards Sleeve Mix)

'Hard To Be Close' Here We Go Magic

'Diagram Girl' Beyond the Wizards Sleeve

'True Love Will Find You in the End' Headless Heroes

'Les Fleurs' Minnie Ripperton

'Principles' Benoit & Sergio

'Time Tough' Toots & The Maytals

'Deuling Banjos' The Original Deuling Banjos

'The Chauffeur' Duran Duran

'Voodoo Ray' A Guy Called Gerald

'My Spine Is The Bassline' Shriekback

'Dark Star' Crosby, Stills & Nash

'Free' Cat Power

'My Girl' Madness

'Man Gave Names to All the Animals' Bob Dylan

'Mushrooms' Marshall Jefferson, Noosa Heads (Salt City Orchestra Remix)

'Scarlet Fantastic' No Memory (Extra Sensory Mix)

'Got To Give It Up' Marvin Gaye

'Every You Every Me' Placebo

'Fearless' Pink Floyd

'Google Eye' The Nashville Teens

'Love Action (I Believe In Love)' The Human League

'Boogie On Reggae Woman' Stevie Wonder

'Close To Me' The Cure

'Look at Miss Ohio' Gillian Welch

'Love and Affection' Joan Armatrading

'Slave To The Rhythm' Grace Jones

'Mirror in the Bathroom' The Beat

'Roast Fish and Corn Bread' Lee 'Scratch' Perry

'Java Jive' The Ink Spots

'Marlene On The Wall' Suzanna Vega

'Protection' Massive Attack

'The Bare Necessities' The Jungle Book

'Here Comes The Sun' The Beatles

'Prelude in C Major BWV 846' Johann Sebastian Bach

'Coney Island Baby' Lou Reed

Acknowledgements

To Polly Powell, my publisher, and all at Pavilion – only they would hatch such an oddity. I really like you lot. To Stephanie Milner, ably assisted by Jane Birch, for your unending patience, ease and well-disguised frustration. To Laura Russell and the photography team, Ellis Parrinder, Rachel Vere and Valerie Berry – I like what you've done ... so much so, I didn't interfere but simply agreed (this is rare).

Tim Bates – the silver fox of publishing. Love spending time with you!

My children, I adore you and love you, as you know. You have taught me much. I only hope to do the same for you. X

My parents, whom I love deeply and learnt so much from. I wasn't easy. Thank you eternally.

To my brother and sister, however you'd describe things, I'd describe us a close!

To Sasha, for your unending calm and patience. I love you and lucky me.

Walter Riddell, Sam and Andy, three good fellows who can always be counted on. You've seen me through one hell of an obstacle course over the last few years.

Everyone who has ever taught me anything and anyone I ever upset (up until now).

Last, but definitely not least (and because I didn't think any one would have put a recipe the aknowledgements before), Kay Plunkett-Hogge and, of course, Fred. Thank you for being such hard task masters and for all the fun and food. You give as good as you get. The recipe below is delicious and is Kay's, from her book *Baan: Recipes & Stories From My Thai Home*, also published by Pavilion.

Kay's Pad Krapow

Serves 2

6 garlic cloves
4–6 bird's eye chillies
1 large red chilli, cut into chunks
Pinch of sea salt
2 tbsp vegetable oil
300 g/10½ oz pork, minced
3 tbsp nam pla (fish sauce)
1 tsp sugar
A very large handful of holy basil leaves
 – the more the merrier

Pound the garlic, chillies and salt together using a pestle and mortar.

Heat a wok until its really hot, then add the oil.

Throw in the chilli-garlic paste and stir-fry for a few seconds.

Add the pork and stir-fry. When it is almost cooked, add the nam pla and the sugar. Stir fry together until amalgamated and the pork is cooked. Then add most of the basil and wilt it in to dish.

Serve over steamed jasmine rice, preferably with a deep-fried egg on top, and the remaining basil leaves scattered on top.

Tip If you can't find holy basil (bai krapow), you can use Thai sweet basil instead. Worst case scenario, I have even made this with European basil. But it isn't quite the same. If you do, just don't call it Pad Krapow ...